THE POEM IN ITS SKIN

BIG TABLE PUBLISHING COMPANY

Paul Carroll

CHICAGO ◨ The Poem
In Its Skin

To Inara—my wife, my friend

Big Table Publishing Company
201 North Wells Street
Chicago, Illinois 60606

Library of Congress Catalogue Card Number: 68-18506

First printing November 1968
Second printing February 1969
Third printing June 1970

ISBN 0-695-87146-3 paper binding
ISBN 0-695-87147-1 cloth binding

TO THE READER

Every good poem is like a person: it has its own skin. Getting to know John Ashbery's "Leaving the Atocha Station" or James Wright's "As I Step over a Puddle at the End of Winter, I Think of an Ancient Chinese Governor" can take as much effort, openness, attention, care, and the ability to put to work one's brains, feelings, intuition and sense of humor as it takes to get to know another person. Everyone who cares about poetry knows this and I mention it only because I know how easy it can be to forget it from time to time and to expect some new poem to illustrate this or that prejudice or preconception I happen to favor at the moment. Our tendency to play Humpty Dumpty by wanting poems to mean what we choose them to mean is natural, I'm afraid; but when confronted by such good poems as we're about to read, the tendency can result in little less than "a vanity and a fruitless solicitude of the mind."

To make an obvious point: Allen Ginsberg's "Wichita Vortex Sutra" is not a Beat poem in the sense that "Howl" or "America" are classic Beat verse; its alleged intention is neither to sabotage *The Oxford Book of American Verse* nor to become a club with which to thump President Lyndon Johnson or Claire Booth Luce: its intention is to release the holy and free and peaceful in both the poet and his fellow Americans by summoning the assistance of saints and deities. Any rewarding discussion of "Wichita Vortex Sutra" will of course explore whether or not the poem succeeds in its alleged intention, which is an ambitious one, to say the least, and which also offers a clue that perhaps here may be a major American poem. Discussion which asks the poem to point a moral or adorn a tale, on the other hand, seems best left (to echo the familiar fin de siècle dogma) in the hands of the servants of criticism: the literary journalists and literary parsons. In other words, I find it fruitless, boring and a waste of time either to praise "Wichita Vortex Sutra" because it appears to support my opinion about the continuing involvement and aggression of the United States in the Viet Nam conflict or to condemn it because its author fails to indicate that

he's read with any profit Cleanth Brooks' *The Well Wrought
Urn* or, worse yet, because he embraces in his private life such
controversial experiences as homosexuality and the use of marijuana and LSD—for which he often is scolded for being the
Rasputin of contemporary American literature.

What has the poet *written?* is of course the only valuable
challenge. To help in trying to meet this challenge by experiencing any poem in its own skin, as it were, the reader today is able
much like a warlock to summon from the world of criticism
such a bewildering and intimidating rout of "lemans, demons,
fallen angels,/and Familiars" (as Isabella Gardner writes in her
elegy for Dylan Thomas "When a Warlock Dies") that at times
he must long as I have for the orthodoxy of such critical positions
as: Every decent poem owns at least one of seven ambiguities;
or even: Poetry is at bottom "a criticism of life," and therefore
it should be evident that Dryden and Pope cannot be called
"genuine" poets because they compose in their "wits" instead
of in their "souls." Critical positions such as William Empson's
or Matthew Arnold's afford the security that one knows at least
where to begin and what to look for when reading a poem. But
I doubt if either Mr. Empson or Arnold would fail to make use
of some of the other ways of looking at a poem which make the
contemporary literary scene the Age of Criticism which the late
Randall Jarrell called it with less flattering connotation than
the one I suggest when I say: the more good critical tools and
methods, the merrier.

And certainly there are almost as many valuable critical
methods available today as there were heresies in the early
Christian Church. Every serious reader of poetry feels grateful
to the New Critics for encouraging our awareness of admirable
intricacies and ambiguities contained in most good poetry; and
to the Neo-Aristotelian critics for educating our appreciation
of the architectural structure of the poem; and to such critics as
Leslie A. Fiedler who have stimulated us not to be insensitive to
what clearly are Freudian realities and mythological dimensions
in more poems than we might have thought.

And of course there are other useful critical methods and
tools. One tool which delights me is the record or tape made by
poets or good actors such as Richard Burton. When studying

"The Waste Land," we can listen to the poet himself dryly but sadly mocking human passion and the longing for rebirth: "April is the cruellest month, breeding . . ." What would Arnold have given to have heard an LP record of Keats or Edmund Kean reciting "Ode on Melancholy?" Wasn't it Yeats who claimed that when the first poem moved from the oral tradition onto the page it was the original bite into the apple of Eden?

As for the critical approach I use in these ten essays, it's probably evident that I try to find whatever help I can in any or all critical schools or tools—including of course records or public readings by the poets—in an effort to see each poem in its own existential reality. The only dogma I like, in fact, is this: No one critical method or school is the True Church which, after all, as Eliot in less devout days reminds us, "remains below/Wrapt in the old miasmal mist." Is there any advice for critics and readers which has the good sense of the one implied by Yeats in the celebrated passage in the letter he wrote to his old friend Lady Elizabeth Pelham a few weeks before he died in 1939? "It seems to me that I have found what I wanted. When I try to put it all into a phrase I say, 'Man can embody truth but he cannot know it,'" Yeats said. "The abstract is not life and everywhere draws out its contradictions. You can refute Hegel but not the Saint or the Song of Sixpence." These ten essays try, in brief, to see what the Saint who is the poem looks like and to hear what he says; and they try to listen to how the Song of Sixpence sounds: I have no use for the Hegel of preconceived critical dogmas.

And if my metaphor of each poem having its own skin makes sense, I trust it's implied I will welcome diverse readings of the ten poems. In fact, I look forward to readings which contradict my own in the hope that such criticism may tell me more about my old friend "A Wicker Basket" or "A Century Piece for Poor Heine" or "April Inventory."

* * *

A word about why these particular poems were chosen for discussion. Originally, I wanted to write a book about the generation of American poets now in their early 40s which is, in my experience, as various, provocative and important as any generation since the Eliot-Pound-Williams generation of 1917; but I decided that close work with poems I've admired for years would be more interesting—and more fun. To feel that one's own generation is as "faire, foul [bawdy] and full of variations," as Robert Burton commended the Latin Elegiac poets for having been, is an understandable vanity. Nevertheless, there are at least a dozen other poets in this generation whose works have given me almost as much pleasure and knowledge as the poems I picked to write about. At one time or another during the early stage of thinking about this book, I considered writing about most of the following poems I admire as much as the ten I have written about: Brother Antoninus: "Annul in Me My Manhood." Paul Blackburn: "Night Song for Two Mystics." Gregory Corso: "Marriage." Edward Dorn: "The Air of June Sings." Alan Dugan: "Love Song: I and Thou." Robert Duncan: "A Poem Beginning with a Line by Pindar." Lawrence Ferlinghetti: "The Great Chinese Dragon." Donald Justice: "Counting the Mad." Galway Kinnell: "The Porcupine." Kenneth Koch: "Taking a Walk with You." Denise Levertov: "The Sharks." Edward Marshall: "Leave the Word Alone." Mark Perlberg: "I Would Like to Say Something Magnificent About Death." Anne Sexton: "The Double Image." Gary Snyder: "Praise for Sick Women." George Starbuck: "Of Late." John Wieners: "A Poem for the Old Man."

Once the ten essays were finished—the process of learning and discovering in the writing of them was so enjoyable I almost regretted it when the manuscript had to be sent to the typesetter and printer—I found I wanted to explore some more general impressions about the ten poets and also about the generation as a whole, which I try to do in the long essay which concludes this book.

Let me stress one thing about this essay. I am neither a critic in the formal sense nor a literary historian: the essay explores my own understanding of this generation of poets. And since it is personal, this will account for the absence of some poets whose work I don't know too well and of other poets who have earned reputations but whose works bore me like Lent.

One of the things which never bores me is literary anecdote and gossip.* In the section "Ten Poets in Their Skins," I make

* This appetite appears only to become more hungry the more it's satisfied. For me it began when I was a student in the Department of English at

use of anecdote or portraiture whenever it seems helpful in describing the man or woman who wrote the poems. But do not expect to read what this poet once in his cups confessed about his proclivity for boys or mongooses or what that one is rumored to have said with a hard mouth from a public platform about his contemporaries once he'd become famous: I detest this type of literary scandal when it becomes public in print or from a platform (although I enjoy it as much as anyone when I hear it as it passes along the literary grapevine).

But I don't want to end on such a sour note. My hope is that what I try to clarify in the essays on the poems and in the one on the whole generation might encourage you either to continue or to begin your exploration of the work of these poets. As Pound wrote to Eliot in 1921: "It is after all a grrrreat littttttterary period."

The University of Chicago in the late 1940s. In the classroom we had been taught that the only respectable concern for the serious student of literature was the Neo-Aristotelian canon as defined and explored by Professors Crane, McKeon, Maclean, and Olson; and I remember I'd sometimes feel guilty when I found myself once again deep in the stacks of Harper Library, poring blissfully over Aubrey or G. B. Harrison's edition of Jonson's *Conversations with Drummond of Hawthorndon* or George Moore's snide side of what Lady Gregory was like. Long after I've forgotten the Aristotelian "form" we were encouraged to contemplate in Eliot's "Gerontion," I remember Lady Ottoline Morrell's observation about the young poet: "I saw T. S. E. again . . . he was ever so Nice—but—I think he is very queer . . . I showed him photographs of Greek IVth and Vth Century statues and he said they gave him the Creeps. They were so akin to Snake Worship. Don't you think it odd of him?—I feel he has Demons on the Brain."

CONTENTS

John Ashbery

LEAVING THE ATOCHA STATION

The arctic honey blabbed over the report causing darkness
And pulling us out of there experiencing it
he meanwhile . . . And the fried bats they sell there
dropping from sticks, so that the menace of your prayer folds . . .
Other people . . .   flash
the garden are you boning
and defunct covering . . . Blind dog expressed royalties . . .
comfort of your perfect tar grams nuclear world bank tulip
Favorable to   near the night pin
loading formaldehyde.   the table torn from you
Suddenly   and we are close
Mouthing the root   when you think
generator   homes enjoy leered

The worn stool blazing   pigeons from the roof
                 driving tractor to squash
Leaving the Atocha Station   steel
infected bumps the screws
     everywhere   wells
abolished top ill-lit
scarecrow falls   Time, progress and good sense
strike of shopkeepers dark blood
no forest you can name drunk scrolls

the completely new Italian hair . . .
Baby . . .   ice falling off the port
The centennial   Before we can

                old   eat
members with their chins
                so high up   rats
    relaxing the cruel discussion
    suds   the painted corners
white   most aerial
        garment crow
                    and when the region took us back
the person left us like birds
    it was fuzz on the passing light
over disgusted heads, far into amnesiac
permanent house depot   amounts he can
            decrepit mayor . . .   exalting flea

for that we turn around
experiencing it is not to go into
the epileptic prank forcing bar
to borrow out onto tide-exposed fells
over her morsel, she chasing you
and the revenge he'd get
establishing the vultural over
rural area cough protection
murdering quintet. Air pollution terminal
the clean fart genital enthusiastic toe prick album serious
        evening flames
the lake over your hold   personality
            lightened . . .   roar
You are freed
            including barrels
head of the swan   forestry
the night and stars fork
That is, he said
        and rushing under the hoops of
equations probable
            absolute mush   the right

entity   chain store   sewer opened their books
            The flood dragged you
            I coughed to the window
last month: juice, earlier
like the slacks   to be declining
        the peaches   more
    fist
sprung expecting the cattle
false loam   imports
                next time around

IF ONLY HE HAD LEFT
FROM THE FINLAND STATION

Whoever reads "Leaving the Atocha Station" for the first or second or even third time must feel as baffled as I am. "Cheshire-Puss," one wants to ask with Alice, "would you tell me, please, which way I ought to go from here?" And one hopes the cat's advice will come true in terms of trying to discover how to read this poem or even if it's worth the effort. When Alice says she doesn't care where she arrives "so long as I get *somewhere*," the cat assures her: "Oh, you're sure to do that if only you walk long enough."

Once one tries to reread Ashbery's poem, however, the cat's warning becomes too true: "In *that* direction," the cat indicates, waving its right paw, "lives a Hatter: and in *that* direction," waving the other paw, "lives a March Hare. Visit either you like: they're both mad."

Indeed, several close readings fail to offer the suspicion of a clue as to what it might be all about. I also feel annoyed: the poem makes me feel stupid. Nobody likes to be for long in a foreign country where one can neither speak nor understand nor read the language. For the knowledgeable reader of modern poetry this could prove especially vexatious. One can't even ask of Ashbery's poem: "Which way to the ambiguity?" or "How many myths at the Mad Hatter's house?" or "Where's the form of the poem? The organic imagery?" Even the most orthodox critical approach seems irrelevant: "How does one get past the heresy of paraphrase?"*

After the original shock of puzzlement or annoyance, however, the sophisticated reader probably responds to what appears to be the challenge thrown down by the poet. Concealed some-

---

* Some readers may not be familiar with all of these allusions to terms or concepts prominent in the dialogue of modern literary criticism. In Appendix One (at the end of this essay) the reader can find a short bibliography of books by critics who have defined and illustrated the salient concepts in the dialogue which is the richest in the history of literary criticism.

where in the title or in the stanzas, one suspects, must be the key which hard scrutiny of the text can discover. Experienced readers of poetry have grown accustomed to feeling something like Alice marooned in the living room on the everyday, "wrong" side of the mirror when they first tried to read "The Waste Land" or "The Pisan Cantos" or "The Wreck of the Deutschland" or the "Altarwise by Owl-light" sonnets of Dylan Thomas. Discovering the key which unlocks the way in which to read good poems can be exciting and rewarding. And it's usually a lot of fun. Everybody likes to solve Zeno's paradox of Achilles and the tortoise—or even to complete a tough crossword puzzle.

So the reader returns with high hope to the title. The Atocha Station sounds not only exotic but possibly significant. If we are in luck, the station might even be historically significant like the Finland Station in Petrograd. On April 16, 1917, Lenin arrived from Germany at the Finland Station, where a vast crowd, waving the red banners of the Bolshevik, greeted him. After an exile of ten years, Vladimir Ilyich Lenin had returned to lead the Bolsheviks in the November Revolution which rang the death knell on the last of the Romanov Tzars. This might be the key. A poem called "Leaving the Finland Station" could be the complete and unexpurgated text of Ashbery's poem but it might lend itself to a sophisticated reading which could argue that the nonsensical stanzas become a parody of drab and bourgeois Soviet reality today when compared to the glorious, muscular paradise on earth for the laborer envisioned by Lenin, Mayakovsky and other old Bolshevik heroes. In this reading, the Bolshevik ideal could be seen as having been smashed into 10,000 trivial or meaningless phrases by the contemporary Communist world. "Leaving the Finland Station" could even be a satire about the decay and final impotency of the revolutionary ideal itself—Marxist, the Spirit of 1776, the Cuba of the Castro Revolution, and so on. What began with the splendor of men demanding freedom ends with the vulgarity of bureaucrats mouthing official gobbledygook.

But what is the Atocha Station? Nothing more than a run-of-the-mill train depot in Madrid.

Still, the title does announce a journey. The journey itself might be our key. After all, the myth of the journey or voyage is one of the foundation stones of modern poetry. One thinks of T. S. Eliot's "Dry Salvages"—that profound reexperience of Christian's earthly pilgrimage—or of St.-John Perse's "Anabasis"—the modern epic of the immemorial migration of mankind weary from "going to and fro in the earth" like the Satan of the Book of Job. Often poems depicting journeys also transform the trip into a metaphor for time or memory. "The past/ Is cities from a train," Robert Lowell writes, "until at least/Its escalating and black-windowed blocks/Recoil against a Gothic church." Or the train itself becomes the symbol for either celebration of the god of technology (such as Whitman's "To a Locomotive in Winter") or indictment of the golden calf of technology (such as Allen Ginsberg's "Sunflower Sutra").

Is there a journey, then, in "Leaving the Atocha Station"? Isolated allusions sprinkled throughout appear to hint that the title means what it says. Fried bats are sold (to satisfy what Babylonian palate one hesitates to ask) in the station where formaldehyde is being loaded onto trains; in the second stanza we appear to be pulling out of the Atocha Station; later, our train might be passing a depot and a "rural area" containing peach orchards and cattle; and the last line itself seems to promise a return trip—"next time around." Time or memory are also here in that past blends into present which merges into past again— and so on throughout the poem. Technology could also be evident in the possibility that the train moving through the Spanish landscape accounts for the fragmentary quality of scenery, pigeons, snatches of conversation (overheard in the corridor?) and perhaps even for the occasional jerky breaks in the lines themselves.

None of these possibilities lead anywhere, however, in the total context of the poem. Occasional allusions either to a trip or to time or memory or to technology remain only isolated fragments in what appears to be an exasperatingly incoherent kaleidoscope of phrases, words, snatches of talk, images and metaphors.

So the reader starts all over again in the search for the elusive key. Suddenly the dead-end of the title seems to make sense when the opening six or so lines are read as pure Dada poetry. Think

of the title as promising a journey and then listen to the babble
of the opening lines:

> The arctic honey blabbed over the report causing
> darkness
> And pulling us out of there experiencing it
> he meanwhile . . .   And the fried bats they sell there
> dropping from sticks, so that the menace of your prayer
> folds . . .
> Other people . . .   flash
> the garden are you boning
> and defunct covering . . .   Blind dog expressed
> royalties . . .
> comfort of your perfect tar grams nuclear world bank
> tulip

Clearly these lines belong in the same family with such Dada
classics as Kurt Schwitter's "Poem No. 48 (1920?)":

> Staggering.
> Earthworm.
> Fishes.
> Clocks.
> The cow.
> The forest leafs the leaves.
> A drop of asphalt in the snow.
> Cry, cry, cry, cry, cry.
> A wise man explodes without wages.

or Philippe Soupault's:

> The airplane weaves telegraph wires
> And the well sings the same song
> Orange tinges the aperitif in the bar of the coachmen
> But the engineers have white eyes
> The lady's lost her smile in the forest

The entire Ashbery poem, in fact, might be a good example of the *ars poetica* described by Tristan Tzara in his 1920 "Manifesto on Feeble Love and Bitter Love":

> To make a dadaist poem
> Take a newspaper.
> Take a pair of scissors.
> Choose an article as long as you are planning to make your poem.
> Cut out the article.
> Then cut out each of the words that make up this article and put them in a bag.
> Shake it gently.
> Then take out the scraps one after the other in the order in which they left the bag.
> Copy conscientiously.
> The poem will be like you.
> And here you are a writer, infinitely original and endowed with a sensibility that is charming though beyond the understanding of the vulgar.

> Example:
> when the dogs cross the air in a diamond like the ideas and the appendix of the meninges shows the hour of awakening program (the title is my own) price they are yesterday agreeing afterwards paintings / appreciate the dream epoch of the eyes / pompously than recite the gospel mode darkens / group the apotheosis imagine he said fatality power of colors / cut arches flabbergasted the reality of a magic spell / spectator all to efforts from the it is no longer 10 to 12 / during digression volt right diminishes pressure / render of madmen topsy-turvy flesh on a monstrous crushing scene / celebrate but their 160 adepts in not to the put in my mother-of-pearl / sumptuous of land bananas upheld illumine / joy ask reunited almost / of has the one so much that the invoked visions / of the sing this one laughs / destiny situation disappears describes this one 25 dances salvation / dissimulated the

whole of it is not was / magnificent the ascent to the
gang better light of which sumptuousness scene me
music-hall / reappears following instant shakes to live /
business that there is not loaned / manner words come to
these people

Obviously Ashbery's poem can be read as a contemporary
example of the poem as pure chance—the accidental encounter
on a page between words and phrases or sentences—prescribed
by Tzara. What is the quality of this type of poem? Certainly one
prominent quality is its merry audacity. After one's original
annoyance at the poem's willful, total unintelligibility and at
the strong possibility that the writer who calls such a work a
poem might be putting the reader on, one can also respond to
how the Dada poem of pure chance snubs its nose, as it were, at
one of culture's most venerable assumptions: namely, an artist
should be coherent and "serious," creating coherent, serious
works which coherent, serious people and critics can contemplate and enjoy, particularly once they've become familiar with
the esthetic theory which the work illustrates—whether that
theory be Neo-Classical or Romantic or Symbolist or Beat. Dada,
in short, wasn't notorious for genuflecting in the cathedral filled
with the faithful in front of the altars of culture.*

A Dada poem of pure chance such as "when the dogs cross
the air" can be read, then, as an exuberant, malicious, comic
attack on the poem as it has existed from Homer to Paul Valéry.
"Leaving the Atocha Station" simply carries the assault into the

---

* Nothing illustrates and also proves the point of the Dada spirit better
than the famous Dada "event" held in April 1920 in Cologne by Hans Arp,
Johannes Baargeld and Max Ernst. As Hans Richter describes it in his
recent *Dada Art and Anti-Art:* "Someone had warned the police that the
Dadaists were worse than the Communists. The authorities lost no time in
closing the 'Event'. It was not hard to find a pretext: the exhibition could
only be entered through the *pissoir* of a beer-hall, frequented by unsuspect-
ing beer-drinkers. The users of the *pissoir*, attracted by the din which came
from the other side, came through and found themselves in the middle of
a Dada exhibition. This Dada-Fair was crammed with all sorts of suggestive
objects, collages and photomontages. People were reciting poems into which
the hearer could project his wildest fantasies. The unexpected shock received by the customers of the beer-hall led to such a commotion that the
police came and closed the Fair. They more or less assumed it to be a
gathering of homosexuals. On closer inspection, it became apparent that
the only morally objectionable object in the exhibition was by a certain
Albrecht Dürer . . . and the Fair was re-opened."

present, spoofing, by implication, such milestones as "The Waste Land" or "Howl." Now, enjoying a poem because its unintelligibility pokes fun at the great, enriching intelligibility of "The Waste Land" and "Howl" may not be everybody's idea of one of the more cultivated pleasures of poetry; but I confess that this quality makes "Leaving the Atocha Station" more precious in my books than any number of well-behaved poems written in the tradition of Eliot or Ginsberg.

Once Ashbery's poem is seen as being a member of the Dada family, the reader begins to notice how it shares certain specific genetic characteristics with the Dada poets and painters.

The most obvious trait is the general sense that the reader has wandered into somebody else's dream or hallucination. Dada and its often ungrateful son Surrealism were of course pioneers in the Indian territory of the unconscious as it manifests itself in dreams, hallucinations, irrational imagery and startling combinations between persons, places and things. As Lautréamont's celebrated simile testifies: "He is as handsome as the accidental encounter on a dissecting table between an umbrella and a sewing machine." So too in Ashbery. Honey might be produced in the Arctic, a menacing prayer "folds," the scrolls are drunk, the prank is an epileptic, the sewer opens "their books"—and so on.

Once I'd seen such images as having come from the tradition of the irrational image of Dada and Surrealism, I wondered whether Ashbery's poem might also be read as either a dream pure and simple or as a text embodying the Surrealist dogma expressed by André Breton's rhetorical question: "What if everything in the Beyond is actually here, now, in the present, with us?"

Is the poem a dream or nightmare? Clearly much of it sounds like a crazy quilt of images from the unconscious of the poet. When I reread the entire poem, however, it sounds almost too studied—this will come as much of a surprise to the reader, I am sure, as it did to me—and too "coherent" and not coherent enough to be exclusively a dream. On the one hand, the poem lacks that dizzy and irrational freedom which most dreams exhibit; and on the other, it doesn't exclusively contain that hidden unconscious wish any dream embodies.

Before we leave the quality of the dream in this poem,

however, we should consider this possibility: "Leaving the Atocha Station" can be read as depicting a traveler dozing and "sleeping in snatches" and dreaming, but awakened abruptly as the train stops or jerks along, and looking out of the window at the garden and at such activity as loading formaldehyde in the Atocha Station (in this reading the train arrives at the Atocha Station, only one of its stops) and at such happenings as the scarecrow falling down in some field and the passing light which contains fuzz—and so on. Then he dozes and dreams again; he awakes again—and so on and on.

Then it is a Surrealist poem? No. When I say that the poem seems too incoherent and at the same time too multiple in its possible readings, the reader may well feel tempted to throw in the towel and perhaps long—as I often have as I've tried to finish this essay—for a poem as old-fashioned in its difficulties as "The Wreck of the Deutschland" or "Howl." But bear with me. Classic Surrealist poems are often texts embodying a fascinating experience of the metamorphosis of the poet as he begins or comes upon himself engaged in the perilous descent into the underworld of the unconscious—or, as an orthodox Surrealist would prefer, into the true reality beyond and below the visible and concrete world we inhabit. "Vigilence" by Breton is a good example. As far as I can see, "Leaving the Atocha Station" contains no such metamorphosis. Indeed, it might even be argued that the concluding phrase "next time around" suggests that the poet sits in a train on the Vico railroad. Everything will be the same once he leaves the Atocha Station next month or next year.

What are some of the other genetic traits "Leaving the Atocha Station" shares with Dada?

Jokes or wit from the unconscious clearly is one such trait. Doesn't the very first line—"The arctic honey blabbed over the report causing darkness"— sound as comic as these classic 1916 Dada lines by Richard Huelsenbeck: "The cows sit on the telegraph poles and play chess/The cuckoo under the skirts of the Spanish dancer"; and "Have you seen the fish that've been standing in front of the opera in cutaways/For the last two nights and days?"; and "If only somebody had the nerve to rip the tail feathers from the streetcar it's a great age"? What makes such lines funny is of course their childlike or dreamlike capacity to combine things not normally associated. Honey from the Arctic is as amusing as the fact that the flea is "exalting" or that the bats on sale are "fried." Then there's such zany, erotic but nonsensical Dada lines as "the clean fart genital enthusiastic toe prick album serious."

Sly parodies of famous modern poems is another genetic trait "Leaving the Atocha Station" shares with Dada. Everybody will remember the superb portrait "LHOOQ" created in 1919 by Duchamp when he drew a graceful moustache and goatee on a print of the "Mona Lisa." Or Picabia's 1920 "Portrait de Cézanne" which consists of a toy monkey tacked to a bulletin board, its tail poking through its legs like an erect penis, and four titles written around the four corners of the board: "Portrait de Cézanne," "Portrait de Rembrandt," "Portrait de Renoir" and "Natures Mortes." In much the same spirit, lines in the Ashbery poem such as "the garden are you boning/and defunct covering . . .   Blind dog expressed royalties" echo and parody the well-known questions addressed to Stetson in "The Waste Land":

> "That corpse you planted last year in your garden,
> "Has it begun to sprout? Will it bloom this year?
> "Or has the sudden frost disturbed its bed?
> "Oh keep the Dog far hence, that's friend to men,
> "Or with his nails he'll dig it up again!

And we smile at Ashbery's clever twist: the menacing wolf in Webster's original lines which Eliot parodies by changing the wolf into "man's best friend" is not only blind (here his master becomes "dog's best friend") but he expresses royalties instead of loyalties.*

* What's being parodied here is of course the *significant* irony in Eliot's passage. The hysterical questions put to Stetson point, you will remember, to the central malady shared by the inhabitants of the wasteland: they can neither die nor be reborn in either the psychological sense of growth out of infantile fantasies and into sexual maturity or in the religious sense of entrance into eternal life. In short, they're the "luke-warm" whom neither God nor Satan desire (and whom Dante observes in the memorable

Another literary parody might be seen in the allusion to Valéry's famous doves pecking on the roof while sunlight blazes incandescently on the ocean in "Le Cimetière marin." In Ashbery's poem the sun becomes a toilet "blazing" (with what deposit one forebears to investigate) while the beautiful doves turn into everyday pigeons: "the worn stool blazing   pigeons from the roof." Still another literary spoof seems contained in images of the coughing person, slacks and peaches in the concluding lines which recall the familiar goat that "coughs at night in the field overhead" in "Gerontion" and Prufrock's white flannel trousers and immortal question: "Do I dare to eat a peach?" And I have a hunch the alert reader will discover still other parodies of famous poems. Is there a joke, for example, intended at the expense of Hopkins' "Márgarét, are you grieving/Over Goldengrove unleaving?" in the sense and sound of "the garden are you boning/and defunct covering"? Do you hear an echo of Pound's miraculous "In the gloom the gold/ Gathers the light about it" in the wryly comic "it was fuzz on the passing light" where fuzz suggests the slang term for police— tracking down bank robbers who've stolen gold? (Such detective work is fun, isn't it?)

Our main job, however, remains to be done: How do all of these various readings—as contradictory as most of them appear —contribute to our experience that we're reading one poem and not three or four or ten different poems?

One thing is evident about both the multiple readings and the fact of the question itself. Both are predicated on the

---

section at the beginning of the *Inferno*). Stetson resembles one of the crew of the *Flying Dutchman* in the sense that not only has he fought in the sea battle at Mylae in 260 BC when the Roman fleet defeated a superior Carthaginian squadron during the First Punic War but he walks over London Bridge one morning during the early 1920s, presumably bound for work in one of the law offices or banks of The City. Stetson's dog becomes, in turn, the ironic antithesis of Webster's wolf mentioned in the famous dirge sung by the mad woman to her son over the corpse of his brother whom he's slain in *The White Devil*: "But keep the wolf far thence, that's foe to men,/For with his nails he'll dig it up again." At least the wolf can find a corpse. There is no corpse of course in Stetson's garden. Inhabitants of the wasteland are neither alive nor dead in any significant way.

assumption that lines which contain the description of the train ride, say, or the Dada jokes or the sense that the poem as a whole is an example of Vico's Eternal Return, form organic and coherent wholes. This assumption itself is grounded on another which we seldom if ever question: namely, lines in a poem remain stationary. No matter how difficult or obscure or ambiguous lines such as "Altarwise by owl-light in the half-way house/ The gentleman lay graveward with his furies," the reader feels assured that their riddle can be solved in the sense that the lines will not mean anything more than what they mean.

The question is: Do the lines in "Leaving the Atocha Station" remain stationary?

Let's look again at the Blind dog/Stetson unit. Notice how we read these lines as if isolated from the stanza in which they occur. But when we reread the stanza itself, one thing becomes clear as early as the opening lines: capital letters begin each of the first two lines but the third opens with a lower case "h," although the punctuation doesn't indicate that the three lines are not part of one sentence. What does this accomplish? One result is that the reader begins to question his original reaction: Why assume that the first two lines make one unit? Lack of a period at the end of line one and the connective "And" prompted me to read both lines as forming one unit; but now I'm not sure.

And I feel even more uncertain when I notice how at first the dots and spaces suggest an ellipsis in the third line below but then how the ellipsis tends to vanish into unrelated phrases:

> he meanwhile . . .   And the fried bats they sell there
> dropping from sticks, so that the menace of your prayer
>   folds . . .
> Other people . . .   flash
> the garden are you boning
> and defunct covering . . .   Blind dog expressed royalties
>   . . .
> comfort of your perfect tar grams nuclear world bank
>   tulip
> Favorable to   near the night pin
> loading formaldehyde.   the table torn from you

Notice how the ellipsis ("Other people . . .   flash/garden")
is both created and spotlighted by the fact that only five spaces
separate both "he meanwhile . . ." from the fried bats and the
"defunct covering . . ." from the blind dog. If these last two units
had eleven spaces separating their parts—as the ellipsis has—
then there'd be no ellipsis. But there does seem to be an ellipsis
which reads something like this: "Here the poet creates a vivid
visual sense of how people and scenery (the garden) —or are
the people in the garden?—seem to flash by his window in the
train."

The problem is that this never occurs again in the poem.
No dots exist in the next three "ellipses" in stanza one and for
no apparent reason six (not five or eleven) spaces separate the
decrepit mayor from the flea at the end of stanza three. Once
again, the reader's natural preconception becomes frustrated.
If the dots and spaces are anarchic throughout the poem, then
can we assume that the original ellipsis exists in the first place?
In addition, the reader begins to question his basic preconception that words or phrases in the same line must somehow
have a relationship with one another. In short, he questions
again if words in a line form a unit at all.

In specific, he might begin to question the Blind dog/Stetson
unit itself. What authority is given by the poem as a *whole* to
consider the first two lines of this unit as creating a unit in the
first place? None. Nothing prevents the reader from discovering
the Blind dog/Stetson parody in the lines; but nothing prevents
him from breaking the "unit" into smaller and totally unrelated units or fragments.

One such unit could read: "the garden are you boning/and
defunct covering . . ." Two more units could be made by splitting
the first unit into: "the garden are you boning" and "and defunct covering." And these two might, in turn, be broken into—
how many even smaller "units"? Five? Ten? The possibilities
multiply in a dizzy way when one realizes that the blind dog
could belong to an entirely different unit than to the original
Eliot one: "Blind dog expressed royalties . . .

        comfort of your perfect tar grams nuclear world bank
            tulip

Favorable to   near the night pin
loading formaldehyde. the table torn from you
Suddenly   and we are close
Mouthing the root

At this point, the reader probably anticipates the next possibility, which is this: nothing prevents Reader A from breaking the words or phrases in any one line into as many combinations as he can create, whereas Reader B may choose to combine the same words or phrases into quite different units, whereas Reader C might want to leave the words and phrases alone and try to read them as they appear in the poem. Reader A can also see the lines at different times in the way in which B or C read them—and vice versa.

Take the very first line: "The arctic honey blabbed over the report causing darkness." How do you read this line? Normally, one tends to read it as a sentence (however nonsensical its meaning). Its subject is "the arctic honey," its predicate "blabbed," and "the report" is clearly the object of the preposition "over." Nothing in the poem, however, stops the reader from reading the line as if it contained five unrelated words and phrases:

The arctic/honey/blabbed/over the report/causing
darkness

or from finding in the line any other combinations:

The/arctic honey/blabbed over/the report/causing/
darkness
The arctic honey blabbed/over/the/report/causing
darkness
The arctic honey blabbed over the report causing darkness

The blind dog, in other words, need not always be blind. Nor are Stetson's dog or the mad mother's wolf always implied because of the parody. Nor do "royalties" always mean: "a payment made to an author or composer for each copy of his work sold or to an investor for each article sold under a patent." Royalties can also mean persons of royal lineage, as well as "rights of jurisdiction granted to an individual or corporation by a sovereign." And so on and on through the other meanings of the word in the dictionary.

Then where are we? "In the thirteenth act of *No Exit!*" some readers may feel tempted to exclaim.

Where we seem to be is face to face with a paradox. At one time, this poem clearly contains such "islands" of significance as the suspicion that we're at times inside a dream or laughing at Dada jokes or literary parodies or observing the shadowy narrative of a train ride through the Spanish landscape. At other times, these islands sink from sight as the lines or words which create them suddenly begin to evaporate and form new and totally independent wholes to which the entire poem contributes or form isolated units or isolated images or phrases or words.

One such whole begins to appear when we begin to respond to the hints of poignancy, often undercut by irony or snide humor, which pervade the entire poem. Notice how good a case can be made for a reading which suggests something like this: "The poem embodies the feelings of someone who is leaving another who clearly is being missed by the traveller."

Images of cold and darkness reoccur, for instance, throughout the three stanzas: the arctic, darkness, the dark blood of shopkeepers on strike, the ice falling off the port, night and the stars—and so on. Images of menace also become apparent: the enveloping darkness in the opening line, the menace of the prayer, the table torn from somebody, rats, vultural, the air pollution, the flood. Moreover, the relationship is (or was) sexual. "Suddenly   and we are close/Mouthing the root" could be a fellatio image. And the goofy Dada line we saw a moment ago—"the clean fart genital enthusiastic toe prick album serious"—can reveal a memory of two lovers, limbs entwined or at least intimately close to one another, enthusiastic over each other but "serious" for a moment as they leaf through some album. Occasional hints of anal sexuality also appear: the worn stool "blazing," the "clean" fart, the sewer.

Finally, the person sitting on the train may also be sore at the beloved. "Absolute mush" could read as an explosive, angry gloss on the relationship; that stark "fist" near the end could mean exactly what it says; and the final phrase "next time around" could be the cynical or bitter feeling with which the speaker comments on love affairs in general.

Here the ambiguity seems to be: How can someone who's remembering a beloved be distracted by so much that's irrelevant, inane or funny? A case might be made, I suppose, that the speaker is napping fitfully or attempting to disguise deep or hurt feelings by permitting such mundane distractions to float through consciousness. In any event, what we have seems to be still another way in which the poem might be read.

To the objection that such readings are too subjective I can only remind us that the poem itself encourages the reader to make of it what he chooses or has the wit to discover. But let me stress this: the reader is encouraged to do this *within* the world of the poem. "Leaving the Atocha Station" isn't a poem which means anything or nothing. What the something which it "means" might be is of course the challenge.

Whatever "Leaving the Atocha Station" might mean, the poem clearly encourages what looks like total freedom within its three stanzas.*

One of the ways in which such freedom is made available is of course through the reeducation of our natural preconception that a poem will in the end reveal only one coherent or organic unity. So far, "Leaving the Atocha Station" reveals at least five or six separate "poems"—and more no doubt exist.

On the one hand, the poem might be read as the description of a journey taken by a person who fears that either a relationship or love affair is over or that it's being menaced in a crucial way. On the other, it can be read as a totally meaningless poem. On still another, it clearly contains a salad of bits of dreams

---

* Or are there four? The text in *The Tennis Court Oath* occupies two pages. "Exalting flea" are the last words on page one. Nothing guarantees, however, that "for the next time around" begins a fresh stanza. Such textual criticism is of course almost Alexandrian in its nicety; but I find this small point fascinating when trying to think about the poem as a whole: it is typical of the ambiguity of readings which pervade the poem.

mixed with prosaic facts from railroad stations and landscape. On yet a fourth hand, the poem might be a wonderful toy containing Dada jokes or parodies of Old Masters that lies in some corner of the nursery otherwise filled by adult and irrelevant or meaningless words such as: "he meanwhile," "your prayer," "when you think," "Time, progress and good sense," "The centennial," "Before we can," "That is, he said," "next time around"—and so on. In this sense, the poem can be said to parody the traditional English or American poem—or, for that matter, the traditional poem as it has been written since Homer's time.

On still a fifth hand, "Leaving the Atocha Station" is clearly a work in which multiple combinations of words and images (islands of significance) continually form, dissolve, and reform again in fresh and totally original combinations, having nothing to do with what they signified the last time one read the poem. Let's look, for example, at the opening of stanza three:

> old   eat
> members with their chins
>   so high up   rats
>   relaxing the cruel discussion
>   suds   the painted corners
>   white   most aerial
>   garment crow
>   and when the region took us
>   back
>   the person left us like birds

Thanks to the freedom made available by the poet, we're free, for example, to isolate the word

> old

and experience it simply by itself. Or the reader might form a unit from the nine lines which could be paraphrased something like this: "Old people care only about eating. They also 'eat' each other. They look like rats. Let's wipe away such a cruel, ugly scene ('relaxing the cruel discussion/suds') by escaping like birds." Or he can enjoy what happens when this smaller unit forms itself: "and when the region took us back/the person left us like birds" in which birds is a simile for the flight of the person. Even this lovely island disappears when one reads the last line as: "The person left us as if we were only fowl;" or: "the person left" and "us" and "like birds" are independent from each other.

And on still a sixth hand, the reader might look at this poem as if he were watching the Six Days of Creation and hadn't been taught yet what to think about what he sees. Let individual words flash by and allow free play for whatever combinations may occur:

> The arctic. Honey. Arctic honey. Blabbed. Over. Reports. Causing. Causing darkness. Darkness. And. Pulling. Us. Pulling us out of there. Experiencing. It. Pulling out out of there experiencing it. He. Meanwhile. And the fried bats they sell there. Fried. Bats. They. Sell. There. Bats dropping from sticks. Bats dropping. Sticks. So. So that. So that the. The menace. The menace of your prayer. Your prayer. Your prayer "folds." Folds. Prayer folds other people.

And so on, miraculously, to:

> Cattle. False. False cattle. Loam. False loam. Loam imports. Imports next time. Next. Time. Around. Next time around. Leaving the Atocha Station. Leaving. The Atocha. Station. The arctic honey blabbed. Over the report.

And so on and on.

In addition, the poem offers—on yet a seventh hand—the possibility of an experience of simultaneity. Nothing prevents the reader from keeping in mind all of the ways of seeing the poem as he rereads it. No one way—either Dada jokes or poignant love affair or Adam looking at Creation or whatever—has priority over or more significance than any other. All exist simultaneously.

A final freedom exists of course in the lack of any one definitive or correct reading. At one time, "Leaving the Atocha

Station" can be read as an anti-poem; at another, as a classroom for the reeducation of the reader (and, by implication, of the poet too) ; and at another, as a parable of the origin of the Tower of Babel or of the existential dogma which states that "existence preceeds essence"; or at still another, as a wonderfully silly toy. In brief, the reader should feel free to do whatever he wants with the words in this poem.

He may even decide never to look at the poem again. Such freedom can be frightening and demanding. How many of us would really want to be Adam—or Eve? Freedom like this can also be frustrating: it remains oblivious of that need felt by many teachers of poetry, critics and graduate students to work on a poem complicated enough to require explication de texte by this or that critical discipline.

But I also suspect some readers will respond to Ashbery's invitation that the reader too become a poet as he rereads "Leaving the Atocha Station." This is of course only another way of suggesting that if the poem had left from the Finland Station, the reader would have been asked to remain in his traditional role as critic observing a poem but not as poet helping to create it.

Finally, what is the image of the poet in "Leaving the Atocha Station"? To see him merely as a magician is not quite accurate. To see him only as heartbroken lover who distracts himself with the toy of this poem is sentimental, it seems to me, and also an easy way to avoid the freedoms within the poems made possible by this artist. I like to think of the poet in the role of Louis Agassiz in the familiar anecdote about the student and the fish which Pound was fond of using as an example of how one might learn to look at a work of art with one's own eyes. Here's the anecdote:

One day in 1860, a student named Samuel Scudder appeared in the Professor's office in what is now the Agassiz Museum at Harvard College and told Professor Agassiz that he intended to devote himself to the study of insects. Instead of an insect, Agassiz presented him with a strong-smelling fish and told him to look at it. "By and by," Agassiz said, "I will ask what you have seen," and left the student with the fish. Here is the young entomologist's own account of what happened to him:

In ten minutes I had seen all that could be seen in that fish. Half an hour passed, an hour, another hour; the fish began to look loathsome. I turned it over and around; looked it in the face—ghastly! From behind, beneath, above, sideways, at a three-quarters view—just as ghastly. I was in despair. At an early hour I concluded that lunch was necessary; so, with infinite relief, the fish was carefully replaced in the jar, and for an hour I was free.

On my return, I learned that Professor Agassiz had been at the Museum, but had gone, and would not return for several hours. . . . . Slowly I drew forth that hideous fish, and, with a feeling of desperation, again looked at it. I might not use a magnifying glass; instruments of all kinds were interdicted. My two hands, my two eyes, and the fish; it seemed a most limited field. . . . At last a happy thought struck me—I would draw the fish; and now, with surprise, I began to discover new features in the creature. Just then the professor returned.

"That is right," said he; "a pencil is one of the best eyes. I am glad to notice, too, that you keep your specimen wet and your bottle corked." With these encouraging words, he added: "Well, what is it like?"

He listened attentively to my brief rehearsal of the structure of parts whose names were still unknown to me . . . When I had finished, he waited as if expecting more, and then, with an air of disappointment, "You have not looked very carefully; why," he continued most earnestly, "you haven't even seen one of the most conspicuous features of the animal, which is as plainly before your eyes as the fish itself. Look again! look again!" and he left me to my misery.

I was piqued; I was mortified. Still more of that wretched fish! But now I set myself to my task with a will, and discovered one new thing after another, until I saw how just the professor's criticism had been. The afternoon passed quickly, and when, toward its close, the professor inquired, "Do you see it yet?"

"No," I replied, "I am certain I do not, but I see how little I saw before."

"That is next best," said he earnestly; "but I won't

hear you now; put away your fish and go home; perhaps you will be ready with a better answer in the morning. I will examine you before you look at the fish."

This was disconcerting. Not only must I think of my fish all night, studying, without the object before me, what this but most visible feature might be, but also, without reviewing my new discoveries, I must give an exact account of them the next day. I had a bad memory, so I walked home by Charles River in a disturbed state with my two perplexities.

The cordial greeting from the professor the next morning was reassuring. Here was a man who seemed to be quite as anxious as I that I should see for myself what he saw.

"Do you perhaps mean," I asked, "that the fish has symmetrical sides with paired organs?"

His thoroughly pleased "Of course, of course!" repaid the wakeful hours of the previous night. After he had discoursed most happily and enthusiastically—as he always did—upon the importance of this point, I ventured to ask what I should do next.

"Oh, look at your fish!" he said, and left me again to my own devices. In a little more than an hour he returned and heard my new catalogue.

"That is good, that is good," he repeated; "but that is not all; go on." And so for three long days he placed that fish before my eyes, forbidding me to look at anything else or to use any artificial aid. "Look! look! look!" was his repeated injunction.

This was the best ontomological lesson I ever had— a lesson whose influence has extended to the details of every subsequent study; a legacy that professor has left to me, as he left it to many others, of inestimable value, which we could not buy, with which we cannot part.

Appendix One

The dialogue which makes modern literary citicism so wealthy and stimulating was created and explored in books such as these: R. P. Blackmur: *Form and Value in Modern Poetry*

(1957). Cleanth Brooks: *The Well Wrought Urn* (1947). Cleanth Brooks and Robert Penn Warren: *Understanding Poetry* (1938). Kenneth Burke: *The Grammar of Motives* (1945) and *The Grammar of Rhetoric* (1950). Ronald Crane: *Critics and Criticism* (1952). T. S. Eliot: *Selected Essays* (1935). William Empson: *Seven Types of Ambiguity* (1930). Ezra Pound: *Literary Essays* (1963). John Crowe Ransom: *The New Criticism* (1941). I. A. Richards: *Principles of Literary Criticism* (1924). Allen Tate: *The Man of Letters in the Modern World: Essays 1928–1955* (1955). Yvor Winters: *In Defense of Reason* (1947).

*   *   *

Among recent critics, the late Randall Jarrell's *Poetry and the Age* (1953) is the most joyous and sane discussion of modern poetry I know. In every sense his criticism is the enemy of much of what parades as literary criticism and which Jarrell attacked for being "astonishingly graceless, joyless, humorless, long-winded, niggling, blinkered, methodical, self-important, cliché-ridden, prestige-obsessed, and almost autonomous."

Two valuable collections which explore many of the poets of the generation discussed in this book are: James Dickey: *Babel to Byzantium* (1968) and Ralph J. Mills, Jr.: *Contemporary American Poetry* (1965). And I hope that Robert Bly—the most stimulating, active and at times exasperating critic today—will soon publish a collection of his essays and book reviews.

Robert Creeley

A WICKER BASKET

Comes the time when it's later
and onto your table the headwaiter
puts the bill, and very soon after
rings out the sound of lively laughter—

Picking up change, hands like a walrus,
and a face like a barndoor's,
and a head without any apparent size,
nothing but two eyes—

So that's you, man,
or me. I make it as I can,
I pick up, I go
faster than they know—

Out the door, the street like a night,
any night, and no one in sight,
but then, well, there she is,
old friend Liz—

And she opens the door of her cadillac,
I step in back,
and we're gone.
She turns me on—

There are very huge stars, man, in the sky,
and from somewhere very far off someone hands me a slice of
      apple pie,
with a gob of white, white ice cream on top of it,
and I eat it—

Slowly. And while certainly
they are laughing at me, and all around me is racket
of these cats not making it, I make it

in my wicker basket.

THE SCENE
IN THE WICKER BASKET

Reading Robert Creeley's "A Wicker Basket" when it first appeared in 1956 was a shock and a delight: here was one of the first poems—if not the first—to describe the experience of getting high on marijuana and the first to speak in the authentic stance and idiom of the hipster. This poem not only brought into American poetry a taboo experience but it did so in a pose cool, sardonic and witty. "A Wicker Basket" is so hip, in fact, that it seems clumsy and square even to wonder about the ambiguity raised by the experience being described, particularly in the final lines:

> And while certainly
> they are laughing at me, and all around me is racket
> of these cats not making it, I make it
>
> in my wicker basket.

What does the speaker "make"? In the context of the ending of the poem, it appears perfectly obvious: he reaches that state of euphoria, that high, which smoking marijuana often creates. Time seems to stand still; the top of one's head feels filled with heaven; and everything seems better and easier to do. And in the context of the poem as a whole, the speaker also makes it in the sense of getting away from the awkward, irritating scene in the restaurant when he felt so dragged that his hands were "like a walrus," his face "like a barndoor's" and he had no head —only two eyes. Finally, there's the possibility that he feels he's made it with "old friend Liz"—not in the sense of having intercourse for he seems alone in the back seat ("my wicker basket") but in the sense of enjoying some kind of pleasant sexual awareness of her, which becomes part of his general euphoric high.

The several meanings of "make" suggested by the poem appear to add up to one experience: the hipster in "A Wicker

Basket" flees a square and unpleasant scene in a fancy restaurant and reaches a good high on marijuana in which he feels secure, superior, comfortable and fed, as well as sexy and grateful toward Liz who has rescued him in her car and turned him on. Creeley's poem, it might be said, describes a kind of miniature Pilgrim's Progress of Hip, moving from the City of Destruction and Square to the Celestial City of High.

Then why does the hip speaker sound increasingly angry and vexed as he tells of making it? Let's listen to how he *sounds:*

> She turns me on—
>
> There are very huge stars, man, in the sky,
> and from somewhere very far off someone hands me a
>   slice of apple pie
> with a gob of white, white ice cream on top of it,
> and I eat it—
>
> Slowly. And while certainly
> they are laughing at me, and all around me is racket
> of these cats not making it, I make it
>
> in my wicker basket.

When read aloud, the long, leisurely, predominately soft or open-vowelled high feeling of the three lines describing the apple pie a la mode is abruptly undercut by the hard, angry sound of the following line. If my ear hears this line correctly, all four words demand a clenched, explosive accent: "ánd Í eát ít." But the euphoric feeling begins again with the soft, seemingly delighted "slowly" and it is enhanced by the soft sounds of "while," "they," "laughing," "all" and "me"—only to be undercut, this time more emphatically, by the harshly muscular sounds of "racket," "cats," "not," "making," "it," "make," "it," "wicker," "basket." Both end and internal (full and half) rhymes only accentuate the feeling that the speaker is sore: "it/it," "racket/it/basket," and "rack/make/wick," "cat/not," "it/it/basket."

Our paraphrase says that this is a poem which ends in good pot feelings of making it; the hipster's voice, however, sounds as though his teeth are grating in rage.

The paradox here comes of course from what Cleanth Brooks so helpfully describes as the heresy or fallacy of paraphrase. No matter how accurate or comprehensive the paraphrase of a poem may be, it can only describe the skeleton of the experience contained in the poem. When it's a question of what the experience *feels* like and (in the deepest sense) is, the paraphrase tells us next to nothing and, in fact, it can often mislead or distort the reading of the poem. In the hands of a good poet like Creeley, what the poem is—its skin, blood and organs, as it were—is embodied in the subtleties of style: imagery, sound, line breaks, rhyme, and even in such elements as the look of the poem on the page, punctuation or lack of it, capital letters or lack of them for the first word of a new line, stanza breaks— and so on. These are the living elements that animate the skeleton, offering that kind of *total* experience which a good poem affords.

Let us return, then, to the paradox that the hipster says he's made it and presumably feels happy, while at the same time he sounds angry. This reopens the original question: What does the speaker "make"? The poem tells us quite clearly. But it doesn't explain or analyze; instead, the poem gives us the experience in all of its complexity and ambiguity of feeling and attitude.

One way the poem does this is through the cunning ambivalence of the central image which dominates the poem: the image of food. For example, why is the only "real" food mentioned a fantasy image created by pot—that marvelous slice of apple pie a la mode? In the opening scene in the restaurant, we never hear about what the speaker ate, much less whether his meal was tasty or mediocre or awful. Even more puzzling: one guesses that if the restaurant has a headwaiter, then it is probably a fairly decent place with a sophisticated menu and wine list. All the reader knows, however, is that the speaker dislikes the restaurant. We don't even know for certain that he ate. Only when he sucks on the stick of marijuana is he fed; but, as we've noticed, he "eats" the fantasy dessert with half-clenched teeth. In a moment I want to return to the image of food. Here we'll notice only that the image contains two things: fantasy and anger.

Ambivalence also seems evident in his feelings about who is feeding him. How does he feel about old friend Liz? At first, he clearly seems to dig her. Liz represents the exact opposite of the square restaurant where he felt stiff and ill at ease. Not only does she have pot but she drives—not the expected Volkswagen or souped-up stock car but one of the icons of the square world: a Cadillac. Irony like this is merry hip. But isn't his mention of her slightly deprecatory—even patronizing?

> but then well, there she is,
> old friend Liz—
>
> And she opens the door of her cadillac,
> I step in back

Why does he get in the back seat? Mention of the "they" who are laughing at him and of the racket of "these cats not making it" may suggest that there are others crowded in Liz's Cadillac; but it isn't clear that they actually are in the front seat. Those who are laughing and the poor "cats" could just as well be figments of a certain mild paranoia which pot sometimes encourages. Whether or not others are in the car, it is evident that the hipster has little or no relationship with Liz. Her only role, in fact, is to rescue him by supplying pot; she remains faceless. And once he's turned on, the relationship with her couldn't be less remote: he's all alone when he makes it in his "wicker basket."

And isn't there an ambivalence too about the other source of food: the mysterious, faceless "someone" who from somewhere very far away brings that slice of apple pie? This is a wonderful, felicitous pot image. But it's also an odd one—as far as the speaker's feelings are involved. An anonymous hand supplies the one item of "real" food in the poem. The hipster views this benefactor as if going through chow line in the Army and not noticing the faceless private who dishes out the soup. Here the ambivalence is in his negation of the personality of "someone": he's even less involved with the "person" who supplies the pie which helps him finally make it than he is with anyone else in the poem.

Why? Once again, the images tell us quite clearly. What does it feel like when he makes it? He's in a wicker basket. Here's another good, witty pot image; but it also suggests that to make the high here is to feel as if he's become an infant again, cozy and safe in the crib. (Puppies and kittens also live in wicker baskets but I think it would be silly and a wrenching of the poem to suggest that the speaker here feels like one of them.) In short, the hipster makes it by fantasizing he's become an infant again. Or it's probably more accurate to say: he experiences a vivid memory of feelings from infancy. Exactly what feelings we'll have to find out. One thing appears certain: they're ambivalent emotions associated with food. On the one hand, he feels cozy, comfortable, secure; on the other, angry, irritable, disrupted.

Let's go back to the restaurant to find out more about where these discordant feelings might have come from.

> Comes the time when it's later
> and onto your table the headwaiter
> puts the bill, and very soon after
> rings out the sound of lively laughter—

One delights in how the speaker here reveals distaste by describing the scene in the restaurant in a mock courtly, almost elegantly old-fashioned style: he "out-Herods Herod," as it were. But the reader never learns what's irritated him. Is it the bill? Lively laughter may suggest that the joke's on him because he gets stuck with a whopping tab; but the laughter could just as easily be seen as part of the general atmosphere in the restaurant or even the speaker's sardonic, cool way to describe annoyance. And with whom has he eaten? Boring company? Or is he alone? Omission of all these facts suggests a strange but obvious conclusion: it doesn't matter whom he's with or what has annoyed him; what matters is that he feels sore at the dinner table. In other words, he's beginning to get angry about food and the fact that others are being fed in an elegant restaurant.

And once he escapes and gets "fed" himself, he feels at first euphoric but ends by being more angry than ever. It sounds

like he's reliving an oral tantrum. Ancient emotions are floating up from memories in the unconscious until they beleaguer
and dominate the present scene. Beginning with the memory
of sour, irritable feelings of being deprived of food, the poem
shifts to an attempt to compensate by eating that fantasy pie,
only to end in the harsh rage of clenched teeth.

Earlier I suggested that "A Wicker Basket" might be a Pilgrim's Progress of High; it now seems more accurate to call it a
Hip Schlauraffenland lost and found and lost again.*

What does it mean, then, when the hipster says: "I make it,/
in my wicker basket"? Clearly it's more complex than we first
thought. He makes it back to an infantile state of irritation,
temporary euphoria and then rage over feeling deprived, fed
and deprived again. Why on earth make it back there? I think
we all know the answer. Not only was the maternal breast the
first but in some ways it remains the most vivid experience of
love and hate when we were simultaneously the center of existence and often abruptly dislocated and fearfully alone.

The ambivalences found a moment ago should seem clearer
now. Look at the image of food. Hors d'oeurves, entreé and
dessert are noticeably absent in the restaurant; the slice of apple
pie a la mode is a fantasy of the miraculous breast returned;
but the euphoria only recalls fierce emotions of a tantrum over
being deprived once again. (The joint of marijuana is, in this

---

* Schlauraffenland ("The Country of the Lazy Ones") is of course the old
German term for the Land of Cockaigne. As far as we know, this mock
country was created by medieval satirists in order to poke fun at the idealis-
tic conceptions of paradise (both religious and secular) prominent throughout the Middle Ages. Traditionally, Schlauraffenland is an island beyond
the horizon where wonders of effortless supply abound. Roast geese chase
themselves down the street, turning over on their backs as they flee, so that
even the laziest person can simply reach out and grab one; broiled fish serve
themselves; roast pigs and geese carrying knives in their sides are always
near at hand; rivers of wine, milk or beer flow forever and at certain times
during the week gentle rains of soup fall; houses are built of cake and other
pastries. In Schlauraffenland men and women are paid to eat and sleep
instead of being paid to work. Conditions are always serene: there are no
deaths or futile disputes and, above all, no ugly females. The most famous
portrait of this good land is the Pieter Brueghel painting "The Land of
Cockaigne" hanging in the Alte Pinakothekin in Münich depicting a
peasant, soldier and scholar sprawled beneath a tree which grows through
a round table on which within easy reach are such delicacies as a broiled
rabbit, pigs' feet, cakes and a jug of wine or milk.

sense, almost like the speaker's muse in a way not dissimilar to the muse invoked by Virgil at the beginning of *The Aeneid*: "Musa mihi causas memora" ("O muse, bring back into my memory the origin (or cause) ".) Then there's the ambivalence about Liz and the anonymous "someone." Both stand for the faceless mother who feeds but deprives.

This chronic ambivalence pervading the poem may help to clarify the final ambivalence: the speaker's attitude. Clearly he feels an increasing sense of paranoia about the faceless "them." Beginning as merely lively laughter, they become the hostile "they" who laugh derisively and also the "cats" surrounding the wicker basket. "They" appear as shadowy but antagonistic as brother or sister or (more ominously) father once appeared to an infant aware that the unalienable right to be fed and loved is not always his alone. But notice how cool, sardonic and witty is his attitude about "them." The hip stance permits him to feel superior to his shadowy enemies; if he's not indeed the cool center of existence, then he's at least (in fantasy) the most superior one around.

But his hip attitude is also very seductive. To whom does he talk, for instance, in lines such as "so that's you, man,/or me"? Clearly the reader. Why? One result is that he invites the reader to join in the tantrum which almost everyone remembers; and, in this sense, the speaker may be trying to excuse his self-indulgence and what sounds like awkward, if not rude, manners in the restaurant and later in the car. But the second result is more basic: he strives to create intimacy. Lack of intimacy is the root of the uncomfortable tantrum. Here he tries to exorcise the uncomfortable feelings. But the intimacy is only an illusion. The reader remains even more faceless than the other people in the poem. "A Wicker Basket" ends in excruciating loneliness.

The poem embodies, in short, the complex experience of an adult suffering the reliving of infantile oral rage, which he tries to escape from (or compensate for) by getting high on pot and creating a fantasy that he is not only fed, cozy and secure, but that he's once again at the center of existence at the gigantic Claes Oldenburg breast. He makes it and he doesn't make it.

Feelings of anger, self-indulgence and irritation are never pretty. Creeley could have "used" them to write another kind of poem—say, a satire or put-down of the square world. That would have been easy. It's entirely to his credit, it seems to me, that he refuses to shun any of the embarrassing or ugly areas of his experience. "A Wicker Basket" calls a tantrum by its right name.

To the reader who may object that this type of psychoanalytical criticism only violates or distorts this good hip poem, I would like to suggest that he look again at another poem which might profit from the analytical approach: Keats' "Ode on Melancholy." Consider, for example, the relationship between the question, Why is the speaker melancholy? and the central image of bitter and joyous food which dominates the poem. You might also want to explore: Who is the Queen "veil'd Melancholy" who can only be seen by "him whose strenuous tongue/Can burst Joy's grape against his palate fine"? By this comparison I suggest no more than this: Creeley, like Keats, does the job of the poet in that he tells the truth of an experience whose origins are rooted in universal infantile experiences of delight and rage.

James Dickey

THE HEAVEN OF ANIMALS

Here they are. The soft eyes open.
If they have lived in a wood
It is a wood.
If they have lived on plains
It is grass rolling
Under their feet forever.

Having no souls, they have come,
Anyway, beyond their knowing.
Their instincts wholly bloom
And they rise.
The soft eyes open.

To match them, the landscape flowers,
Outdoing, desperately
Outdoing what is required:
The richest wood,
The deepest field.

For some of these,
It could not be the place
It is, without blood.
These hunt, as they have done,
But with claws and teeth grown perfect,

More deadly than they can believe.
They stalk more silently,
And crouch on the limbs of trees,
And their descent
Upon the bright backs of their prey

May take years
In a sovereign floating of joy.
And those that are hunted
Know this as their life,
Their reward: to walk

Under such trees in full knowledge
Of what is in glory above them,
And to feel no fear,
But acceptance, compliance.
Fulfilling themselves without pain

At the cycle's center,
They tremble, they walk
Under the tree,
They fall, they are torn,
They rise, they walk again.

THE SMELL OF BLOOD
IN PARADISE

Due to the lucid, unambiguous vocabulary in "The Heaven of Animals," the quiet authority in the voice speaking, and the almost simplistic description of the environment (which in its naïveté recalls the Arcadian harmonies of Edward Hicks' painting "The Peaceable Kingdom") it is perhaps entirely natural to ignore the central issue which this poem raises: What kind of a heaven do we find ourselves in?

"Why, it's a paradise for beasts," is the answer, it would seem. By a marvelous expansion of imagination Dickey has depicted an eternal Eden for animals; and with an "art which conceals art," he has made it possible for the reader to see this heaven as if he were one of the creatures.

Notice, for example, how the landscape is seen. One may question at first the lack of vivid description in the environment in stanza one and in lines such as "The richest wood,/The deepest field." These hints of landscape appear even flatter and less colorful than the text in a reader for four-year olds (where at least basic adjectives like "green" or "tall" might render grass or wood more visible) ; and to tell us that wood and field are "richest" and "deepest" is to tell us nothing; in fact, we probably feel annoyed because such bald, declarative writing makes us do most of the work by demanding that we imagine what the richest wood or deepest field look like. This is of course quite deliberate. The unadorned description depicts how the animals themselves view their new environment: the reader is invited to see and feel through their senses. Here is cunning, if not brilliant, writing. Dickey does not encourage us to view this heaven as if we were present either as Adam naming the original animals in the Garden before the Expulsion or as men after the Fall—as hunters and masters of lions, deer, antelopes, zebras, wildebeests or cows.

No doubt this also accounts for that other curiosity: none of the beasts is named. A lion or deer opening its "soft eyes" in this eternal landscape, having come "beyond its knowing," would not catalogue the other animals by name. The careful reader will point out that the poet emphasizes the soft eyes of the animals by twice calling our attention to their opening; and the point may be raised: "Here we are not really seeing through their eyes; we are gazing *at* them." But this is, in fact, merely another piece of good writing by Dickey. Frequently when we look at animals, either at the zoo or in the front yard or living room, we do tend to look into their eyes, striving in this way to establish contact and to enter as far as possible into their existence. In "The Heaven of Animals" the soft eyes, then, are the bridge provided by the poet which permits us (whether or not we are completely aware of what is happening) to enter into their skins.

In short, the reader shares in the privilege of being in a heaven for animals only. To be here as an animal is a privilege in the sense that there seem to be no great complexities such as we remember in, say, the "Byzantium" of William Butler Yeats, with its ambiguous metamorphosis of human into artificial bird or those awesome " fresh images" created by the breaking of the "bitter furies of complexity" on the Emperor's marble dancing floor. Yet Dickey's heaven isn't a child's world. The eternal cycle of victim and slayer involves mature, perfected and powerful creatures. But the absence of complexities in either the animals' natures or in the eternal cycle of their activities suggest that this heaven is as naïve but clearly outlined as a great primitive painting by Rousseau or Edward Hicks: we always know where we are.

And the internal harmonies one discovers in this heaven are also reassuring. The total absence of conflict or discordancy suggests an orderly, even tranquil and universal concord. Both the beasts whose "reward" is to be slain over and over again and the killers who descend on their bright backs in a "sovereign floating of joy" fulfill themselves in the cycle which is perfect in the harmony of its operation. In fact, the harmony and order in this heaven recalls nothing so much as the celestial harmony evident among the spheres in the paradise of *The Divine Comedy*. In much the same way that the reader learns to see through the eyes of the animals in Dickey's poem and even comes to participate in the harmony of the cycle of slaughter and rebirth and slaughter again, Dante learns gradually how to look at the heavenly spheres as one of the immortals and finally comes to understand the universal harmony of the cycles of creation.* Each heaven possesses a harmonious order in which the creatures act according to their natures without conflict either in will or in desire. In the *Paradiso* the souls of the blessed move over "the immense ocean of Being" toward their final destination and ecstasy in the contemplation of the Beatific Vision—the "Love that moves the sun and other stars." In "The Heaven of Animals" the beasts move in an eternally harmonious cycle of prey and killer.

But is the harmony in Dickey's poem all that harmonious? The attentive reader may have noticed the two or three minor but discordant elements within the poem which, when seen together, raise the suspicion that if we're in a heaven, it's a peculiar heaven, to say the least.

Notice, for example, that all the stanzas contain five lines— except the very first one, which curiously has six. Granted that this is only a small discordancy but it prepares the reader for more important ones. Take the jarring, ambiguous intrusion of the adverb "desperately" in the third stanza:

> To match them, the landscape flowers,
> Outdoing, desperately
> Outdoing what is required:
> The richest wood,
> The deepest field.

Something is out of joint here. The unnaturalness of nature's processes in this landscape—the *desperate* effort to create a perfect environment—not only severely qualifies the celestial perfection of both that richest wood and that deepest field but also raises an important ambiguity with respect to the serenity and natural perfections suggested by the opening of two

---

* Dante's experience of the celestial harmony is of course far more complex than the reader's gradual knowledge of what it feels like to be one of the immortal beasts in "The Heaven of Animals." See Appendix One for a paraphrase of the complexity in the *Paradiso*.

stanzas—the resurrection of the animals in natural habitats and
their blooming, perfected instincts.

And when the poem is read aloud, another subtle but harsh
discordancy obtrudes. Basically, the meter appears to be a three
beat iambic line with occasional two or four beat lines. (There's
also the possibility that the opening line contains five full
stresses.) But certain central lines appear to demand a most
harsh, wrenching beat which disrupts the general metric
harmony. Consider the second and third lines here:

> To match them, the landscape flowers,
> Outdoing, desperately
> Outdoing what is required

or the final two here:

> For some of these
> It could not be the place
> It is, without blood.

Of course, there may be other ways to scan these lines; but if
my reading makes sense, the intrusion of the heavy beat in the
lines could be said to have the disruptive effect of a slap on the
face. At the very least, these lines contribute to one's growing
suspicion that a countercurrent of discordancy runs throughout
the poem. The suspicion of discord is only heightened by a
closer look at the last line quoted above. In addition to the
excess of beats, the cunningly contrived enjambment of "it is"
which is wrenched from its normal speech unit—"It could not
be the place it is"—combines with the hard sounds of "it,"
"out" and "blood" to create an intense, piercing moment of
harshness.

How are we to understand the growing sense of discordancy
suggested by the several harsh elements within this otherwise
orderly and harmonious heaven? One thing seems certain: the
several discordant elements combine to create a malevolent

tension. It's almost as if the discordancy were the serpent in what is otherwise an Eden; the serpent may be out of sight, hidden behind the shrubbery near the Tree of the Knowledge of Good and Evil: but he is there. The serpent is, in fact, as integral a part of Eden as the original parents, the Tree and the harmony of creation in the garden.

In Dickey's poem the discordancy is integral, it seems to me, when seen as part of the central event in the heaven of animals: the ecstasy of violence. This event is described with consummate lucidity by the most memorable lines in the poem, depicting the descent of the eternal hunters:

> And their descent
> Upon the bright backs of their prey
>
> May take years
> In a sovereign floating of joy.

What is stunning is that these lines mean exactly what they say. On earth, predatory beasts hunt only to find food; in heaven, they hunt only for the joy of it. Even more stunning perhaps: the victims also enjoy their role in the hunt; in fact, it is their "reward: to walk/Under such trees in full knowledge/Of what is in glory above them," and they feel no fear but instead accept with compliance being torn over and over again forever by "claws and teeth grown perfect."

And when we realize that the cycle of hunters tearing victims who rise to be torn again is, in fact, the *only* event in this heaven, we see that the discordant elements we've noticed contribute to the sense that we are in the middle of a nightmare—radiant, dignified but a nightmare, nonetheless. Think of some of the other events the animals could be enjoying—sexual intercourse, eating, running, swimming, playing, and so on. None of them occur in this heaven. Here is a paradise of joyous violence only.

Here is a heaven, in truth, in which—however harmonious its perpetual cycle, however beautiful, simple and lucid its environment, however joyous its hunters and victims—one wouldn't choose to remain too long. I confess this heaven in the end frightens me. If the reader becomes one of the animals—and we've seen that he does in that he sees only through the eyes of an animal and responds only with the instincts of an animal—then the reader too becomes one of the actors in the perpetual cycle of maimer and maimed.

One way to view "The Heaven of Animals," in fact, is to think of this heaven as a richly intricate metaphor for human life. Not only is each of us often either a victim or a "killer" but each of us is capable of the wonder of rebirths depicted in the poem. (Each of us has the possibility of "rebirth" in so many emotional or intellectual areas.)

Another way to experience the poem is to take the heaven of beasts as a literal place. But if this is indeed a heaven, then what kind of a god made it? Only by implication is his (its?) nature suggested by the poem. But that nature is weird—to say the least. Either the god is one who appears interested only in creating an eternal and ceaseless cycle of maiming, rebirth, and maiming again, or he too is a nature which contains both victim and hunter and like some great beast he is unable to alter what he is.

However one decides to read the poem, it should be evident that Dickey has succeeded in offering an experience which is (as far as I know) totally original in American poetry. One may end by feeling fascinated by the possibilities raised: Would I choose to be hunter or victim? Or one may end by recoiling in fear or even hatred. But I doubt if anyone will soon forget this poem.

Appendix One

In the first canto of the *Paradiso,* Dante and Beatrice are suddenly transported to the sphere of fire located between the earth and the moon; there Dante becomes so "transhumanized" that he is able to hear the music of the spheres but at first he feels bewildered: he doesn't realize they have left the earth. Even after Beatrice explains, he confesses he is perplexed to know how he has risen, more swiftly than air or fire, against the laws of gravitation. Beatrice takes pity on the confusion of his earthly intellect and explains to Dante the law of universal gravitation

which orders all things material and spiritual. Then in one of
the great metaphors in the poem—the immense ocean of Being,
the *immensum pelagus essentiae* of which St. Thomas Aquinas
wrote—she describes how all things seek their true place:

> "All things whatsoever observe a mutual order;
> And this is the form that makes
> The universe similar to God.
>
> In this the exalted creatures trace
> The impress of the Eternal Worth—
> The goal of the ordinance I speak about.
>
> In this order all created things incline
> By various degrees, either near or farther away
> According to their principle
>
> Wherefore they move to diverse ports
> Over the immense ocean of Being,
> Each one with instinct given it to bear it on."

Then Beatrice elaborates how in the order of the universe
each created part—planet, animal and human—has its own
function and acts according to the order within its own nature:

> "This one bears the fire towards the moon;
> And this, the mover in the hearts of things that die;
> This draws the earth together and unites it.
>
> And not only creatures lacking intelligence
> Are shot by this bow,
> But those who possess both intellect and love."

Isabella Gardner

THE WIDOW'S YARD

"Snails lead slow idyllic lives . . ."
The rose and the laurel leaves
in the raw young widow's yard
were littered with silver. Hardly a leaf lacked the decimal scale
of the self of a snail. Frail
in friendship I observed with care
these creatures (meaning to spare
the widow's vulnerable eyes
the hurting pity in my gaze).

Snails, I said, are tender skinned.
Excess in nature . . . sun rain wind
are killers. To save themselves
snails shrink to shelter in their shells
where they wait safe and patient
until the elements are gent-
ler. And do they not have other foes?
the widow asked. Turtles crows
foxes rats, I replied, and canned
heat that picnickers abandon. Also parasites invade
their flesh and alien eggs are laid

inside their skins. Their mating
too is perilous. The meeting
turns their faces blue with bliss
and consummation of this
absolute embrace is so
extravagantly slow
in coming that love begun
at dawn may end in fatal sun.
The widow told me that her
husband knew snails' ways and his garden had been Eden for them. He
said the timid snail could lift three
times his weight straight up and haul
a wagon toy loaded with a whole
two hundred times his body's burden.
Then as we left the garden
she said that at the first faint chill
the first premonition of fall
the snails go straight to earth . . . excrete
the lime with which they then secrete
the opening in their shells . . . and wait for spring.
It is those little doors which sing,
she said, when they are boiled.
She smiled at me when I recoiled.

THE POETRY
IS NOT IN THE PITY

To the question, "Who is talking to us in a poem?" should be added another not often asked even by knowledgeable readers of poetry: "How far should we trust or believe the speaker?" When the woman in Isabella Gardner's tense, terse "The Widow's Yard" confesses at the beginning of the poem that she has made a close study of the habits of snails inhabiting the back yard of her neighbor, the "raw young widow," because

> Frail
> in friendship I observed with care
> these creatures (meaning to spare
> the widow's vulnerable eyes
> the hurting pity in my gaze)

should we believe her? One's inclination is to reply: "Yes, of course. Why not? Why look for ambiguities or lies?" And of course there's no reason to create complications. Most good poems are complicated enough. When the poem itself invites us to doubt what its speaker claims, however, then that's another matter.

How many readers have been taken in, for example, by the man speaking in Robert Frost's "Mending Wall?" (I was for years.) Remember how he leads us to believe that he's the shrewd, slyly humorous humanitarian who is the opposite of his Yankee neighbor, wary and hidebound by tradition, who wants the wall mended every spring, thus keeping the two farms apart—and, by implication, the two neighbors as well? Yet the speaker clearly reveals that he's not as free-spirited or as much of a humanist as he'd have the reader (and himself?) believe. Listen again to *what* he says:

> The gaps I mean,
> No one has seen them made or heard them made,

> But at spring mending-time we find them there.
> I let my neighbor know beyond the hill;
> And on a day we meet to walk the line
> And set the wall between us once again.

The speaker, in truth, wants the wall up and in good shape as much as his neighbor whom he teases for being such a slave to tradition as to believe "Good fences make good neighbors." The speaker's actions reveal that he too believes in the old saying. But the reader must be alert to realize that he believes it because his wit and obvious "humanity" tend to beguile both reader and himself into taking at face value the speaker's own opinion of himself as a better man than his somewhat cloddish neighbor.*

In other words, it seems sensible when reading a poem to use that shrewd, if often unconscious, judgment we employ every day when we meet and talk with new people or even with a friend or loved one. Often we make up our minds—perhaps without consciously realizing it at the time—exactly how far we're willing to believe what we hear. And how frequently is it a question of *how* the speaker says it and not what he or she says? As everybody knows, "I love you," for example, can mean anything from "I really don't feel like talking now" to "Let's go to bed and make love the way I like it" to "I love you."

Should we believe the woman in "The Widow's Yard," then, when she explains that she's observed the snails with care in order to avoid causing further suffering to the young widow (by showing "the hurting pity in my gaze")? If we do believe her, then the poem clearly is about that awkward, shy experience of not knowing what to say when confronted by the grief of someone who may be a friend or practically a stranger. And if this be so, we're right in sympathizing with the speaker when the young widow lashes out in what sounds like bitterness:

> It is those little doors which sing,
> she said, when they are boiled.
> She smiled at me when I recoiled.

* See Appendix One for a discussion of how Frost's poem can be violated by over-simplification by that teacher or critic who wants to believe the speaker's own opinion of himself as one who strives to become a better and closer neighbor.

In such a reading, one's empathy is with the speaker, whereas the raw widow, although one may feel pity for her loss, is hardly very attractive. Bitterness never is.

But is this reading accurate? Let us look more closely at the opening stanza. Although we're told about the delicate *The New Yorker* or *Town & Country* sensibility of the speaker (I am assuming of course that the speaker is a woman) in that she wants very much not to inflict more pain on her neighbor, it is equally evident that the center of attention is on the woman speaking and not the bereaved widow. At first, this may not seem peculiar; but I suspect that as we continue finding out more about the speaker it will become clearer that the poem is really about her in a special and in the end unattractive way.

What is she like? Look at how she handles, for instance, the awkward situation of talking socially with a young widow who seems almost a stranger. On one's first reading of the poem, the woman speaking appears to deal with it well: she expresses sympathy and understanding through the central image of the snails, which she uses as a discreet analogy to the current lot of the widow. That is to say, she doesn't talk directly about the sore fact that the widow's husband is dead and buried. Moreover, she seems sensitive, intelligent and discreet in her use of the snail analogy. Not only has she taken the trouble to do research on snails—as the opening quotation (presumably from an encyclopaedia or old college textbook) indicates—" 'Snails lead slow idyllic lives' "—but her careful observation of the widow's snails has given other, less "idyllic" facts which she puts to good use in what sounds like an attempt to soothe her neighbor's pain. In stanza two, for example, her litany of sympathy for the snails—and, by prudent analogy, for the widow as well—catalogues how snails are tender-skinned and are menaced by natural excesses such as too much sun, rain or wind. Then she offers her pity in a subdued Eastern Girls' School pep talk:

> To save themselves
> snails shrink to shelter in their shells
> where they wait safe and patient
> until the elements are gent-
> ler.

Even the line break for the sake of the rhyme seems to contribute to the feeling of sympathy and good advice: "gent-/ler"
asks to be read with a slight catch in the throat, a break, an
intake of breath. And it may be noticed that the break high-
lights "gent"—a quiet allusion perhaps to the deceased husband.

And when the widow asks if snails do not have "other foes?"
the speaker warms to her task, becoming more down-to-earth,
assuming a practical but still sympathetic tone as she mentions
other enemies: turtles, crows, foxes, rats, the canned heat abandoned by picnickers, parasites, and even the snails' mating
itself. At first, this looks admirable. The speaker sounds like a
caring, civilized woman who seems to be warm or at least
sympathetic by talking about the hardships and hazards of
being a snail instead of talking directly about the dead husband
and thus becoming a possible source of fresh pain. She also
sounds adult as she offers discreet but good female advice: "We
women are 'tender skinned' and easily hurt," she seems to
imply, "but we must learn how to survive until the 'elements
are gent-/ler.' And we must also beware of those who might
hurt us or reopen wounds"—presumably those "friends" who,
unlike the speaker, might rub salt in the wound by bringing up
the stark fact of the death of the husband. (Isn't there also a
hint here of a Katharine Hepburn type of "Keep a stiff-upper
lip, girls. Let's not allow cruel adversity to encourage too pro-
longed pity for ourselves"? One almost hears the ghost of the
speaker's genteel aunt or headmistress applaud: "Well done,
girl!")

And it would be correct to applaud her if it weren't for the
suspicion of an odd perversity raised by the speaker's final
example of the "perils" of the snail:

> Their mating
> too is perilous. The meeting
> turns their faces blue with bliss
> and consummation of this
> absolute embrace is so
> extravagantly slow
> in coming that love begun
> at dawn may end in fatal sun.

What's so perilous about that? Even if the sun kills the copulating snails, it sounds great to have intercourse until faces turn "blue with bliss." Is there a better way to die? But why does the speaker bother to mention erotic delight in front of a woman who's recently lost her sexual partner? And notice how the sexual delight ends in death. To the widow, sex and death can only translate into: my husband. Such a tactless and perhaps unconsciously cruel reminder asks the reader to take another and sharper look at the person who has brought it up in this way.

For example: Why is she so anxious to talk about snails in the first place? To put the question in another way: What doesn't she say when she and the widow meet in the backyard? She doesn't say: "I'm sorry." Nor does she speak that other cliché so often used in awkward encounters such as this one: "You must be feeling terrible. I think I know what it's like. I've lost. . . . ." Both of these common clichés are also skeletons of possibly genuine feeling and are entrances to what may be a real relationship. After the cliché is spoken, there comes that existential moment where you either show your real feelings and establish some type of bond or you do not show them and remain behind your mask. But to show her real feelings is exactly what the speaker avoids.

As she hides behind encyclopaedic items about snails, she gives, in truth, little or nothing of herself. And she ends (in that image of the bliss of snails) with the temporary self-congratulatory security that she is superior to the widow—at least so far as *freedom* to enjoy sexual pleasure is concerned.

When she confesses at the beginning that she is "frail in friendship," we should have believed her. She probably is not as consciously aware of how frail in friendship her words and attitudes reveal her to be but the reader (and the widow too, as we'll see in a moment) notices that she offers neither deep feelings of sympathy nor any effort to establish a meaningful relationship with her neighbor. In fact, the reader begins to suspect that it is herself whom the woman speaking spares and protects.

How does she *sound*, for example? She speaks in short, clipped lines which are couplets. The line lengths suggest a certain tenseness, which is natural, given the situation; but the couplets create the feeling of a certain hard formality and even artificiality: they could suggest a woman in tight control of herself, as well as one who's hiding, in a sense, inside a shell of civilized but artificial manners. The sound of what she is saying, in short, certainly doesn't encourage the reader to consider her as a warm, sympathetic person.

And how does the widow react to her neighbor?

Her first response seems innocent enough—"And do they [the snails] not have other foes?"—until one discovers that she knows a great deal about snails herself. This puts her original question in a more ironical light. The widow knows perfectly well that snails suffer from "other foes"; and, in fact, her original response can be read both as ironic and as an expression of impatience or even irritation at her neighbor's rather sentimental description regarding the vulnerability of snails and, by implication, of women. It sounds as if the widow intuits that her neighbor is hiding behind a shell of civilized, formal and rather artificial "sympathy."

When the widow speaks again—right after the fulsome, voluptuous description of snails' sexual bliss—her remarks sound even more ironic and sharp. In direct and I think pointed contrast to her neighbor's catalogue of perils in the life of the snail, the widow offers tough, practical facts about snails: their herculean strength, their way of survival in winter, their sound when being boiled.

It becomes clear, it seems to me, that "The Widow's Yard" depends in an important way on what is *not* said but is instead implied. The widow, for example, is really speaking between the lines, saying something like this to her well-meaning but in the final count insincere neighbor: "Oh, come off it. Face it, darling: you're more interested in hiding your feelings than in trying to console me."

In this reading, the image of the snails serves a double and ambiguous role. The speaker thinks she's talking about snails as a polite way of offering advice and sympathy, using their lives as an analogy for the shock and perils of widowhood; but she hides behind a shell by not offering genuine sympathy or warmth. The speaker is a snail more than the widow is one.

The irony here seems acute. The speaker thinks she's offering sympathy and that in the encounter in the backyard she cares more about the widow than about herself; what she actually accomplishes, however, is to protect herself from any vital relationship. It sounds as if she desires to eat her cake and still have it: she wants the satisfaction of feeling she's helped another person who is crippled by grief but she doesn't want to pay the price of what such help costs—namely, giving and sharing real feelings and real warmth.

The widow intuits this and tells off her neighbor in that final, bitter couplet of how snails "sing" when boiled. The widow boils the speaker in her own shell.

Then what is "The Widow's Yard" about? It is about the reluctance or fear behind the everyday failure to communicate. ("People have *nothing* to say to each other," Celine writes in a great phrase.) And it is about how we often deceive ourselves by thinking we feel sympathy and empathy for others, whereas it is ourselves we care about and protect. "The Widow's Yard" is a cunning delineation of civilized narcissism.* Here the poetry is not in the pity; it is in the courageous exposure of one of the uglier or less flattering roots of what we like to call pity.

Appendix One

The tendency to ignore what the speaker in Frost's poem reveals about himself is a good example of one of the bad habits of reading poetry which many of us learned from often well-intentioned but poor teachers. They were poor teachers when they asked poems to "point a moral" and so ended by simplifying the human complexity of a good, crooked poem like "Mending Wall." When I first read this poem in high school, I remember the teacher saying something close to the reading suggested by Louis Untermeyer in his study *Modern American Poetry*: "In 'Mending Wall' we see two elemental and opposing forces" whom he identifies as the speaker, the "seeker after causes," and his Yankee neighbor, the "literal minded lover of tradition."

---

* See Appendix Two for a discussion of some other ways in which this poem has been read by such perceptive critics as Robert Bly and John Logan.

The two farmers represent, Mr. Untermeyer concludes, "the essence of nationalism versus the internationalist: the struggle . . . between blind obedience to custom and questioning iconoclasm." And we were encouraged by our teacher to put the poem to work by applying its "lesson" to questions such as: "What are the walls that separate nations?" "Should they be kept in repair?" "What is the history of the long unfortified border between the United States and Canada?" "What are some of the other 'walls' that keep people apart?"

Behind the reading by Untermeyer and behind the type of discussion guided by the Carmelite Father who taught our class is of course the assumption that the speaker in "Mending Wall" is to be believed when he implies that he's against keeping the wall between his apple orchard and his neighbor's pine trees. And he obviously is against the wall and whatever it stands for in fact as well as in his neighbor's mind; but he also is the one who initiates the mending ("I let my neighbor know beyond the hill") : he could refuse to repair the wall. In this sense, the poem is more than a dramatic monologue depicting a shrewd, humorous Yankee—the symbol of "questioning iconoclasm"— whom the reader may flatter himself he resembles, as contrasted to the neighbor and his literal-minded devotion to the old ways. The poem is also a subtle, foxy study of the duplicity and smugness of the man speaking. He likes to feel superior to his neighbor by pretending *his* hands aren't grasping the boulder they are in fact grasping, which makes him look as much like "an old-stone savage armed" as his neighbor. In short, the speaker is probably more full of mistrust (and even ill will) than the neighbor because he at least knows one can go beyond the walls of tradition; but he clearly doesn't want to beyond them: he wants to mend the wall and keep it there.

Appendix Two

In his controversial and by now well-known essay "Prose vs. Poetry" (*Choice #2* (1962)) Robert Bly offers a reading of Miss Gardner's poem which reaches a conclusion about the speaker and the "raw young" widow in which their roles are in every respect the reverse of the reading I've suggested. The reader might want to compare the two views of the poem. Here is Bly's reading (it appears as part of a review of Miss Gardner's *The Looking Glass* in which Bly singles out "The Widow's Yard" for detailed discussion) :

> The scene is the backyard of a widow's house, upon whose trees Miss Gardner notices the tracks of snails. The two women begin to talk about snails. Miss Gardner explains their enemies are sun, wind, rain, turtles, foxes, and the canned heat left by picnickers. Also, snails make love so slowly at night that they are sometimes caught by the rising sun, whose light kills them. It turns out that the widow's husband knew all about snails. Just as the details Miss Gardner have told have silently evoked her situation, the situation of the younger or vulnerable woman in love, so now the details chosen by the widow evoke her painful loneliness and widowhood. In her turn she describes how at the first chill of fall the snails head for earth, excreting a lime that walls off any opening in their shell. So far the vulnerable woman, the woman with less experience, can follow the conversation. Suddenly the widow says something totally unexpected: "It is those little doors which sing, she said, when they are boiled." The younger woman suddenly feels her inexperience and feels alone; yet, at the same time she is aware of a sensitivity and compassion which she still possesses. The widow has noticed nothing. "She smiled at me when I recoiled." This is a fine poem . . . The pleasures of Miss Gardner's poems lie in their content. In the best poems there is a femininity and humanity that have weight.

In his essay "The Poetry of Isabella Gardner" (*Sewanee Review*, Summer 1961) John Logan finds the snails themselves to be the most compelling element in the poem. Here is his interesting and surprising analysis:

> The "raw widow" of "The Widow's Yard" has lost her husband and is victimized by the pain of this, but she

possesses a relic of him—the snails he loved and cared for, which curiously creative as they are "litter with silver . . ./ the rose and laurel leaves" in her yard. Stronger than Sisyphus struggling with the rock of his heart's grief these snails are able to haul "a wagon toy loaded with a whole/two hundred times [their] body's burden."

It seems to me these heroic, silver leaving "tender-skinned" creatures are figures for the poet himself (herself) and that the conclusion of the poem expresses the desire all artists share—that the misery resulting from their extraordinary sensitivity and from the burden of their gift will issue in the beautiful litter of their art, in a kind of song: "at the first faint chill . . .

the snails go straight to earth . . . excrete
the lime with which they then secrete
the opening in their shells . . . and wait for spring.
It is those little doors which sing,
she said, when they are boiled.

Allen Ginsberg

WICHITA VORTEX SUTRA

Face the Nation
Thru Hickman's rolling earth hills
       icy winter
         grey sky   bare trees lining the road
     South to Wichita
       you're in the Pepsi Generation   Signum
             enroute
Aiken Republican on the radio
    60,000 Northvietnamese troops now infiltrated but over
          250,000
  South Vietnamese   armed men
             our Enemy—
                Not Hanoi our enemy
                Not China our enemy
                     The Viet Cong!
          McNamara made a "bad guess"
"Bad Guess" chorused the Reporters?
    Yes, no more than a Bad Guess, in 1962
              "8000 American Troops
                handle the Situation"
                Bad Guess
    in 1956,   80% of the
       Vietnamese people would've voted for Ho Chi
       Minh

    wrote Ike years later "Mandate for Change"
             A bad guess in the
                Pentagon
And the Hawks were guessing all along
          Bomb China's 200, 000, 000
          cried Stennis from Mississippi
          I guess it was 3 weeks ago
Holmes Alexander in Albuquerque Journal
    Provincial newsman
       said I guess we better begin to do that Now.
    his typewriter clacking in his aged office
    on a side street under Sandia Mountain
      Half the world away from China
Johnson got some bad advice Republican Aiken sang
to the Newsmen over the radio
    The General guessed they'd stop infiltrating the South
      if they bombed the North—
        So I guess they bombed!
    Pale Indochinese boys came thronging thru the jungle
        in increased numbers
      to the scene of TERROR!
While the triangle-roofed Farmer's Grain Elevator
    sat quietly by the side of the road
      along the railroad track—
    American Eagle beating its wings over Asia
     million dollar helicopters
     a billion dollars worth of Marines
       who loved Aunt Betty
      Drawn from the shores and farms shaking
    from the high schools to the landing barge
    blowing the air thru their cheeks with fear
      in Life on Television
Put it this way on the radio
Put it this way in television language
            Use the words
            language, language:
              "A bad guess"

Put it this way in headlines
    Omaha World Herald—   Rusk Says Toughness

Essential For Peace

Put it this way
      Lincoln Nebraska morning Star—
                Vietnam War Brings Prosperity
Put it this way
      Declared McNamara,   speaking language
      Asserted Maxwell Taylor
      General, Consultant to the White House
      Vietcong losses leveling up three five zero zero
                per month
      Front page testimony February '66
      Here in Nebraska same as Kansas same known in Saigon
      in Peking, in Moscow, same known
      by the youths of Liverpool three five zero zero
      the latest quotation in the human meat market—
                Father I cannot tell a lie!

A black horse bends its head to the stubble
    beside the silver stream winding thru the woods
      by an antique red barn on the outskirts of Beatrice—
          Quietness, quietness
       over this countryside
          except for unmistakable signals on radio
           followed by the honkytonky
             tinkle of a city piano
    to calm the nerves of taxpaying housewives of a Sunday
    morn.
          Has anyone looked in the eyes of the dead?
U.S. Army recruiting service sign Careers With A Future
    Is anyone living to look for future forgiveness?
Water hoses frozen on the street,
    Crowd gathered to see a strange happening in the
    garage—
      How red the flames on Sunday morning
          in a quiet town!
Has anyone looked in the eyes of the wounded?
    Have we seen but paper faces, Life Magazine?
    Are screaming faces made of dots,
      electric dots on Television—

fuzzy decibels registering
the mammal voiced howl
from the outskirts of Saigon to the console model picture
tube
in Beatrice, in Hutchinson, in El Dorado
in historic Abilene
O inconsolable!

Stop, and eat more flesh.
"We will negotiate anywhere anytime"
said the giant President
Kansas City Times 2/14/66: "Word reached U.S. authorities that Thailand's leaders feared that in Honolulu Johnson
might have tried to persuade South Vietnam's rulers to ease their
stand against negotiating with the Viet Cong.

American officials said these fears were groundless and
Humphrey was telling the Thais so"
A.P. dispatch
The last weeks paper is amnesia.
Three five zero zero is numerals
Headline language poetry, nine decades after Democratic
Vistas
and the Prophecy of the Good Grey Poet
Our nation "of the fabled damned"
or else . . .
Language, language
Ezra Pound the Chinese Written Character for truth
defined as man standing by his word
A word picture: a forked creature
Man
standing by a box with birds flying out
representing speech of the mouth
Ham steak please waitress, in the warm cafe.
Different from a bad guess.
The war is language,
language abused
for Advertisement,
language used
like magic for power on the planet

Black Magic language,
          formulas for reality—
                    Communism is a 9 letter word
                         used by inferior magicians
with the wrong alchemical formula for transforming earth into
          gold
                         —funky warlocks operating on guesswork,
                              handmedown mandrake terminology
                                        that never worked in 1956
               for grey-domed Dulles,
                                   brooding over at State,
                    that never worked for Ike who knelt to take
                         the magic wafer in his mouth
                                   from Dulles' hand
                              inside the church in Washington:
Communion of bum magicians
               congress of failures from Kansas & Missouri
          working with the wrong equations
          Sorcerer's Apprentice who lost control
               of the simplest broomstick in the world:
                                   Language
O longhaired magician come home and take care of your kid
               before the deluge of radiation floods your living-
                         room
                              your magic errandboy's
                              just made a bad guess again
               that's lasted a whole decade.

N B C B S U P A P I N S L I F E
          Time Mutual presents
               World's Largest Camp Comedy:
                              Magic In Vietnam—
          reality turned inside out
               changing its sex in the Mass Media
               for 30 days, a bedroom farce
                              in the TV den
          Flashing pictures of Senate Foreign Relations Committee
               room
               Generals faces flashing on and off screen

mouthing language
State Secretary speaking nothing but language
McNamara declining to speak public language
The President talking language
Senators reinterpreting language
General Taylor Limited Objectives
Owls from Pennsylvania
Clark's face Open Ended
Dove's Apocalypse
Morse's hairy ears
Stennis orating in Mississippi
half billion chinamen crowding into the
polling booth,
Clean shaven Gen. Gavin's image
imagining Enclaves
Tactical Bombing the magic formula for
a silver haired Symington:
Ancient Chinese apothegm:
Old in vain
Hawks swooping thru the newspapers
talons visible
wings outspread in the giant updraft of hot air
loosing their dry speech in the skies
over the Capitol
Napalm and black clouds emerging in newsprint
Flesh soft as a Kansas girl's
ripped open by metal explosion—
three five zero zero   on the other side of the planet
caught in barbed wire, fire ball
bullet shock, bayonet electricity
bomb blast terrific in skull & belly, shrapnelled
throbbing meat
While this American nation argues war:
conflicting language, language
proliferating in the airwaves
filling the farmhouse car, filling
the City Manager's head in his oaken office
the professor's head in his bed at midnight
the pupil's head at the movies

blond haired, his heart throbbing with
desire
for the girlish image bodied on the screen:
or smoking cigarettes
and watching Captain Kangaroo
that fabled damned of nations
prophecy come true—
Though the highway's straight,
dipping downward through low hills,
rising narrow on the far horizon
black cows browse in the caked fields
ponds in the hollows lie frozen
in quietness
Is this the land that started war on China?
This be the soil that thought Cold War for decades?
Are these nervous naked trees & farmhouses
the vortex
of oriental anxiety molecules
that've imagined   American Foreign Policy
and magick'd up paranoia in Peking
and curtains of living blood
surrounding far Saigon?
Are these the towns where the language emerged
from the mouths here
that makes a Hell of riots in Dominica
sustains the aging tyranny of Chiang in silent Taipeh city
Paid for the lost French war in Algeria
overthrew the Guatemalan polis in '54
maintaining United Fruit's banana greed
another thirteen years
for the secret prestige of Dulles' family lawfirm?
Here's Marysville—
a black railroad engine in the children's park,
at rest—
Next the Track Crossing
with Cotton Belt flatcars
carrying autos west from Dallas
Delaware & Hudson gondolas filled with power stuff—
a line of boxcars far east as the eye can see

carrying battle goods to cross the Rockies
into the hands of rich longshoremen loading
                        ships on the Pacific
        Oakland Army Terminal's lights
                blue illumined all night now—
Crash of couplings and the great American train
        moves on carrying its cushioned load of metal
                doom
Union Pacific, Norfolk & Western, linked together
                        with your Hoosier line
followed by passive Wabash rolling behind
        all Erie carrying cargo in the rear,
                Central Georgia's rust colored truck proclaim-
                ing
                        The Right Way, concluding
the awesome poem writ by the train
                across northern Kansas,
        land which gave right of way
        to the massing of metal meant for explosion
                        in Indochina—
Passing thru Waterville,
                Electronic machinery in the bus humming with
                        prophecy—
paper signs blowing in cold wind
                mid-Sunday afternoon's silence
                                        in town
        under a frost-grey sky
                        that covers the horizon—
That the rest of earth is unseen,
                        the outer universe invisible,
                Unknown except thru
                        language
                                airprint
                                        magic images
        or prophecy of the secret
                        heart the same
                        in Waterville as Saigon one human
                        form:
When a woman's heart bursts in Waterville

a woman screams equal in Hanoi—
On to Wichita to prophecy! O frightful Bard!
　　　into the heart of the Vortex
　　　　　　where anxiety rings
　　　　　　　　the University with millionaire pressure,
　　　　　　lonely crank telephone voices sighing in dread,
and students wake trembling in their beds
　　　　　　with dreams of a new truth warm as meat,
　　　　　　little girls suspecting their elders of murder
　　　　　　　　committed by remote control machinery,
　　　　　　boys with sexual bellies aroused
　　　　　　　　chilled in the heart by the mailman
　　　　　　　　with a letter from an aging white haired
　　　　　　　　　　　　　　General
　　　　　　　　Director of selection for service in
　　　　　　　　　　　　　　deathwar
　　　　all this black language
　　　　　　writ by machine!
　　　　　　　　O hopeless Fathers and Teachers
　　　　　　　　in Hue　　do you know
　　　　　　　　　the same woe too?

I'm an old man now, and a lonesome man in Kansas
　　　but not afraid
　　　　　　to speak my lonesomeness in a car,
　　　　　　because not only my lonesomeness
　　　　　　　　it's Ours, all over America,
　　　　　　　　　　　　O tender fellows—
　　　　　　　　& spoken lonesomeness is Prophecy
　　　　　　　　in the moon 100 years ago or in
　　　　　　　　　　the middle of Kansas now
It's not the vast plains mute our mouths
　　　　　　　　that fill at midnite with ecstatic language
　　　　　　when our trembling bodies hold each other
　　　　　　　　breast to breast on a mattress—
　　　Not the empty sky that hides
　　　　　　　　　　　the feeling from our faces
　　　nor our skirts and trousers that conceal
　　　　　　the bodylove emanating in a glow of beloved skin,

white smooth abdomen down to the hair
between our legs,
It's not a God that bore us that forbid
our Being, like a sunny rose
all red with naked joy
between our eyes & bellies, yes!
All we do is for this frightened thing
we call Love, want and lack—
fear that we aren't the one whose body could be
beloved of all the brides of Kansas City,
kissed all over by every boy of Wichita—
O but how many in their solitude weep aloud like me—
On the bridge over Republican River
almost in tears to know
how to speak the right language—
on the frosty broad road
uphill between highway embankments
I search for the language
that is also yours—
almost all our language has been taxed by war.
Radio antennae high tension
wires ranging from Junction City across the plains—
highway cloverleaf sunk in a vast meadow
lanes curving past Abilene
to Denver filled with old
heroes of love—
to Wichita where McClure's mind
burst into animal beauty
drunk, getting laid in a car
in a neon misted street
15 years ago—
to Independence where the old man's still alive
who loosed the bomb that's slaved all human consciousness
and made the body universe a place of fear—
Now, speeding along the empty plain,
no giant demon machine visible on the horizon
but tiny wooden trees and wooden houses at the sky edge
I claim my birthright!
reborn forever as long as Man

in Kansas or other universe-Joy
reborn after the vast sadness of War Gods!
A lone man talking to myself, no house in the brown vastness
to hear,
imagining the throng of Selves
that make this nation one body of Prophecy
languaged by Constitution as
Happiness!
I call all Powers of imagination
to my side in this auto to make Prophecy,
all Lords
of human kingdoms to come
Shambu Bharti Baba naked covered with ash
Khaki Baba fat bellied mad with the dogs
Dehorahava Baba who moans Oh how wounded,
how wounded
Citaram Onkar Das Thakur who commands
Give up your desire
Satyananda who raises two thumbs in tranquility
Kali Pada Guha Roy whose yoga drops before the void
Shivananda who touches the breast and says Om
Srimata Krishnaji of Brindaban who says take for your
guru
William Blake the invisible father of English
visions
Sri Ramakrishna master of ecstasy with
eyes
half closed who only cries for his
mother
Chaitanya with arms upraised singing & dancing his own
praise
Sacred Heart my Christ acceptable,
Preserver Harikrishna returning in the age of pain
Durga-Ma covered with blood
destroyer of battlefield illusions
million faced Tathagata gone past suffering
Allah the Compassionate
Jaweh Righteous One
all Knowledge-Princes of Earthman, all

ancient Seraphim of heavenly desire, Devas, yogis
        & holymen I shall chant to
        come to my lone presence
                into this Vortex named Kansas—
I lift my voice aloud,
    make Mantra of American language now,
    pronounce the words beginning my own Millennium—
        I here declare the end of the war!—
                        Ancient days' illusion!
Let the States tremble,
        let the nation weep,
            let Congress legislate its own delight
                let the President execute his own desire—
this Act done by my own voice,
                nameless Mystery—
published to my own senses,
                blissfully received by my own form
        approved with pleasure by my sensations
            manifestation of my very thought
            accomplished in my own imagination
                all realms within my consciousness fulfilled
        60 miles from Wichita
                near El Dorado,
                    The Golden One.
    In the chill earthly mist
            houseless brown farmland plains rolling heavenward
                            in every direction
        one midwinter afternoon on Sunday called the day of the
                        Lord—
            Pure Spring Water gathered—in one tower
                    where Florence is
                        set on a hill.
                stop for tea & gas
    Cars passing their messages along the country crossroads
                to populaces cement-networked on flatness,
                    giant white mist on earth
                and a Wichita Eagle-Beacon headlines
                    "Kennedy Urges Cong Get Chair in Negotiations"
    The War is gone,

Language emerging on the motel news stand,
                the right magic
        Formula, the language that was known
        in the back of the mind before, now in the black print
                        of daily consciousness
Eagle News Services Saigon—
        Headline Surrounded Vietcong Charge into Fire Fight
                the suffering not yet ended
                                for others
        The last spasms of the dragon of pain
                shoot thru the muscles
            a crackling around the eyeballs
                of a sensitive yellow boy by a muddy wall
Continued from page one   area
        after the Marines killed 256 Vietcong captured 31
        ten day operation Harvest Moon last December
                        Language language
        U.S. Military Spokesmen
                Language language
                        Cong death toll
            had soared to 100 in the First Air Cavalry
            Division's Sector of
                Language language
                Operation White Wing near Bong Son
Some of the
        Language language
                Communist
                        Language language soldiers
charged so desperately they were struck with six or seven bullets
                                before they fell
        Language language M 60 Machine Guns
                Language language in La Drang Valley
        the terrain is rougher and infested with leeches and
                                        scorpions
                The war was over several hours ago!
Oh at last again the radio opens
        blue Invitations!
                        Angelic Dylan singing across the nation
                        "When all your children start to resent

                                        you
                              Won't you come see me, Queen Jane?"
                   His youthful voice making glad
                                   the brown endless meadows
                   His tenderness penetrating aether,
                         soft prayer on the airwaves,
                               Language language, and sweet music too
                               even unto thee,
                                     hairy flatness!
                               even unto thee
                                     despairing Burns!
         Future speeding on swift wheels
                         straight on the heart of Wichita!
         Now radio voices cry population hunger world
                                     & unhappy people
                         waiting for Man to be born
                               O man in America!
               you certainly smell good
                                     the radio says
                   passing mysterious families of winking towers
                   grouped round a quonset hut on a hillock—
                               feed storage or military fear factory here?
         Ooh! sensitive lights of Hamburger & Skelley's Gas
                                     feed man and machine:
                   Kansas Electric Substation aluminum robot
                         signals thru thin antennae towers
                         above the empty football field
                                     at Sunday dusk
               to a solitary derrick that pumps oil from the unconscious
                               working night & day
                         & factory gas flares edge a huge golf course
                               where tired businessmen can come and play—

         Cloverleaf, Merging Traffic at East Wichita turnoff
                         McConnell Airforce Base
                               nourishing the city—
                   Lights rising in the suburbs
                   Supermarket Texaco brilliance starred
                                     over streetlamp vertebrae on Kellogg,

green jewelled traffic lights
confronting the windshield,
Centertown ganglion entered!
Crowds of autos moving with their lightshine,
signbulbs winking in the driver's eyeball—
The human nest collected, noon lit,
and sunburst signed
for business as usual, except on the Lord's Day—
Redeemer Lutheran's three crosses lit on the lawn
reminder of our sins
and Titsworth offers insurance on Hydraulic
by De Voors Gurad's Mortuary for outmoded bodies
of the human vehicle
which no Titsworth of insurance will customise
for resale—
So home, traveller, past the newspaper language factory
under the Union Station railroad bridge on Douglas
to the center of the Vortex, calmly home:
to Hotel Eaton—
Carrie Nation began the war on Vietnam here
with an angry smashing axe
attacking Wine
Here fifty years ago, by her violence
began a vortex of hatred that defoliated the Mekong
Delta—
Proud Wichita! vain Wichita
cast the first stone!—
that murdered my mother
who died of the communist anticommunist psychosis
in the madhouse one decade long ago
complaining about wires of masscommunication in her
head
and phantom political voices in the air
besmirching her girlish character.
Many another has suffered death or madness
in the Vortex from Hydraulic
to the end of the 17th—
enough!
The war is over now—

Except for the souls
          held prisoner in Niggertown
still pining for love of your tender white bodies O children of
     Wichita!

"I LIFT MY VOICE ALOUD,/MAKE MANTRA OF AMERICAN LANGUAGE NOW . . ./ I HERE DECLARE THE END OF THE WAR!"

Is "Wichita Vortex Sutra" a major American poem? The great act of imagination at the core of this long work seems to demand that the reader consider the poem either as a notable and even monumental achievement or as a roaring and pretentious failure. Either this poem is incandescent in that Allen Ginsberg succeeds in assuming the role of poet as priestly legislator and as Baptist of a mantra whose dispensation brings peace and love or it is opaque in that he fails to become little more than mock creator of a harangue whose dispensation brings bad rhetoric and banality.

This is of course relentlessly univocal. Yet the poem demands such univocal judgement due to the sheer heroism and daring of its declared intention. With admirable sincerity and making no bones about it, Ginsberg attempts to assume the role called for by Shelley in the celebrated if somewhat petulant assertion that poets are "the unacknowledged legislators of the world."* Ginsberg assumes this role when he attempts to legislate by declaring the end of hostilities in Viet Nam in these astonishing lines which occur about two-thirds of the way through the poem:

> I lift my voice aloud,
>> make Mantra of American language now,
>> pronounce the words beginning in my own Millen-
>>> nium—

* W. B. Yeats offers more practical advice to poets who want to think of themselves as legislators. Shortly before retiring from political life—he served as Senator in the Irish Senate from 1922 to 1928—Yeats admonished his old friend Ezra Pound: "Do not be elected to the Senate of your country. Neither you, nor I, nor any other of our excitable profession can match those lawyers, old bankers, old business men, who, because all habit and memory, have begun to govern the world." Poets would be as much out of place in a Senate and in political life in general, Yeats continued, as would "the first composers of Sea-chanties in an age of Steam."

I here declare the end of the war!—
Ancient Days' illusion!
Let the States tremble,
let the nation weep,
let Congress legislate its own delight
let the President execute his
own desire—
this Act done by my own voice,
nameless Mystery—

What makes this assertion so original is the means by which
Ginsberg strives to give validity and authority to his act of
legislation: he declares the end of the war by making a mantra.
More specifically, it is a mantra of the American language. The
central implication seems clear. If the mantra of the American
language "works," then it should be able in some vigorous, magical or religious way to end the slaughter in Viet Nam. But first,
what exactly is a mantra?

The dictionary explains that mantra comes from the San-
skrit term for sacred formula or counsel and defines it as "a
mystical formula or invocation or incantation in Hinduism or
Mahayana Buddhism"; but since I am ignorant about Eastern
religions, I asked Ginsberg if he would explain his understanding of mantra, as well as to indentify some of the important but
obscure allusions to Hindu or Buddhist mysticism—for example,
the litany of gurus, swamis, yogis, saints and demigods whom he
invokes in the section beginning: "I call all Powers of imagina-
tion/to my side in this auto to make Prophecy . . ." In August
1966, the poet generously replied in the form of a letter and
notes written in the margins of a xerox copy of the poem.* Here

---

* The text of the letter and notes appears in Appendix One. At first, I
thought that the proem to "Wichita Vortex Sutra" mentioned by the poet
in his letter should be included in an essay exploring the poem; but when
I learned that both the proem and poem were portions of an extremely
long poem-in-progress tentatively called "These States," I decided to limit
my remarks to a discussion of the poem which has impressed me as a
complete and self-contained work of art since it first appeared in *The
Village Voice* (April 28, 1966). The reader might be interested to know
that the entire text of "These States" comes from an almost literal transcription of the tape recording made by the poet as he wandered around
America as a Guggenheim Fellow in Poetry during the fall of 1965 and
winter of 1966.

is Ginsberg's definition of mantra: "a short magic formula usually invoking an aspect of the Divine, usually given as meditation exercise by guru to student, sometimes sung in community or 'kirtan'—the formula is considered to be identical with the god named, and have inevitable power attached to its pronunciation. Oft used in chanting or invocation."

The mantra made in "Wichita Vortex Sutra," then, seems to consist of three parts. First, there is the litany beginning "I call all Powers of imagination," invoking the holy men, demigods and gods from whom the poet asks assistance in the making of his mantra. Then there is the creation of the mantra itself: "I lift my voice aloud,/make mantra of American language now . . ." Finally, the mantra is put to work as the poet announces his act of declaring the end of the war and then pronounces benediction on the United States, Congress and President Johnson; and then as part of the mantra he ritualistically enumerates the five "leaps" or "skandas"—the areas of apportionment of consciousness mentioned in the Buddhist Sutras: the liberation of his own form, sensations, thought, imagination, and "all realms within my consciousness."

The intention of the mantra is heroic and ambitious. If it works, it functions as a magic formula whose power can end the war and also as the formula which invokes that which is eternal and divine and free in the poet himself, as well as that which is holy and free in the members of Congress and in the President. Clearly here is one of the supreme moments of imagination in American poetry. There has been nothing to equal its grandeur, it seems to me, since Whitman's "Passage to India."

What is impressive about this mantra is that it isn't merely a Hindu or Buddhist prayer for peace and for the liberation of the holy in the poet and in his fellow Americans. Instead, Ginsberg attempts to make a mantra out of the American language itself. What exactly could this mean? The poet explains in his reply to my original letter in which I mentioned that I'd been thinking of his poem as fulfilling Shelley's assertion that poets are the unacknowledged legislators of the world: "Not *only* a question of legislator as Shelley's formula. Merely that the war has been created by language . . . & Poet can dismantle the language consciousness conditioned to war reflexes by setting up (mantra) absolute contrary field of will as expressed in language. By expressing, manifesting, his DESIRE (BHAKTI in yoga terminology—'adoration')."

Here, then, is the dramatic and crucial tension created by the making of the mantra: the poet expresses his desire for peace and the liberation of the divine and free in himself and his countrymen by creating a mantra made with American words; but the mantra will succeed in bringing peace and liberating the holy and free in Americans only if its language can oppose and finally dismantle the corrupt and evil language which has conditioned the American people to "war reflexes"—the corrupt and evil language which (according to the poet) created and sustains the current Viet Nam war. In brief, the mantra is one of true or beatific language; its job is to dissipate and annihilate the slaughter and moral barbarism created by false or evil language. In this sense, "Wichita Vortex Sutra" is primarily a poem embodying an experience of contemporary American language and what that language can or cannot accomplish.

When read in the light of this tension between false and true language, the poem divides into three parts. The first section is the longest, containing five stanzas of some 365 lines, all of which document in one way or another aspects of the false and evil language which created and sustains the Viet Nam war. The second section, beginning with the stanza "I call all Powers of imagination/to my side in this auto to make Prophecy . . ." depicts in some 50 lines the creation of the mantra. The final section opens in "the chill earthly mist" 60 miles from Wichita and contains some 130 lines in two stanzas in which the mantra of true language is put to work in opposing the false words of the first section.

Let us look at some of the outstanding examples of the false and evil use of the American language in the first section and attempt to see how such perverted uses drive the poet to declare: "The war is language,/language abused/for Advertisement,/ language used/like magic for power on the planet/Black Magic language,/formulas for reality . . ."

At the very beginning of the poem, the poet encounters an example of black magic language as he hears the voice of Senator Aiken [Republican, Vermont] on the interview program

"Face the Nation" coming over the radio in his Volkswagen driving on a Sunday morning in February 1966 past Hickman, Nebraska, along Route 77, bound south for Wichita. The Senator claims that Secretary of Defense McNamara made "no more than a Bad Guess" when he predicted in 1962 that only "8000 American Troops [could] handle the/Situation." Here are at least two examples of misused or twisted "formulas for reality." By calling McNamara's miscalculation only a bad guess, the Senator distorts what that miscalculation in all events actually was: namely, a calculated sop thrown to pacify the American people and soften or quiet whatever moral opposition they may have felt against our involvement in Viet Nam, as well as a sop to mollify whatever objection they might feel in the near future to the increasing escalation of aggression by American pilots against Viet Cong troops and civilian villages. What makes the Senator's description false is that the Secretary of Defense might possibly have known in 1962 that America would increase its "commitment" and aggression on the large scale that it actually did.

A minor but equally false perversion of language occurs when Senator Aiken describes the war as "the Situation." To call napalm bombing, machine-gunning and destruction of helpless villages by United States pilots—not to speak of the massacre of our own soldiers by the Viet Cong—a "situation" is precisely that kind of official gobbledygook which refuses to call an event by its correct name (however ugly that name is) and by so refusing only helps to blunt moral perceptions of what that reality might be.* Bombing with intent to destroy and kill, intricate tactical strategies, abortive attempts to negotiate peace, and swelling rosters of dead or wounded on both sides: this is not a "situation:" this is war.

* A copy of the first draft of the essay on his (or her) poem was sent to each poet in the hope that comments and/or variant readings would help to clarify awkward or wrong interpretations. In a letter dated November 22, 1967, Ginsberg offers variant readings of several crucial passages in "Wichita Vortex Sutra." Although his comments proved helpful and stimulating when I rewrote the essay, I decided to keep my original reading of most of the passages in question. But in case the reader might want to compare the two readings, I have included the poet's comments in Appendix Two. The first comment concerns the lines about Senator Aiken's statement to the reporters about Mr. McNamara's "bad guess."

Other examples of perverted use of words bombard the poet as he reads newspaper headlines. "Rusk Says Toughness Essential for Peace" declares the *Omaha World Herald*. Toughness? What's accomplished by the use of this virile noun? Such a word only flatters a nation's image of itself and helps to dissipate whatever reservations Americans may have about the morality of our slaughtering in Viet Nam by conjuring the image of the American as Wild West hero who refuses to let anybody push him around or make a sissy out of him. What the use of the word tends to ignore or varnish over is the moral reality: What right do Americans have to act "tough" with Oriental peasants who are fighting for what is, after all, their own country? Thirty years ago, a German newspaper could have said: "Hitler Says Toughness Essential for Final Solution"—meaning the extermination of countless Jews who were in no rational or legal sense enemies of the Third Reich. Then there's the headline: "Vietnam War Brings Prosperity." Here the perversion exists in the word "prosperity." By claiming that the war brings prosperity, the headline implies that the aggression is not only reasonable and valuable but condoned by the god of capitalism. No sensible man denies that prosperity is a good thing; but the use of the word here blunts the vital issue: Prosperity at what moral cost? Antebellum slavery brought prosperity to Southern planters and to the entire economy of the South. Barbaric working conditions and immoral wages brought prosperity to owners of Chicago meat packing houses and New England textile mills in the late 19th century. And so on.

Examples of perverted black magic language heard over the radio or read in the newspapers continue to assault the poet throughout the long first section of the poem as he comes to know how persuasive and corrupting the perversion has become. One example is the old misuse of the word "Communism" to encourage a growing "war reflex" both in American statesmen and military men and in the citizens as a body. While eating ham steak in the warm cafe, the poet broods how "Communism is a 9 letter word/used by inferior magicians" and funky warlocks which resulted in the "Communion of bum magicians/congress of failures from Kansas & Missouri/working with the wrong equations/Sorcerer's Apprentice who lost control/of the simplest broomstick in the world:/Language . . ." whose perversion may erupt in the "deluge of radiation" flooding the living rooms of America.

Nor is the black magic language limited only to the present. In one of the most memorable passages in the poem, Ginsberg recalls an episode of the perversion of the Word which occurred in 1956 when President Eisenhower "knelt to take/the magic wafer in his mouth/from Dulles' hand/inside the church in Washington . . ." Here the "magic" communion wafer given by Dulles (acting as lay presbyter) seems to symbolize all of the abuses and perversions of the American language: it is the Word abused. Presumably the wafer represents the false advice given by the then Secretary of State that America should continue its involvement in the Viet Nam civil war, although on strictly moral grounds this country had no justification whatsoever for its increasingly active participation in that Asian conflict.

Misuses of language also occur in the examples from mass communication (symbolized by the almost comic monster NBCBSUPAPINSLIFE) and from the advertising industry. Not only does "Time Mutual" present the "World's Largest Camp Comedy" by turning the Viet Nam reality inside out but the poet also notices the pathetic but droll misuse of words by advertising companies. One billboard informs him that his generation is not the Lost Generation or the Generation of 1776 or the one of Manifest Destiny: it is "the Pepsi Generation"; another billboard tells him how Marines are "in love" with a local bread made by a Pop Art icon called Aunt Betty.

On a more profound level, one also notices how the poet himself suffers from the abuses done to the American language by fork-tongued politicians, hysterical columnists, mass media and by those Barnums of exaggerated and phony language—the gentlemen of advertising. What could be more trite, flat and prosaic, for example, than his own description of the Nebraska landscape: "icy winter/grey sky   bare trees lining the road/South to Wichita"? Here is an ultimate indignity created by false language: it leaves a contemporary American poet with only shabby equipment with which to try to do his job. Even his grasping at those masters of the spoken American idiom—Walt Whitman and Ezra Pound—as possible antibiotics to counteract the infections in our language turns into a buffoon episode in which the only words Ginsberg has are: "Ham steak waitress please."

What do all of these examples of perverted black magic language add up to? The poet tells us clearly in the desperate passage quoted a moment ago, beginning: "The war is language . . ." All of the perversions of black magic language in the opening section, the passage implies, not only helped to encourage and condone the original involvement of America in the internal affairs of Viet Nam but the false, evil idiom helps to perpetuate that involvement by distorting the bald reality that United States troops are engaged in a murderous aggression waged against Oriental peasants who have never threatened or harmed America in any way whatsoever.*

Then what must the mantra accomplish? It must oppose and dismantle the "war reflexes" conditioned by the false, evil misuses of the American tongue. How? Through language. Fire must fight fire.

For one thing, the true and beatific language must call events and moral realities by their correct names. And it must accomplish this tough task by embodying a vocabulary which is not only accurate but powerful and *magical* in the profound and mysterious sense of that word. Indeed, this true language must be something like the idiom used by the mystical alchemists of the Middle Ages—those extraordinary men who (as Jung documents in his important study *Psychology and Alchemy* (1953)) were hardly concerned with such trivial, childish goals as discovering how to transform cheap iron or matter into gold; rather, they were striving to create out of gross matter nothing else than the God Incarnate.

The true and beatific language, in short, must be brilliant and memorable enough to create and sustain the "absolute contrary field of will" which alone can cure the moral disease

---

* See Appendix Three for a discussion of the relationship between words and the morality of war.

resulting from the false and evil idiom and, by so doing, end the war in Viet Nam. The language of the last 180 lines must be the language of great poetry.

Is it?

The language of the creation of the mantra certainly is if not great, then memorable poetry. In strong, vivid and lucid words Ginsberg not only creates the possibility of an original super-natural reality for the American consciousness but he calls for the liberation of the holy and free in himself and in his fellow countrymen.*

But what about the language in the stanzas following the making of the mantra? Does it have the ring of great or mem-orable poetry?

No.

On the contrary, the shocking thing seems to be that the language of the final section of "Wichita Vortex Sutra" sounds much the same if not even worse than the black magic vocab-ulary of the first section. One hears the same flat, boring descrip-tions of the landscape, the same type of newspaper headlines, the same Rand-McNally catalogue of Kansas towns and cities, ending with a doggedly accurate map of Wichita streets and the names of office buildings, gas stations, the McConnell Air Force Base and the Lutheran Church of the Redeemer past which the poet's Volkswagen drives, heading for the Hotel Eaton on Douglas Street.

Not only is the language undistinguished and prosy but in

---

* I will never forget the feeling that swept over me as I heard the poet recite the lines of the creation of the mantra at The University of Chicago one evening in February 1967. Here was an American poet calling—for the first time in our literature perhaps and certainly for the first time since Whitman—for the possibility of the existence of the ancient verities in the life of these States. Ginsberg was calling for communion with the gods and for release of love and peace in the souls of Americans. He was calling, in truth, for the realization by himself and by all of us that the Kingdom of God is within everybody. And as I remember the figure of the poet chanting his prayer on the stage of Mandel Hall, I hope that never again will I have to hear or read the wide-spread but boring criticism of Ginsberg which scolds or condemns him because he is supposed to be the Rasputin of American Poetry: the degenerate who is out to subvert or tarnish the Stars and Stripes, Mom, Home, and the Boys of the 4-H Club, as well as *The Oxford Book of American Verse*. The man on stage that evening was a holy man.

several crucial instances the diction disintegrates into bad or
flashy rhetoric. Take the section in which Bob Dylan is invoked
as an Angel of Glad Tidings. As the Volkswagen speeds past the
"endless brown meadows" and the small Kansas town of Burns,
the folk-rock singer's voice floats over the radio, singing "Won't
You Come See Me, Queen Jane?" Here is the entire Dylan
section:

> Oh at last again the radio opens
> blue Invitations!
> Angelic Dylan singing across the na-
> tion
> "When all your children start to resent
> you
> Won't you come see me, Queen Jane?"
> His youthful voice making glad
> the brown endless meadows
> His tenderness penetrating aether,
> soft prayer on the airwaves,
> Language language, and sweet
> music too
> even unto thee,
> hairy flatness!
> even unto thee
> despairing Burns!

In what sense is Dylan "angelic"? And why does his voice
gladden the brown, endless meadows? Why should the town of
Burns be in despair? And even if its citizens are suffering from
despair, why should Dylan's "soft prayer" and "sweet music"
alleviate their unhappy condition? Answers to such questions
remain in my mind a total blank: the poem does nothing to
clarify them. Instead, it seems to fall back on an adolescent
rhetoric in which the mere mention of Dylan and the epithet
"angelic" are supposed to persuade the reader that here is an
angel of language who embodies the true and beatific American idiom which puts to rout the effects of the earlier language
of black magic. Even worse: Burns is in despair presumably
because its small-town natives are writhing in unhappiness (the
reader is encouraged to imply) because they don't hear Dylan

often enough. Unfortunately, the melancholy effect of such rhetoric is to make the reader suspect that such writing is no better in kind than the rhetoric of Senator Aiken and the copy writer who describes the "love" of Marines for Aunt Betty's loaves of bread.

An even more glaring example of bad rhetoric occurs in the (by now) celebrated final lines:

> The war is over now—
>> Except for the souls
>>> held prisoner in Niggertown
> still pining for love of your tender white bodies O
>> children of Wichita!

Even if one understands children here in the metaphorical sense which translates into "white citizens," one doubts if it is their bodies for which the ghetto Negro pines: it is more likely their necks. In a less melodramatic sense, it's neither white bodies (the hoary Caucasian fantasy that black men possess magical sexuality which if not castrated will lure white females away forever) nor white necks for which most Negroes "pine": rather, it's the more mundane opportunity to obtain and earn the jobs, prestige and buying power taken for granted by the majority of whites. Here I'm not interested in the compassion of Allen Ginsberg (he clearly is the speaker in the poem) for the American Negro; I am concerned with why the concluding lines disintegrate into piously liberal but sentimental rhetoric. Nothing in the body of the poem justifies the switch from Viet Nam to the Negro Revolution. Even less organic is the creation of the figure of the Loving Negro.*

Notice that until these lines the poem hasn't once mentioned civil rights or the Negro Revolution. Then why does the speaker switch horses, as it were, in midstream? To argue that, after all, both the Viet Nam conflict and the Black Revolution are both

---

* Nor can the final lines be understood (as far as I can see) as an example of the "impure" discussed in the concluding essay and in the essay on Frank O'Hara's "The Day Lady Died." The concept of the impure doesn't apply here because the final lines clearly are intended by the poet to be the conclusion of what is an extremely well-structured and organic poem.

"wars" and that the victims of both are victims of White American aggression and that the poet here attempts to end all types of war and aggression: this is pious liberal sentiment which has nothing to do with this poem as a poem. What the sudden and unprepared introduction of the loving Negroes of Wichita accomplishes, on the other hand, is to create the nagging suspicion that the speaker himself feels his mantra has failed, despite his assertion that "The war is over now," and that he tries to gloss over or even to ignore the suspicion of failure by turning to that last resort of the rhetorician: the instant cliché or self-righteous sentimentality. The conjuring of the loving Negroes is part of the same kind of rhetoric one hears from a rhetorician of the John Birch Society who invokes the cartoon of the Pilgrim Father with the White Face or the Henry Ford of Free Enterprise in an argument attempting to annihilate all that is not white or capitalistic or Protestant Christian.

Still a third example of bad rhetoric occurs in the Carry Nation section. The reader is asked to believe that the crusader for temperance—who in the 1890s marched into saloons throughout Kansas to hurl vituperations at the drinkers and smash furniture and fixtures with her hatchet ("hatchetation" of "joints," as she put it) — is responsible for beginning the "vortex of hatred" evident in Wichita today. Moreover, this vortex now defoliates the Mekong Delta and also murdered the poet's mother by driving her insane "one decade long ago." One accepts the existence of the vortex discovered by the poet in the same sense that one accepts the wasteland discovered by Eliot. No reasons exists within "Wichita Vortex Sutra," however, to clarify how Miss Nation created the vortex or why the vortex is responsible either for the war in the Mekong Delta or for the insanity of Mrs. Naomi Ginsberg. (I trust this doesn't sound flippant: I don't intend it to be.) Obviously his mother's insanity is a moving memory for Ginsberg—as the reader may recall from that great elegy "Kaddish"—but he still fails to perform the ancient task of the poet: to render why or how any connection whatsoever exists between her insanity and Carry Nation or between the two women and the current aggression of the United States against the Viet Cong. To feel that the connection should be obvious merely because of the poet's wounded feelings is not enough, in my opinion. Such a reading, in fact, only responds to the sentimental rhetoric of the lines and not to the lack of genuine poetry in them.

And this brings us to a final and perhaps profound issue: Why does the language fail to be great poetry? One approach to a possible answer would be to explore still another question: Does the mantra "work"?*

As far as additional news of war is concerned, the mantra seems to be working: we hear only of conflicts which happened a few days or even few hours ago as the poet reads an edition of the *Wichita Eagle-Beacon* of the 100 Viet Cong deaths near Bong Son and how soldiers "charged so desperately they were struck with six or seven bullets/before they fell." And he tells us clearly that he feels the mantra is working because:

> The War is gone,
>> Language emerging on the motel news stand,
>>> the right magic
>>> Formula, the language that was known
>> in the back of the mind before, now in the
>>> black print
>>> of daily consciousness

Even though we hear no more of present conflict, however, there seem to be several more subtle ways in which the poem itself suggests doubts that the mantra is "working" not only in the sense of the cessation of war but also in the sense of releasing the holy and free in both the speaker and in his countrymen. The most obvious of these doubts occurs when we hear what does come over the radio now that there's no more news of war. What the poet hears are the voices of angels.

We've seen how the voice of the first angel—Bob Dylan as

* I am dismissing without discussion another possible answer as to why the language fails. This is that answer which those readers and fellow poets who dislike (or envy) Ginsberg and his poems might be tempted to argue: namely, that the language fails because Ginsberg is a bad poet. I dismiss this view with the most basic observation. Any poet whose imagination could have created the mantra in the first place is one I will bear with and follow to the end, assured that he will take the poem into areas in which few American poets have dared to explore.

the Angel of Glad Tidings—fails in an important way to embody the incandescent language promised by the making of the mantra: his "blue invitation" disintegrates into sentimental rhetoric. Then the poet hears the voices of the Angels of Apocalypse—"Now radio voices cry population hunger world/& unhappy people"—who also prophesy the nativity of the new American Adam who presumably will overcome the Whore of Babylon of Famine and who also seems to fulfill the prophecy made in the first section of the poem: "I claim my birthright!/ reborn forever as long as Man/in Kansas or other universe— Joy/reborn after the vast sadness of War Gods!" But the new Adam is parodied and rendered merely comic by the voice of the mock Angel of Advertising which suddenly floats over the air waves with a fragment from a soap commercial: "you certainly smell good/the radio says . . ." False or evil language, in short, infects what at first appear to be the healthy voices of the new dispensation made possible by the creation of the mantra.

On still another level, the poem corrodes one's hope that the mantra is working in the sense that it has released the divine and free in the speaker and, by extension, in his countrymen. And that is: it ends in a loneliness or lack of love more exacerbating than the loneliness and hatred which pervades the opening section and which the poet discovers in himself and in his fellows and which he cries out against in the moving stanza beginning: "I'm an old man now, and a lonesome man in Kansas/but not afraid/to speak my lonesomeness in a car,/because not only my lonesomeness/it's Ours, all over America,/O tender fellows . . ."

Loneliness pervades all of the stanzas leading up to the creation of the mantra. One notices how desolate the loneliness feels in that the Nebraska landscape through which the speaker drives is without people. All one hears are faceless voices. In fact, the only faces seen are in the grotesque photo in *Life* depicting adolescent Marines "blowing the air thru their cheeks with fear." And it is this loneliness which compels the speaker to feel:

> All we do is for this frightened thing
> we call Love, want and lack—

> fear that we aren't the one whose body could be
>   beloved of all the brides of Kansas City,
>   kissed all over by every boy of Wichita—
> O but how many in their solitude weep aloud like
>   me . . .

But is this acute American loneliness and lack of love allevi-
ated by either the making of the mantra or the realities experienced once the mantra begins its dispensation?

At first, it appears that both loneliness and lack of love are
dispelled—particularly in the intimacy between poet and the
Indian holy men summoned in the litany at the beginning of
the creation of the mantra. Notice the vividness of detail in the
summoning of the ten saints: "Shambu Bharti Baba naked covered with ash/Khaki Baba fat bellied mad with the dogs/De-
horahava Baba who moans Oh how wounded,/how wounded"—
and so on. This is the kind of specific, intimate knowledge of
another person that only a close friend or lover has. But the
reader may also begin to notice a paradox: once the speaker
begins to summon the supernatural beings whom the saints
worship, the sense of intimacy evaporates. The poet calls on
them in increasingly formal and depersonalized epithets: "Allah
the Compassionate/Jaweh Righteous One"—and so on. Here
the irony is that the speaker seems to end lonelier than he began.

And the loneliness only becomes more exacerbated as he
continues driving toward Wichita. Even voices disappear as he
enters Wichita itself and sees only a gas station, factory, super-
market, "crowds of autos moving with their light shine," an
insurance company and the De Voors Gurad's funeral home. At
the end his only companions are ghosts and faceless abstractions
—the ghosts of Carry Nation and his mad mother, and the
anonymous souls of Negroes and the bodies of the "children" of
Wichita. The poem ends, in truth, in a nightmare vortex of
loneliness.

Still a third way in which the poem suggests that the mantra
hasn't worked its "right magic/Formula" is in the spiritual
vacuum which pervades the final section. As we've seen, the
mantra promises a release of the divine in both speaker and
fellow countrymen. Instead of continued communion with

the gods or an awareness of divinity in Americans, however, the poet sees statues commemorating the only god this country knows: the god of the pragmatic, concrete, materialistic present. It is as if Wichita itself becomes a cathedral filled with "statues" of signs advertising hamburgers and Skelley gas, the Kansas Electric Substation, Texaco, the Lutheran Church, the (felicitously named) Titsworth Insurance Company, the funeral parlor—and so on. And instead of the release of divine energy in Americans, the poet experiences only the re-release of hatred (in the figure of Carry Nation), paranoia (his mother), and racial violence (the Negroes of the ghetto). In short, the concluding stanzas depict a spiritually empty whirlpool, irresistible and catastrophic in power, in which the poet suffers the desolation of existence in a nation without gods or spiritual realities.

All of these doubts of the mantra's efficiency raised by the poem contribute to suggest that "Wichita Vortex Sutra" fails to achieve the intention stated by the poet: namely, to dismantle "the language consciousness conditioned to war reflexes by setting up (mantra) of absolute contrary field of will as expressed by language."

But does the poem itself fail? The answer might seem obvious. If the mantra fails and the language continues to be diseased by false or evil idioms, then Ginsberg's act of legislation fails too and obviously the poem itself is a failure.

But such a verdict depends of course on discursive analysis. Such analysis can help to reach an intelligent grasp of some aspects of a poem but it is almost useless if not a hindrance once the reader moves (as he should move) beyond what the poem *appears* to be saying and begins an adventure into the deeper and more obscure areas of the complex of experience which the poem may *in reality* embody.

In short, it should prove valuable to explore: *Why* does the mantra fail?

How could it have succeeded? When we examine the irony created by the meeting of the two equal but separate powers in the final section—the poet as holy man and America as secular nation—it should become clear how and why the mantra must fail.

On the one hand, there's the religious act of the poet as

holy man. As priestly legislator, he invokes saints and deities to help in the creation of the mantra; and then as Baptist, he announces the dispensation of the mantra by calling on "Proud Wichita! vain Wichita" to repent of its sin in having sustained the vortex of hatred, and he announces in the composite figure of the Loving Negro and the white "children" of Wichita the advent of the Lamb of peace, love and brotherhood. The Lamb is of course the new American Adam proclaimed earlier by the Angel of Apocalypse. The Baptist arrives in Wichita, in short, to make the prophecy announced in several passages throughout the poem.

But to whom? The America to whom the Baptist speaks is, on the other hand, clearly alien if not hostile ground for such a dispensation and Messiah.

How is America depicted in the poem? As we've seen, it seems a wilderness containing expanses of fields and meadows vacant of people but infested by the voices of "angels" of evil or false language, and containing small towns and the secular cathedral called Wichita—both of which are also empty of people (with the exception of the faceless crowd in Beatrice, Nebraska). In addition, Wichita contains statues commemorating the gods of commerce and technology, as well as a vortex of hatred filled with war reflexes, paranoia and ghettoes.

To think of this America as merely the wilderness surrounding the Jordan, however, would be an understandable but serious error. Notice how the poet himself responds to the alien reality, strength and beauty contained not only in the farmlands of Nebraska and Kansas but also in some of the small towns and in Wichita itself. Rural elegance is acknowledged in lines such as: "A black horse bends its head to the stubble/beside the silver stream winding thru the woods/by an antique red barn on the outskirts of Beatrice—/Quietness, quietness/over this countryside"; and in the view glimpsed through the chill earthly mist of "houseless brown farmland plains rolling heavenward/ in every direction." And the excitement of a happening is contained in the haiku of the burning garage in Beatrice: "Water hoses frozen on the street,/Crowd gathered to see a strange happening in the garage—/How red the flames on Sunday morning/in a quiet town!" Wichita too contains elegance and a kind of muscular or existential beauty: the poet responds to its "mysterious families of winking towers" grouped around the quonset hut on the hill, the aluminum robot of the Kansas Electric Substation signalling through thin antennae towers to the solitary derrick that "pumps oil from the unconscious/working day and night," the "green jewelled" traffic lights, the Texaco sign "starred/over streetlamp vertebrae"—and so on.

In short, the America here is the everyday middle class America which in its natural resources, standard of living, and commercial and technological genius is the most prosperous nation men have ever known. The "alien gods" of this country are of course the gods of the practical, existential present. And the implication seems clear, in my opinion, that such gods condone this nation's continued commitment to the South Vietnamese in their civil war with the North for the most obvious reason: it might be most practical to protect this American middle class life by helping to defeat Communism in Viet Nam and truncate its potential growth.

The irony, in brief, is this: the Baptist announces the coming of the Lamb in a country which neither desires nor recognizes the authority of such a Messiah.

And the irony cuts of course both ways. As we've seen, the Baptist is himself a distinguished victim of the black magic language which created the vortex of war and hatred he would oppose with the Lamb of peace and brotherhood: the Baptist speaks in the idiom of the New Testament Pharisee and not in the tongue of the Old Testament prophet. And the irony at the expense of middle class America cuts as deep. The greatest nation in the sense of material prosperity and power the world has known is capable of producing a language which is perhaps among the most barbaric the world has ever heard. Contemporary American language not only conditions "war reflexes" which result in a harvest of slaughter among Oriental peasants but in its banality, its glut of clichés and adolescent vocabulary with which to express complex adult feelings and ideas, this language affords no decent words with which a powerful American poet might express desire for peace and love and brotherhood.

The mantra fails, then, because it couldn't possibly have succeeded. If the mantra had "worked," the poem would have been false. How could the religious act of the poet, which is doomed to expression in language which embodies worship of alien gods, affect that language and what it has created and sustained?

One problem still remains: Does the failure of the mantra contain all of the complex of experience within this poem? What prompts me to raise the question is the heroic quality in the final image of the poet as Baptist.

Although the concluding lines with the image of the Loving Negro and the white children contain an ironic example of that false rhetoric which the mantra attempts to oppose, the lines when read from another view also contain genuine poetry. What makes the final lines moving, it seems to me, is the fact that they are spoken at all. Everything opposes this last and almost desperate attempt to make the mantra effective: the poet stands as Baptist crying in a false language in a secular wilderness; yet he refuses to stop his attempt to dismantle the vortex of hatred and death which seems about to envelop him.

In this sense, "Wichita Vortex Sutra" can be read as a poem of noble desire. The desire it embodies is the ancient one: that the Lamb of God come among this people, bringing peace, love and salvation. This desire not only seems to inspire the creation of the mantra in the first place but also encourages the poet to continue trying to build a Jerusalem of peace and brotherhood in the teeth of such a hostile or indifferent environment. In a striking sense, this is the same desire which we have heard in Blake's famous lines from "Milton":

> And did those feet in ancient time
> Walk upon England's mountains green?
> And was the holy Lamb of God
> On England's pleasant pastures seen?
>
> And did the Countenance Divine
> Shine forth upon our clouded hills?
> And was Jerusalem builded here
> Among these dark Satanic Mills?
>
> Bring me my bow of burning gold!
> Bring me my arrows of desire!

Bring me my spear!   O clouds, unfold!
Bring me my chariot of fire!

I will not cease from mental fight,
Nor shall my sword sleep in my hand,
Till we have built Jerusalem
In England's green and pleasant land.

Finally, the nobility of the desire of the poet who refuses
to cease from mental fight accounts, it seems to me, for some of
the memorable passages throughout the poem which in their
intensity and magnanimity seem unequalled by any American
poet since Whitman.

Reread that passage on United States Foreign Policy, for
instance, which occurs a little over half way through the first
section as the Volkswagen nears Marysville, Kansas, beginning:
"Is this the land that started war on China?" and ending with
the indictment of the Dulles law firm for the alleged greed
which prompted its support of the overthrow in 1954 of the
Guzmán regime in Guatemala which had favored agrarian
reform and encouraged Communists to hold key posts in government. Then there's the section depicting the Human Mystical Body which begins as the station wagon passes through
Waterville, Kansas and which ends: "When a woman's heart
bursts in Waterville/a woman screams equal in Hanoi." Or
take the Loneliness of Americans section (which some might
censure for its sentimentality but which I find genuine poetry
because of the incandescence of the desire) which opens with the
confession: "I'm an old man now, and a lonesome man in
Kansas" and continues with the meditation on God the Creator
and concludes with the poet searching for the language "that
is also yours."

In the light of such passages embodying Ginsberg's desire for
peace and brotherhood, we should reread the Indictment of
Wichita section, beginning with the entrance of the Volkswagen
into the "Centertown ganglion" and ending with the final
exhortation to the children of Wichita. When seen in the
broader context of the poem as statement of desire, this section

no longer seems, in my opinion, as rhetorical or sentimental as it once did. Now it blazes with compassion.

When the entire poem is seen as being a statement of desire, it seems irrelevant to circumscribe our critical appreciation by such questions as: Does the mantra fail? or Is this an anti-Viet Nam poem? What matters is that the poem embodies and sustains throughout the statement of Ginsberg's complex desire to assume the function of poet as priestly legislator and as Baptist announcing the dispensation of peace, compassion and brotherhood for all Americans. In this sense, then, "Wichita Vortex Sutra" is a major work.

Appendix One

NEW YORK CITY, AUGUST 1966

Dear Paul:

A proem part to this poem will be published in *Ramparts*. No fair making me do all that scribbling. Please hang on to this in case someone else asks me.

Not *only* a question of legislator as Shelley's formula. Merely that the war has been created by language (as per Burroughs analysis for cut ups) (or Olson's complaint about abuse of language) (or W.C.W.'s) & Poet can dismantle the language consciousness conditioned to war reflexes by setting up (mantra) absolute contrary field of will as expressed in language. By expressing, manifesting, his DESIRE (BHAKTI in Yoga terminology—"adoration").

This poem is a collage of news radio paper optical phenomena observed & noted in field of vision outside car window, at stops, etc. + fantasy + imagination, memory of history, desire, etc.

In haste—
Allen

[Note: Reference in the poem appears first, in *italics*; the poet's comment on the image, allusion, quotation or whole passage follows the reference.]

Face the Nation: radio interview show

Hickman: town in Nebraska

Signum enroute: Latin for sign (yes, billboard)

Aiken: Vermont Senator

"bad guess": quote Aiken on Face the Nation show Feb. 20 or so

Stennis: Senator

Holmes Alexander: columnist

to the Newsmen over the radio: on the Face the Nation show

Farmer's Grain Elevator: sign on elevator

Aunt Betty: a billboard sign, local bread I think

Marines . . . blowing the air through their cheeks with fear: a photo in *Life*

Rusk Says Toughness Essential for Peace: literal headline front page

Vietnam War Brings Prosperity: literal headline front page

youths of Liverpool: Beatles and all the other kids there

Beatrice: a town in Nebraska on Rt. 77

Hutchinson, El Dorado: Kansas

historic Abilene: Ike museum, Kansas

"of the fabled damned": Democratic Vistas (#97 Modern Library Edition, p. 314. Otherwise end of 4th par. from conclusion)

for Ike who knelt to take/the magic wafer in his mouth/from Dulles' hand/inside the church in Washington: this is literal also from TV—an incident during Ike's time

NBCBSUPAPINSLIFE: this is the abacadabra formula for
Black Magic Hypnosis communication in America

NBC

CBS

UP

AP

INS

LIFE etc.

Clark's face Open Ended: Senator Clark of Pa. who described
the war as unfortunately "open ended" (i.e. possible war
on China)

Stennis: Senator from Mississippi

Gen. Gavin: suggested enclave formula for U.S.

Enclaves/Tactical Bombing: retreat suggested then strategy

*Napalm and black clouds emerging in newsprint (and fol-
lowing lines):* all Feb. '66

Captain Kangaroo: pop song of the day

Dulles' family lawfirm: Dulles family lawfirm handled
United Fruit

Marysville: Kansas, across Neb. border—where [the poet
Michael] McClure was born

Oakland Army Terminal: there had been Berkeley attempts
to picket and leaflet this place

The Right Way: sign on train

Waterville: Kansas town

millionaire pressure: Mr. Love, 2nd biggest backer of Birch
Society, from Wichita

lonely crank telephone voices: When we came to read at
Kansas State U. in Wichita there were crank phone call
complaints to our sponsor the Philosophy Dept. Feb. '66

an aging white haired General: Hershey & the Draft

Hue: town in Vietnam site of Buddhist/Student Protests—
students were blister-gassed by Diem soldiers 1963

Republican River: Kansas City river, runs to Junction City

the old man's still alive: Truman

Shambu Bharti Baba: Naked sadhu I saw much of in Benares, lives in burning ground

Baba: Brother

Khaki Baba: 19th Century N. Bengali Saint who wore khaki & lived w/dogs

Dehorahava Baba: I met in Benares; yogi who said those words to me

Citaram Onkar Das Thakur: Vaishnavite Guru I met in Benares who said to me "Give up desire for children"

Satyananda: Swami I met who had freak 2 thumbs on one hand in Calcutta who said "Be a sweet poet of the Lord"

Kali Pada Guha Roy: Tantru Yogi guru from Benares who told me that, like Poetry, formal yoga also ends in Light of God

Shivananda: Swami of Rishihesh who told me "Your own heart is your guru"

Srimata Krishnaji: A living lady saint of Brindiban (home of Lord Krishna) who said I shd. take Blake for guru—she translated Kabir, a 14th cent. Blake-like Hindu poet saint, & many other saint poets, into English

Sri Ramakrishna: 19th century saint—go ask the Vedanta Society. He wept for Mother Kali

Chaitanya: 15th or 16th century Bengali Saint, worshipper of Krishna, who circulated Hari Krishna Mantra which I sing also—often pictured dancing half naked in ecstasy & supposedly himself an incarnation of Krishna

Preserver Harikrishna: One name for Vishnu the Preserver's incarnation (in Bhagavad Gita) as Krishna. Hari is name of Vishnu

Durga-Ma: Shiva's Force, or a 10 armed Female Principle wife of Shiva, Mother Durga, who destroys evil with violence

Tathagata: Buddha the "passer-through"

Devas: Hindu gods

yogas: a yogi is a man who does yoga

Mantra: a short magic formula usually invoking an aspect of the Divine, usually given as meditation exercise by guru to student, sometimes sung in community or "kirtan"— the formula is considered to be identical with the god named, & have inevitable power attached to its pronunciation. Oft used in chanting or invocation

my own Millennium: 1000 year period of bliss

My own form . . . sensations . . . . thought . . . imagination . . . . consciousness: the 5 "leaps" or 5 skandas (areas, apportionments, of consciousness, mentioned in Buddhist Sutras)

El Dorado: a town near Wichita on Rt. 35

Florence: small town in center of which is a watertower with large sign "Pure Spring Water"

"Kennedy Urges Cong Get Chair in Negotiations": literal headline Feb. 14, '66

Eagle News Service Saigon: Wichita Eagle story

Surrounded Vietcong Charge Into Fire Fight: this is the headline

Continued from page one: continued from Feb. 14 *Wichita Eagle*

after the Marines killed . .: these quotes are all exact: "some of the communist soldiers charged" etc

Angelic Dylan singing across the nation/"When all your children start to resent you . .": coming in on car radio

Burns: tiny town near Wichita

"you certainly smell good": that's what radio said that instant

Skelley's Gas: Skelley's Gas Station

Kellogg: (street) main drag in Wichita

Titsworth offers insurance: [to author's query, "Insurance firm? *some* name!" Ginsberg notes]: Yes, obviously

Hydraulic: street

De Voors Guard's Mortuary: Funeral director firm—the data is all there writ out in the poem

newspaper language factory: Wichita Eagle-Beacon office

Douglas: street

Hotel Eaton: on Douglas, near the beatnik Vortex Gallery

Mekong Delta: river—site of most of the present fighting (guerilla) in Vietnam & defoliation raids by napalm etc.

17th: street, near the University

Niggertown: area of Wichita between Hydraulic & 17th Street

Appendix Two

Aiken Republican on the radio: In my own mind Sen. Aiken's "bad guess" was just straight forward facts—that the whole $50 billion a year war machine was operating (comically enuf) on sheer subjective guesswork (like Laurel & Hardy trying to find oil). That's all I meant. "Bad Guess" as distinct from Orwellian pseudoscientific think-touch-Time-Life con that all higher decisions are options taken by Men of Distinction on basis of inevitable non-subjective Necessity.

that never worked for Ike who knelt to take/the magic wafer in his mouth/from Dulles' hand: Two grown men with destinies of planet in hand were dealing w/each other in a magic-subjective intimate way. Poem makes claim that much magic's going on unnoticed in US & I cited the above fact to nail it down in awareness, since taking sacrament's so common no one notices the anthropological fact of weird magic practices going on there. Also it's an evidence of white Christian Black magic conspiracy against nonchristian World.

Ham steak please waitress: Ham steak not intended as buffoon episode—merely a nailing down of common lunchtime fact in midst of overheated imagination runs re Pound + language. Rueful, but not buffoonish, in my opinion.

Sacred Heart my Christ acceptable . . . Jaweh Righteous One: Re the gods: & selected *aspects* of each God, i.e. sacred heart, compassionate, & righteous—in which I had personal faith, wherein I made personal identification, or found the ancient forms equivalent to the saints I met or my own heart's desire. This selection of aspects is done in this context at variance or oddness with most commonly held images of—say, Christ. Who as Christian gets really hung on the red-meat *Sacred Heart?*

the end of the war: "I here declare the end of the war" is a fact, whether the war ends for everyone or not. I end the war in me and anyone who's affected by my gesture . . . I didn't pronounce the mantra to work on all literal levels automatically. I pronounce it w/faith—& cast bread on waters.

Oh at last again the radio opens/blue Invitations!/Angelic Dylan singing across the nation: I think Dylan's "Queen Jane" is a great lyric poem, done as it is in blues style, an invitation to return to relationship—of course interpretation of this does depend on knowledge of lyrics & music by Dylan and in this particular song the passage means exactly what it says . . . Angelic because he looks like an angel & has spiritual or transcendental instinct & manifests them in music and poetry. If you feel there's no place for this type in Xtian [Christian] Angelology I'm sure we could find some variant Angelology in the new book by Davidson that wd. fit. After all, there is not "literally" an angel. Or better, Dylan is as literally angelic type as anything in history or literature.

despairing Burns: N.Y. Times today says whole Midwest is restive and unhappy and I was simply noting a Judgment: and given the Shelley and Warbroadcast data in the poem a judgment surrounded by facts.

the souls/held prisoner in Niggertown/still pining for love of your tender white bodies O children of Wichita!: As far as poesy & accurate language, my own favorite line in the poem is the last about pining for tender white bodies . . . I really dig the ending line as the perfect inspired element, switch, & focussing of the problem of awareness of Sacred Heart right on Wichita Streets. Quite flatly: my understanding is that present race hostilities is obviously frustrated relationship, frustrated love. The *ground* is desire. All hate energy is a conversion of that desire when blocked. That's obvious intellectually. I simply put it in the lover-like language it basically deserves: "still pining . . ."

Appendix Three

Moral realities are always among the first victims of the perversion and prostitution of language documented by "Wichita Vortex Sutra." Something rotten happens, for example, when a United States bomber pilot drops napalm on a defenseless Viet Cong village, assassinating or maiming children and women, and he's encouraged by current Army idiom in Viet Nam to call the napalm "cola." (Current here means the winter and spring of 1968.) "Cola" sounds as if he were dropping refreshments—indeed, the word recalls the familiar Coca-Cola slogan: "The pause that refreshes"—instead of napalm which scorches and destroys human flesh. "Hawks" is another example of sick language. Men who demand that America increase the barbarity of killing or the use of nuclear warheads on an "enemy" which has none: such men are not powerful, handsome, masculine hawks; they are vultures.

When language is twisted and deprived of its primary function—that is, to describe the truth of men and events—then a nation may well be on the road toward barbarism, immoral aggression and slaughter for the sake of slaughter. When language describing the morality of a war is accurately used, on the other hand, there remains the possibility that a great nation engaged in war may insist on the actuality of the tremendous phrase by Yeats—namely, the actuality which holds "reality and justice in a single thought."

The objection that the United States is engaged in hostility in Viet Nam in order to secure a needed toehold and possible airbases in Asia and that our real foe is not the Viet Cong peasant but Red China and possibly the USSR, is a legitimate and fascinating speculation: but it is another issue and it should not distract from our concern with the misuse and abuse of language documented in Ginsberg's poem.

John Logan

A CENTURY PIECE FOR POOR HEINE (1800-1856)

To Paul Carroll

> Give up these everlasting complaints about love;
> show these poets how to use a whip.
>
> MARX
>
> My forefathers were not the hunters.
> They were the hunted.
>
> HEINE

1

Heine's mother was a monster
Who had him trained
In business, war and law;
In the first she failed the best:
At work in his uncle's office
He turned a book of Ovid's
Into Yiddish. And Harry's memories
Don't even mention the family's
Chill and scare at the chance
Of a fortune from a millionaire. But a grown
Heine fainted and wept
If an uncle failed to provide;
And there was no money in the house when he died:

2

Except what he got from mother.
Syphilis brought
Its slow and fictional death—
Still he never would tell
His folks how sick he was of sex.
He wrote her frequently
To give no cause for alarm
Dictating because of a paralyzed
Arm, into the willing
And ready ear of some
Lady fair, reporting
For today, criticizing his wife
And telling the details of nearly-married life.

3

He called his mother a dear old
"Pussy cat";
His wife was a "wild cat";
She was the stupid Cath-
Olic opposite of the Jewish
Other—and cared even less
For his verse, being unable
To read and listening little,
Which is worse. Their need for love
So shocked him, he ran away
To a princess friend—like his sister
A rather crystalline dolly
Charitable toward sexual folly.

4

Two weeks after his mother
I mean his wife
And he were married, having harried
Each other for a number of years,
He put himself in a fight
With a man he got a cuckold;
He chose the absolute pistol,
But found he was only shot

In the thigh—and his own weapon
Of course went high.
So he went to visit his mom
After years of exile from home
Because of politics he put in a pome.

5

He left his mother I mean
His other at home
With her nervous bird and her
Shrieking tantrums—or else
He left the bird with the wife,
Et cetera—he wrote her a letter a
Day like a scolding parent
Afraid she'd become a Paris
Whore as he hoped she would
(And as he was) but she stayed
Till death, tho she shattered a glass
In her teeth, and all the rest—
Such as throwing a fish in the face of a guest.

6

As soon as he left himself
To the needs of a wife
He was shook to find in the face
In the mirror the eyes of his father
When his flesh had started to fade:
He began to be blind, and gave in
To a kind of paralysis that made him
Lift the lid of his eye
By hand to see his wife.
At the end, cones of opium,
Burned on his spine, helped him
To dream of a younger father
Doing his hair in a snow of powder;

7

He tried to kiss his father's
Hand but his pink
Finger was stiff as sticks
And suddenly all of him shifts—

A glorious tree of frost!
Unburdened of the sullied flesh.
His father died before him
Leaving him free to be
The Jew—he had fled their flight
To that of the protestant fake
Exacted in Christian states,
But pain had him lucid (or afraid)
Till the ancient covenant with God was made.

8

But his tough old mother stayed on
And he never became
The husband; he took to his marriage
Couch interesting women,
Remaining a restless, curious virgin.
In the last years of his life
He wept at the pain of lust
Stirred in his tree-like limbs
Already dry. And he left
Framing with paralyzed lips
One more note to his mother.
Only the ambiguous Dumas cried
At the holy rite they danced when he died.

9

His soft old flesh slipped
Inside its great
Trunk with a sound he held
Too long inside his skull.
God absolve his mother,
His wife and him: after all
As Heine said, thrusting
Again that Freudian wit
He showed to prove to friends
And self his sanity had not
Come to the fate of potency—
"It is God's business to have mercy."

10

There is no need to forgive
His saintly poems
As there is for the work of another,
To whose New York park
The marble Lorelei fled—
Banned with the books of her maker—
To mock and lure at him
And us from a Catholic plot
Like a baptized, voluptuous mother
Powerful over the figure
Of the frantic Harry, and over the
Three mother-fishes:
Melancholy, an idol of the Hebrew Smart,

And one with the mended, broken arm of Art.

After Antonina Valentin
and after a memorial to Heine
in Kilmer Park

WAS FRAU HEINE A MONSTER? OR YUNG AND EASILY FREUDENED IN DÜSSELDORF, HAMBURG, BERLIN, PARIS AND NEW YORK

Even before the reader who has only the most casual familiarity with Heine's biography arrives at less than half way through "A Century Piece for Poor Heine," he may feel puzzled if not actually appalled at the increasing number of errors of fact in the poem. True, John Logan's wry wit and compassion for his subject may delight, engage and perhaps even distract; but the reader can also hardly help but notice as early as in stanza four, for example, at least three outstanding errors.*

The first error occurs in the sly Freudian slip in the opening three lines. To hint that there was little distinction between Heine's mother, Frau Betty van Geldern Heine, and his mistress and eventual wife, Crescentia Eugénie Mirat, is a bald distortion of fact. Frau Betty Heine was a cultivated, poised and intelligent person; Heine's wife (whom he insisted on calling Mathilde) was illiterate, childish and stupid.

And the second distortion of fact is even more glaring. Eight days after the poet had married Mathilde on August 31, 1841 he did fight a duel with a Herr Solomon Strauss in the duelling

---

* I confess I feel some reluctance about using the word "error of fact" because it implies some negligence or lack of correct information on the part of the poet, whereas, as I hope we'll see, the errors are what help to make Logan's poem so memorable. My reluctance comes from an illuminating remark I heard John Logan make about the act of writing "A Century Piece for Poor Heine." In his recollection of what went into writing the poem in 1956, Logan explained, he cannot find any memory of having consciously distorted or falsified the biographical facts he had read in Antonina Valentin's *Heine: Poet in Exile* (1956).

Certain passages which captured his attention were marked in his copy of the biography, Logan continued, but when he sat down to write the poem a few months later, he didn't feel that it was important to check the veracity of this or that biographical event or fact. And readers of poetry should feel grateful that he did not bother. Otherwise, we may have had an "accurate" but in all events perishable biographical poem about Heine instead of this good poem which, if my reading of it is at all near the mark, embodies a deep but anguished experience. Here we are confronted of course with the mystery of the creative act. And we'll leave it at just that.

area near Saint-Germain in Paris; but Heine hadn't cuckolded
Strauss: he'd merely slandered the gentleman and his wife.*
The slanders occurred in a book Heine had published earlier
that year called *Das Buch Börne* which contained a vitriolic and
somewhat libelous attack against one of the poet's old enemies,
Ludwig Börne, a political journalist and agitator who for years
had been the leader of the liberals among the German exiles in
Paris and who happened to be the lover of Frau Strauss. When
Das Buch Börne appeared in Germany and Paris, its snide and
tasteless insinuations about the love affair between Börne and
Frau Strauss caused such a furor that Heine's Hamburg publisher, Julius Campe, complained in a letter to the poet: "Even
Börne's old political opponents have gone over to his side because they respect his honesty, sincerity and incorruptibility of
character. Your book has produced exactly the opposite effect
from what you intended. Some people commit suicide by their
own free will: your literary suicide is something new." Indignation against Heine grew and eventually Strauss challenged
him to a duel of honor. After considerable squabbling over the
choice of weapons—Strauss favored swords, Heine pistols—the
contest took place at 7 a.m. on September 7th. And as Logan
accurately describes, Heine received a flesh wound in the hip—
Strauss had been given first shot because he was both challenger
and offended party—and when his turn came the poet chose to
fire in the air, ending the duel.

The final distortion in stanza four is subtler and more curious. It is true that a few weeks after the duel Heine travelled
by stage coach from Paris to Hamburg in order to visit his
mother for the first time in twelve years; but it is false to assert
that he'd been exiled from Germany due to "politics he [had]
put in a pome." His exile, which began in May 1831, was entirely voluntary. Earlier that year, Heine's prose book *Nachträge
zu den Reisebildern* was banned in Prussia as being "pernicious,
blasphemous and obscene"—stock epithets of the day for any-

* True, the verb Logan chose in the phrase "a man he got a cuckold" seems
to encourage an ambiguity: it could mean, on the one hand, that Heine had
merely caused Strauss to be called a cuckold by exposing in print his wife's
infidelity; or it could mean that Heine had actually cuckolded him. In the
context of the stanza as a whole (which we'll look at in a moment) I incline
to favor the second reading.

thing liberal or unorthodox—and a few months later the poet had taken leave of his fatherland in a preface he'd written for a book by one Robert Wesselhöft called *Kahldorf über den Adel* in which Heine had voiced his fury against the suppression of the Polish insurrection of 1831 by the German States and against the reactionary governments of Germany, Austria and Russia. As a result of these and other radical activities, Heine became and remained persona non grata in his native land and his name frequently appeared near the top of this or that roster of political undesirables circulated by one or another of the German States, most regularly on rosters originating in Metternich's government in Austria. But the fact remains: his long exile was voluntary; and it did not result from any poem of his.

How are we to understand these errors and distortions? If they were the only ones in "A Century Piece for Poor Heine," we might dismiss them as oddities of poetic license in much the same spirit that any reader of poetry learns to ignore Keats' famous error at the end of "On First Looking into Chapman's Homer" which states that stout Cortez was the first European to see the Pacific from the heights of Darien in Panama, whereas history tells us that it was Balboa. A closer look at other lines throughout the poem, however, reveals that the errors and distortions are chronic, particularly whenever an aspect of the relationship between Heine and his mother is mentioned or explored.

What was that relationship like? To learn something about it, we should look first at how Heine's mother is portrayed in the poem.

In the very first line, for example, Frau Heine is slandered by still another distortion of fact: "Heine's mother was a monster . . ." This simply was not true. However antagonistic one may feel toward mothers, the fact is that Frau Betty Heine was a decent person who favored her eldest son Harry above his two brothers and sister throughout his life. This sober and practical woman discouraged Harry's early precosity in writing to the extent that, as Miss Valentin records, "she snatched all books of fiction from him, kept him from going to the theatre, and strictly controlled his circle of acquaintances"; but it is obvious that such guidance (however misguided) was meant more in the spirit of hope for her brilliant son than in the spirit of malevolence. At first, Frau Heine encouraged Harry to become a scientist, then a businessman and, for one brief period, to seek his destiny as a professional soldier; once Heine had become a celebrated poet and man of letters, however, Frau Heine gave the attention and recognition which only a good parent can give: she followed all her son's works, "asked endless questions about his literary projects, and complained if the news he gave her was not detailed enough."

In other words, still another error occurs in stanza three when the implication is made—with considerable wit and cunning—that Betty Heine and the poet's wife Mathilde shared a stupidity and indifference regarding Heine's work. Of Mathilde, Logan writes:

> She was the stupid Cath-
> Olic opposite of the Jewish
> Other—and cared even less
> For his verse, being unable
> To read, and listening little,
> Which is worse.

It is true that Betty Heine didn't encourage her son to become a poet; but once he had, she did care about what he accomplished and took pride in the praise and attention his work earned in the literary and intellectual scenes of the day. To give Frau Heine the accolade she merits, one has only to recall other mothers of boys who became celebrated poets. Think of Madame Vitalie Rimbaud—that pillar of stern, destructive will as far as her son Arthur was concerned. Or Baudelaire's vain and seductive mother who paid no attention whatsoever to her son's poetry. Then there's Mrs. Grace Hart Crane. Almost to the end of his life, her son was still trying in vain "to explain himself to his mother," as Allen Tate remembers, "and to force from a peculiarly stupid and selfish woman the recognition and love of what he was."

But the poem continues to slander Frau Heine in crafty lines like: "And there was no money in the house when he died:/Except what he got from mother." Here the first line is accurate. In the months before the poet died in his wretched 5th floor apartment at Number 3 Avenue Matignon in Paris, his household (consisting of Mathilde, her parrot and dog and the faithful maid Pauline) lived from hand to mouth—as the poet had done most of his adult life. And on the day of his death there literally was no money in the house. (A friend paid for the funeral.) But the poet, scarcely able to move his paralyzed lips, consoled his wife by promising there soon would be money: a person whom he identified as Little Zacherie would come presently "with a sack full of silver coins." And so it happened. On the day after Heine's funeral—held on February 20, 1856 in a Montmartre cemetery—a dwarf dressed in black appeared at the apartment and with a low bow introduced himself as Monsieur Zacherie from the publishing house of Michel Levy. Clutched in his hand was a canvas sack containing the money due from the French edition of Heine's works published by Levy. In addition, Heine's widow could anticipate the annual allowance bestowed on the poet by his cousin Karl Heine, son of the millionaire Salomon Heine, the banker of Hamburg. Although the allowance was niggardly, it usually arrived on schedule. In short, there was "no money in the house" when Heine died: but soon there would be some. But not from mother. This is a barefaced lie. Even if she had wanted to send Harry some money Frau Heine couldn't have done so: she was almost stone broke at the time of his death. But the reader is encouraged to believe that the "monster" of a mother promoted financial dependency upon herself in much the same wicked spirit that she had insisted that her son be trained in "business, war and law."

Even this last charge contains a distortion. It was Uncle Salomon who persuaded Harry to read law. After observing his young nephew take less than a year to plunge into bankruptcy the cloth firm of Harry Heine & Company (which Salomon had subsidized) the uncle agreed to pay for the poet's study at the University of Bonn—but only on the condition that the studies would promise a definite utilitarian goal. Law and medicine were the only "liberal" professions open to Jews at that time in Germany; and since Heine showed no interest in becoming a doctor, law was the only possibility left. (Heine earned the degree of Doctor of Law in 1825 but he never practiced.)

And still another distortion occurs in the very next lines: "At work in his uncle's office/He turned a book of Ovid's/Into Yiddish." This is a charming, ironic scene. And given the date (Heine lived in Hamburg from 1816-1819 and for a brief period worked in his Uncle Salomon's bank in that city) it can be seen as an archetype of a scene soon to become all too familiar: the young poet trapped in the hostile or enervating business world. (One thinks of the young T. S. Eliot lost behind the teller's cage in Lloyd's Bank or Hart Crane grinding out ad copy extolling the glories of Arrow Shirts or fertilizer or young Allen Ginsberg slaving over market research reports.) But the actual scene probably never occurred. It is true that Heine hated his job in the bank and that his uncle tried to discourage his ambition to become a poet and, indeed, soon fired his nephew; but the translation of Ovid was made several years before Heine lived in Hamburg. According to Miss Valentin, the poet put some of Ovid into Yiddish when he was a student at the Technical School in Vehrendampf. And who had enrolled Heine in this trade school? That's right: it was mother. So what does this minor distortion accomplish? It points to an odd inference. Even in small episodes, the poet feels as if mother were present. Although Frau Heine was living in Düsseldorf, she is present in her son's feelings and fantasy as he sits on his stool in Uncle Salomon's bank. Moreover, the distortion suggests that to Heine trade school and bank were one and the same place: it is where mother forbids him to write verses translated from a naughty poet.

What do all these distortions, lies and slanders about Frau Heine add up to?* They picture her as a witch. Her evil spell over her son Harry seems to be that her presence dominates all

* The errors and distortions might help to answer another problem which the alert reader may have wondered about: Why did Logan choose to write a poem about Heine's anguished but yet comic and finally pathetic relationship with his "dear old pussy cat" of a mother instead of doing the job in an essay? The poem is clearly about Heine's Oedipus Complex. Why not explore it in an essay? The reader can find a discussion of this problem in Appendix One.

of his activities (even when, in reality, she has little or nothing to do with them). Biographical facts show that she was hardly to blame for the fact that Harry had to waste his time studying law or working in the bank or that he took a stupid wife who had no interest in his work or that he died broke. But to Heine the spell of the witch was intricate and binding.

To see how intricate and binding, let's look again in stanza four at the marriage, the duel and the trip home. Are the three events related? To Heine they are. But how? Surely a duel over an affair of the heart is a peculiar kind of honeymoon; and this duel in particular: Heine feels as if he's fighting because he's stolen another man's wife (whereas, in fact, Börne did the deed). Here the emotional implication seems to be: "Marriage is fighting and punishment." But why? The clue is of course in the opening lines: "Two weeks after his mother/I mean his wife/And he were married, having harried/Each other for a number of years . . ." When "marriage" is translated into "I feel married to mother" it becomes clear. This is of course the classic Oedipal triangle: mother, son, dad; love, betrayal, fighting. Here we must applaud Logan's brilliant pun in the verb "harried." As a little boy in the family circle, Heine was called Harry; and the union through rhyme of "harried" and "married" suggests that to Heine his relationship with Mathilde was probably one more replay of the old Oedipal melodrama in that the poet in all events engineered a lot of the chronic and Homeric turbulence, angers and scrapping between himself and his wife.

The melodrama plays on. As a result of the duel (it matters little in fantasy who actually wins or loses) Heine does indeed "win" mother back: he goes home to her. And how does he feel about it? The poem tells in an ironic, sly way. Notice how the comic spelling of "pome" creates an off-rhyme with "home" and "mom." But we've seen that Heine was not exiled from Germany because of his political verses. Why does it seem to him that he was? He could write poetry better than almost any man alive. So he is exiled because of what he can do as a man. Thus, the triple rhyme above translates into emotional terms somewhat like this: "I've been punished (exiled) because I'm a man. But now I'm wounded. Nobody would dare hurt me. I can go home. Mother's mine again." Heine returns, feeling like a little boy again. Notice how his acts as a man, for example, are negated in the stanza. Little boys have fantasies that they're married to mother; men get their own wives. Little boys fight with father in the fantasy they're dueling over mother; men wage wars for profit, land or power. Little boys write "pomes" about homes and moms; men compete for literary recognition and prizes by writing literature.

Heine indeed is bewitched. No matter what he does as a man—get married or duel or write poetry—it appears to him only as one more replay of the ancient but trite melodrama.* What does the replay feel like in the stanza just discussed? It seems to be a malevolent feeling of thwarted sexuality, violence and punishment, accompanied by the spurious delight that the little boy once again has mother all to himself. It is the feeling which pervades the whole poem.

No wonder Frau Heine is shown as a fascinating witch. Her grown son can never escape from her spell. But she's a witch only in his fantasy life; in reality, Betty Heine was not only a loving person but she led her own life quite independent of her son Harry.

But what about the other facts mentioned in the poem which are not directly related to Betty Heine? All of them are accurate. In stanza five, for example, we hear how Mathilde "shattered a glass/In her teeth" and rudely threw a fish in the face of a guest. And so she did. Her temper tantrums were equal to if not more ferocious than Heine's own fits. And in the following stanza, we meet the splendid episode of the dying poet

---

* I should make it clear that I'm not insensitive to the suffering and tragic waste involved in such a melodrama. Heine must have felt terrible a lot of the time; and he may not have known why. Neurosis is a crafty enemy: it can disguise itself as successfully in battles with a man of genius as it can in battles with you and me. And the waste in time and energy is pathetic. I hope it is also clear that the remarks above are only glosses on Logan's poem; they're not intended to present a case history of Heine's emotional problems. On the other hand, we are within bounds, I think, when we respond to the comedy and irony in Logan's portrait of Heine. Notice how the three events in stanza four, for example, are depicted as if they took place in a Keystone Kop Komedy. There is something droll and ironic in the figure of a great poet engaged in what is, after all, an emotional hangover from childhood.

dreaming of his father as being a "glorious tree of frost." This too happened. In a moving passage written a month or so before Heine died, he tells how he dreamt he saw his handsome father Samson sitting before a mirror, his hair a cloud of powder, his pink face all smiles. Heine confides that as a child he'd often seen his father like this when the barber came to powder his wig. In the dream he tried to run toward his father in order to kiss his hand; but as he touched the fingers he felt horror: "Father's fingers were dead branches. He had become a leafless tree. Hoar-frost covered all his limbs."

It would seem, then, that in Heine's fantasy life—for that is of course the heart of the poem—distortions occur only when mother is involved and that the poet is free to see facts about Mathilde and Samson Heine for what they are. But in what sense are such facts accurate?

Let's look at how Mathilde is pictured in the poem. Every mention of her is biographically correct. When we first meet her (at the end of stanza two) Heine is criticizing her in letters written home to mother which complain about "the details of nearly-married life." And he had ample reason. In almost every respect Mathilde was a bad bargain as a wife: a poor house-keeper, a spendthrift and a second-rate companion, particularly when it came to taking any interest in her husband's career as a man of letters; and in her frequent tantrums she was indeed "a wild cat." In short, Mathilde was "the stupid Cath-/Olic opposite of the Jewish/Other." In only one respect is her portrait inaccurate: Mathilde was terrific in bed. According to copious testimony in Heine's journals and letters, she loved sexual pleasure as much if not more so than he apparently did. But the reader would never guess this from the poem. Why not? Heine's other sexual exploits are given sufficient mention.

An odd fact about her portrait in the poem should help to account for this striking omission. When is Mathilde seen in any place but in the shadow of her mother-in-law? Every mention of her, moreover, puts her in the most unfavorable light—even in the one episode when she seems to stand on her own. At the end of stanza five we hear how Mathilde "stayed/Till [Heine's] death" but we notice how what might have been a good or even noble act of self-sacrifice is followed by mention of one of her innumerable tantrums and her rude behavior as hostess; and we also notice how all of these facts are contained within the frame of a stanza whose most prominent section describes Heine in mother's home, writing scolding letters to his wife. In short, Mathilde has no face or place of her own: she is always only a foil for the omnipresent witch of a mother.

The irony of this is subtle but telling. Mathilde Mirat's skill in giving sexual pleasure is the only thing she can do better than Betty Heine—at least, as far as Harry is concerned. Omission of this fact keeps Mathilde forever inferior to mother. The irony is of course at Heine's expense too. Omission of sexual pleasure infers that in his deepest feelings he may not have allowed himself to enjoy the rich, satisfying sexual scenes he had (or could have had) with his wife. The omission suggests, finally, that Heine probably never felt married. In addition, he doesn't have a genuine relationship with any other woman except mother. In the poem he keeps company with several ladies fair (including that wonderfully classic European type: the princess who was a "rather crystalline dolly/Charitable toward sexual folly"); but all of them remain as shadowy as Mathilde. In a letter to Wesselhöft written when Heine was 32, he expressed this sad plight: "I'm condemned to love only the most stupid or lowest type of female." (Translate "love" to "desire sexually" and the reader probably has a good description of the dynamics of all of his "romantic" attachments.)

Even the accurate facts about Mathilde, then, can be seen as only one more tentacle of the octopus who dominates the poem: Heine's fantasies about himself and mother.

But in what sense are either his dream of his father or his promiscuous sexual affairs (still another "accurate" biographical fact, by the way) tentacles too?

The dream about Samson Heine in stanzas six and seven is one of the few touching episodes in this otherwise relentlessly sad poem. As the poet lays dying, he dreams of "a younger father/Doing his hair in a snow of powder"; but when he attempts to kiss his father's pink fingers, suddenly "all of him shifts—/A glorious tree of frost!/Unburdened of the sullied flesh." The reader knows from Heine's journals that this dream actually occurred but in the poem itself it seems ambiguous.

Exactly who becomes transformed into the tree of frost? It could be Heine as well as his father. The ambiguity is revealing. If it is Heine, the tentacle is obvious: in fantasy the poet becomes the handsome rival who once stole mother from the little boy. But if it's indeed the father Samson, then the tentacle is even more tenacious. Notice how the image of the glorious tree of frost decays (in the following two stanzas) into a grotesque and pathetic tree as we see Heine weeping in his declining years at the pain of lust "Stirred in his tree-like limbs/Already dry" and hear how the poet's badly paralyzed body is like a great tree trunk. The contrast between the glorious tree and the grotesque one forces a comparison: "Father was a handsome, glorious man; I am a damaged grotesque." This comparison is a curious one—to say the least. Although Samson Heine was charming and good-looking, he was a compulsive failure and bankrupt throughout life; his son was not only handsome too (until he became partly paralyzed and grew corpulent) but he was one of the great successes in the literary world of his day. But the comparison suggested by the two trees suggests that even on his death bed (and presumably throughout life) Heine felt inferior and impotent when compared to Samson. Why? The answer is obvious: father can be mother's lover; the little boy cannot.

Both possible readings of the glorious tree of frost image can of course be accurate. In fantasy, Heine sees himself as both the rival who replaces father and the little boy who's punished for such a terrible deed by pretending he's a damaged tree.

The image of the damaged tree reoccurs throughout the poem in various ironic allusions to Heine's "tree-like" arms and hands. One notices how in each allusion the one limb Heine puts to good use in reality—by writing his books—is described as being either punished or damaged or impotent. Moreover, all of the allusions reveal some type of sexual failure. In stanza one, for example, the young Heine is punished by having to work as a bank teller when he'd rather spend all of his time in translating one of the masters of erotic literature. In following stanzas the reader hears how his arm is paralyzed as the result of intercourse and how Heine impotently misses the mark when it comes his turn to fire "the absolute [phallic] pistol"—and so on.

Here is of course a brilliant use of image. It suggests that in Heine's fantasy his achievement as a man is damaged, impotent or inferior: the damaged limb becomes a metaphor of how he tends to see himself not as a man but as still a little boy.

What about the one other aspect which appears to show Heine as a man in the poem? His sexual conquests. Ample mention is made of them; but how does Heine *feel* about sex?

The poem tells us. Or more accurately, it suggests how he felt. The reader hears how "sick he was of sex" and how indeed he dies as a result of syphilis contracted during intercourse (it was probably during his student days, according to hints in his letters). To find out how Heine felt, however, we should look at a puzzling phrase in stanza eight and at a peculiar adjective in the final stanza.

The phrase is the one in which he's called a virgin: ". . . he took to his marriage/Couch interesting women,/Remaining a restless, curious virgin." Exactly how was he a virgin? The lines imply that a multitude of sexual adventures cannot in themselves cause a person to lose his virginity—except in the strictly biological sense. To lose one's virginity is to be no longer a child. But adult sex involves adult people. A lot more is involved than the physical act. One who engages in intercourse but neither shares himself as a person nor wants his partner to be a person in her own right is one who remains an emotional virgin: he remains a child. Heine remained a "virgin," finally, because "his tough old mother stayed on"—in his memory and in what look like his deepest feelings. To betray her would be to lose his virginity by finding another woman (in the full adult sense of the word).

Another side of the same feeling is suggested by the peculiar adjective used in the last stanza to describe his poems: they are called "saintly." Saintly? One might accurately describe as "saintly" the poems of John of the Cross or Gerard Manley Hopkins or even, in a curious way, the lyrics of the late Theodore Roethke; but whatever else Heine's poems are they are neither holy nor marked by profound religious sensibility. (His late, anguished "religious" lyrics are another matter which, I am afraid, we cannot explore here.) Nor are Heine's poems distinguished for either their faith, hope or charity. If anything,

Heine's poems are profane, often ribald, despairing. The dominant amatory feeling in Heine's most successful poems hardly celebrates the joys of love, much less the delights of sexual pleasure; on the contrary, as Heine himself confessed, at the height of his frantic and apparently voluptuous sexual bouts with Mathilde: "How strange it is that overwhelming love writes no verses. It scarcely permits one to write prose." In truth, the prevailing experience of love in Heine's lyrics is bittersweet, frustrated, ironic, disillusioned.

The experience is close in spirit, in fact, to a portrait of Heine which appeared in a poem by one of his classmates at the University of Göttingen in the early 1820s. Philip Spitta, who later became an author of pious verses, wrote the poem, which reads: "One day the Devil went forth into the world. Eventually he discovered a cottage covered by flowers in which Love dwelt. Love was ill and nursed by Angels. The Devil assumed his post by Love's bedside. Ever after, those who passed by heard the Devil's malevolent laughter mingling with the voices of the Angels and they glimpsed his infernal face framed by the roses of Heaven." "The portrait is very like me," Heine is said to have admitted as tears filled his eyes, according to contemporaries who were present. It's unclear whether Heine meant Sick Love or the Devil: perhaps he meant both. In any event, Spitta's rather trite and rococo poem contains two elements which could well have affected Heine. Love is victim of both physical malady and diabolical possession. In other words, Love cannot function and is doomed to misery. One way to view this is to see a man who feels he cannot enjoy a rich and meaningful sexual life with the beloved because he's under a spell.

It is accurate, incisive and ironic, then, to call Heine's poems "saintly" if by saintly Logan implies that characteristic of the traditional saint which ignores or hates or fears the delights or fulfillment possible in adult sexuality. Indeed, what is generally considered Heine's happiest love poem—"Du bist wie eine Blume"—was inspired by a young Jewess who was still a child when Heine was moved to write the lyric. (He met her during the summer of 1823 when he visited the estate of the young Polish nobleman, Count Eugene von Breza.)

And when the reader begins to wonder about to whom Heine's love poems were addressed, I think he'll see how they are "saintly" in another but related sense. Innumerable ladies fair served as the immediate stimulation for most of Heine's best lyrics: his haughty cousin Molly, her sister Therese (the subject of the exquisite "Die Kleine gleicht der Geliebten") and during the later Paris years, the shadowy women whom we know only by their first names—Angelique, Diane, Hortense, Yolanthe, Maria. What seems curious, however, is that regardless of how numerous or different from one another these women may have been, Heine explores again and again the same complex of feelings when writing verses to them. And that complex is (as I suggested a moment ago) bittersweet, frustrated, ironic, disillusioned. What I imply here should be obvious: I do not presume to say that Heine didn't desire or lust after the women to whom he addressed his lyrics; I merely suggest that the love he documents with each and every female bears a curious but sad resemblance to the one experience of love which dominates "A Century Piece for Poor Heine": the frustrated and bittersweet feeling that he cannot achieve either a lasting or satisfying sexual relationship with the beloved. And if the experience is always the same one, then the beloveds in the poems may be only substitutes for the one archetypal figure with and for whom the poet first experienced the complex of feelings of affection, frustration, anger and disillusionment which he was later to write so memorably about. That figure is of course the Madonna of childhood. In their consistent devotion to the Madonna, then, his poems are "saintly." (By writing so devotedly about this cluster of feelings, however, Heine may have enjoyed at least one dubious pleasure. In verse he could conjure back emotions associated with mother and, in this sense, he could bring her into the present and "keep" her with him for a while.)

Then how does the Heine in the poem feel about sex? The two passages we've explored seem to point to one melancholy conclusion. Even in his most vivid sexual feelings, Heine continues to see himself as a naughty but restless (and probably often frustrated and angry) little boy. Since he could never consummate his sexual feelings with their first and lasting object, he had to be "content" with second best: he keeps himself a little boy sexually by remaining a virgin and writing love poems about only his feelings for the Madonna.

Other aspects of the poem reveal how Heine may have felt

in the deeper parts of his unconscious about the octopus of everlasting involvement with mother. Take the peculiar sequences
of time.

In a standard biography the reader could expect a clear pro-
gression of events beginning with the poet's childhood in
Düsseldorf, and continuing through the Waterloos and Pyrrhic
victories of adolescence—the unrequited passion for his cousin
Amalie (the "Molly" of the early lyrics) and the fiascos in
commerce in Frankfurt-am-Main and Hamburg; the study of
law at Bonn and the more congenial reading of literature under
A. W. Schegel at Göttingen, the cynical "conversion" to Chris-
tianity in 1825, the early celebrity earned by *Buch der Lieder*;
and then the developing years of mature fame in Berlin as the
"German Voltaire"; the triumphs, follies and frustrations of the
Paris years, including the love affairs and the Punch-and-Judy
marriage with Mathilde; and ending with the agonized, sordid
but curiously heroic death by syphilitic paralysis.

In Logan's chronology, however, we notice how Heine dies
and resurrects several times. As early as the last line of stanza
one Heine dies broke. In the next stanza he is dying from "the
slow and fictional death" of syphilis but he recovers sufficiently
to be able to escape in stanza three to the castle of his "princess
friend." By stanza five he's dead again—at least by implication
in the statement that Mathilde "stayed/Till [his] death." Three
stanzas later he finally dies the official death, framing "one more
note to mother," and is buried. By the end of stanza nine, however, Heine has recovered to the extent of being able to amuse
his friends, himself and the reader with his famous aphorism:
"It is God's business to have mercy." And in the final stanza we
meet the poet who is "alive" enough (even though he's a statue)
to feel "frantic" because the marble Lorelei "mock and lure"
at him in the Heine Memorial Statue. Notice one other distortion of the calendar. By the end of stanza two and throughout the next stanza Heine is solidly married and obviously has
been married for some time; yet at the beginning of stanza
three he's been a husband for only two weeks.

Why is there such scrambling of years and dates? The answer
seems to be a sad one. The several deaths and resurrections and
the crazy calendar of other events point to the suggestion that

for Heine there is no sense of growth. He seems to see himself stunted in a changeless world of childhood.

This suggestion is strengthened, I think, when we consider what Logan omits from the poem. Although the title tells us that it will be about Heine, we must wait until the very last stanza for any mention of his achievement as a writer. To appreciate what Logan accomplishes by this omission we need only recall some famous poems addressed by one poet to an admired master: Wordsworth's sonnet on Milton or Auden's elegy on Yeats or Dante's tribute to Virgil throughout most of *The Divine Comedy,* and so on. Logan's omission is chilling in its inference. It suggests that Heine in the most alive recesses of his emotions may have taken scant satisfaction from the one role in which he succeeded as few men have succeeded: the writer who became one of the masters of world literature. The reader hears about Heine's work, in fact, only in so far as it has some connection with the relationship with mother: the Ovid translation, the exile allegedly because of a political poem, the "saintly" poems, and the distortion of fact which claims that both Heine's mother and wife didn't pay attention to his books. No mention is made of the poet who wrote *Die Nordsee* cycles and classics like "Die Lorelei," "Du bist wie eine Blume" or "Erstorben ist in meiner Brust" or the grand and anguished religious poems of the last years or even "Atta Troll," the influential poem which in the eyes of many critics sounded the death knell of Romantic poetry. Nor is there any mention of the compassion and macabre satire in his best prose. One reference is made to his celebrated wit but the poem clearly isn't interested in presenting the great Heine humor which led Havelock Ellis to exclaim: "Heine's humor is a modern development of the mad king and the fool in *King Lear*—that humor which is the last concentrated word of the human organism under the lash of fate."

Why not? Heine must have known that he had a genius for literature. But "A Century Piece for Poor Heine" implies by omission that in his eyes the genius and the recognition he received remained secondary to the primary fact of his life: the young mother and little Harry.

How is this great poet depicted, for instance, in the very last stanza describing the Heine Memorial Statue which stands in

Joyce Kilmer Park in New York City? Here the irony is again telling and pathetic. Although a century has passed since his death (Logan's poem was written in 1956) Heine remains frantic under the spell of the "voluptuous" Lorelei mother. And notice the adroit use of the present tense (the rest of the poem is in the past) in the description of the terrible spell of the mother: she "mock[s] and lure[s] at him." The implication is: "And so it shall always be." In addition, the final image contains an irony which Heine would have been among the first to appreciate. One of the supreme lyric poets of the world ends (as a result of the Nazi barbarism against the Jews) in the park named after one of the worst poets of the world. Moreover, the author of "Trees" provides the final and bitter nuance to the image of Heine as a damaged tree. The man who wrote:

> I think that I shall never see
> A poem lovely as a tree;
>
> A tree whose hungry mouth is prest
> Against the earth's sweet flowing breast;
>
> A tree that may in Summer wear
> A nest of Robbins in her hair;
>
> Upon whose bosom snow has lain;
> Who intimately lives with rain.
>
> Poems are made by fools like me,
> But only God can make a tree.

is surely the ironic Döppelganger of the great poet whose most persistently profound feelings have been suggested by this poem to be haunted by memories of the "sweet-flowing breast" and the god-like father who can "make" the mother.

Even in the look and sound of "A Century Piece for Poor Heine," the reader may sense something of Heine's life-long bondage to memories of early emotional fantasies. Notice how the poem at first looks harmonious and orderly as if it were about one thing and one thing only. And so it is. But is the poem that harmonious? The harmony is in important ways an illusion. Notice the slightly jarring, if not jangling, effect evident as early as the end of stanza one: the sentence ends at the beginning of stanza two—an effect which reoccurs at the end of stanza six and the first line of stanza seven. Even more jarring is the meter itself. Basically a loose iambic trimeter, the meter again and again contracts to a two-line beat, helping to suggest the feeling of discordancy within what only looks like harmony. Then there's the incongruity of the style itself. The tale of a great lyric poet is told in a style which often passes over into doggerel. This seems deliberate: the doggerel parodies the pathos and gravity of the central fact of the poem—the crippling relationship with mother.

When these elements of style are seen as a whole, it suggests the feeling of a man grating his teeth, trapped inside a tree or prison cell, as it were, free to move only within the confines of the trunk or cell from which he cannot escape. One remembers the Wood of the Suicides in Canto XIII of the *Inferno*. Dante unwittingly plucks a branch from one of the trees and the trunk begins to bleed because it is really the "body" of a damned soul. But the difference between Dante's tree and the tree which is Heine in Logan's poem seems basic. In the *Inferno* the suicides have been metamorphosed into trees (whose leaves and branches Harpies gnaw and mutilate forever) because they forfeited their real bodies by doing the ultimate violence to themselves: their suicide is out of despair of God's mercy. In "A Century Piece for Poor Heine" the poet becomes a tree because he has never allowed himself to grow: his suicide is a suicide of the emotions.

Why Heine committed a suicide of the emotions must remain a tragic mystery. One cannot presume to psychoanalyze him and Logan is to be commended, in my view, because he stops short of such pretension. Instead, he succeeds with consummate result in depicting the plight of a great poet who remained a prisoner in the Venusberg of memories and fantasies from childhood.

I conclude with a confession and with what I hope will serve as a mild exorcism or antidote because I am not unaware of the irony inherent in our entire discussion. The subject of this essay was, after all, one of that rare company whose love lyrics and unfailing, spectacular humor have brought delight and truth to countless men and women. Our discussion, on the other hand, has been sober, even grim. Still, while we were exploring some of the ways in which Logan delineates and dissects what Heine may have suffered from in the more obscure and less accessible areas of his unconscious, I tried to keep in mind the man himself, and I confess that from time to time I entertained the happy suspicion that Heine might have appreciated the wit, irony and compassion lavished on him by Logan. And I also wonder whether he might have enjoyed at least one attempt at irony in this essay. I allude to the phrase from *Finnegans Wake* buried in the title. "Yung and easily freudened" occurs, you may remember, in a passage in which Joyce seems to be having a merry time mocking (among other things) the more ponderous and humorless critics who having absorbed some of the Freudian discipline turned their attention to Lewis Carroll in the hope of discovering a happy hunting ground in his novels and in such juicy biographical episodes as Carroll's relationship with young Alice Liddel. By way of tribute and admiration to Heine, then, and to the poet who wrote with such affectionate understanding about him, here is the passage from Joyce:

> And, speaking anent Tiberias and other incestuish salacities among gerontophils, a word of warning about the tenderloined passion hinted at. Some softnosed peruser might mayhem take it erogenously as the usual case of spoons, *prostituta in herba* plus dinky pinks deliberatively summersaluting off her bisexycle, at the main entrance of curate's perpetual soutane suit with her one to see and awoh! who picks her up as gingerly as any balmbearer would to feel whereupon the virgin was most hurt and nicely asking: whyre have you been so grace a mauling and where were you so chaste my child? Be who, farther potential? and so wider but we grisly old Sykos who have done our unsmiling bit on 'alices, when they were yung and easily freudened, in the penumbra of the procuring room and what oraculer comepression we have had apply to them!

Appendix One

The problem arises of course from the obvious but slippery fact that Logan selects only those aspects which depict some facet of Heine's relationship with his mother, his wife and, in one episode, his father; but he deliberately ignores the rich possibilities inherent in Heine's other experiences as well as in his poetry, prose and thought. To this problem Heine himself seems to offer one answer in the following lines from one of his familiar lyrics:

> Es ist eine alte Geschichte,
> Doch bleibl sie immer neu;
> Und wem sie just passieret
> Dem bricht daz Herz entzwei.

> ("It's the same old story/Although it's always new;/And for him to whom it's just occurred/It can break the heart anew.")

Now, an essay exploring Heine's Oedipus Complex would concentrate on the truth of the first line above but it would have no tolerance for errors or distortions in the poet's biography. The skeleton of such an essay might look something like this: the poet's acute Oedipus Complex not only kept him emotionally tied to mother's apron strings but it also, sadly, prohibited Heine from becoming an adult with respect to sexual and financial matters.

Our essay might continue by developing some of the implications suggested by Heine's complex. One such implication might be the question: What was the relationship between his emotional problem and the source of his poetry and his macabre, stinging "Freudian" wit? And such a question could lead, in turn, into broader but related areas. For example: To what degree are the anguished roots of a lot of lyrical poetry grounded in the poet's involvement with memories of mother and childhood? Here one thinks of Baudelaire or Rimbaud or Hart Crane or the Dylan Thomas of "Fern Hill" and "Poem in October"; the figure of the mother in Whitman's life and in the "Kaddish" of Allen Ginsberg also comes to mind. Investigation of the relationship between the image of the mother and the source of some of the great poems by these writers could take us, in turn, into an exploration of a less romantic view of some of the masterpieces of the poetry of love. Was it simply by chance, for example, that the beloved of Catullus or Petrarch or (even) Dante was the wife of another man?

Another area which the essay on Heine's emotional problems might examine would be that occupational hazard of many poets: the galling financial dependency. Heine himself suffered from it all of his life. Why have so many other poets also existed in such demeaning or dependent straits? Here the roll call extends as far back as many of the poets of antiquity and includes Villon, Coleridge, Baudelaire, Rimbaud, Verlaine, Dylan Thomas, Crane, César Vallejo—as well as many contemporary poets. Our essay might discover that the comforting bromide, which blames the myopic and/or pigheaded world for refusing out of ignorance or jealousy to reward the poet, might be adolescent; and that a more rewarding and intriguing strategy would be to study some of the facts of the biographies of poets. Time and again, the facts would reveal the puzzling and often disturbing reality that many of the poets cultivated and even perpetuated dependent if exacerbating scenes whenever it came to the question of money.

But a good poem will tend to ignore such considerations and questions. In particular, it will resist an abstract paraphrase like: "'A Century Piece for Poor Heine' tells about the poet's Oedipus Complex." Of course it does. But the salient difference between an essay and a poem both dealing with Heine's emotional problems is that the essay would explore the origin of the complex, whereas the poem would be far more concerned in embodying the sweat, the lies, the profoundity of feeling and the pathos of what such a complex might have felt like to one man named Heinrich Heine.

W.S. Merwin

LEMUEL'S BLESSING

You that know the way,
Spirit,
I bless your ears which are like cypruses on a mountain
With their roots in wisdom. Let me approach.
I bless your paws and their twenty nails which tell their own
      prayer
And are like dice in command of their own combinations.
Let me not be lost.
I bless your eyes for which I know no comparison.
Run with me like the horizon, for without you
I am nothing but a dog lost and hungry,
Ill-natured, untrustworthy, useless.

My bones together bless you like an orchestra of flutes.
Divert the weapons of the settlements and lead their dogs a
      dance.
Where a dog is shameless and wears servility
In his tail like a banner,
Let me wear the opprobrium of possessed and possessors
As a thick tail properly used

To warm my worst and my best parts. My tail and my laugh
    bless you.
Lead me past the error at the fork of hesitation.
Deliver me

From the ruth of the lair, which clings to me in the morning,
Painful when I move, like a trap;
Even debris has its favorite positions but they are not yours;

From the ruth of kindness, with its licked hands;
I have sniffed baited fingers and followed
Toward necessities which were not my own: it would make me
An habitué of back steps, faithful custodian of fat sheep;

From the ruth of prepared comforts, with its
Habitual dishes sporting my name and its collars and leashes of
    vanity;

From the ruth of approval, with its nets, kennels, and taxi-
    dermists;
It would use my guts for its own rackets and instruments, to play
    its own games and music;
Teach me to recognize its platforms, which are constructed like
    scaffolds;

From the ruth of known paths, which would use my feet, tail,
    and ears as curios,
My head as a nest for tame ants,
My fate as a warning.

I have hidden at wrong times for wrong reasons.
I have been brought to bay. More than once.
Another time, if I need it,
Create a little wind like a cold finger between my shoulders, then
Let my nails pour out a torrent of aces like grain from a thresh-
    ing machine;
Let fatigue, weather, habitation, the old bones, finally,
Be nothing to me,
Let all lights but yours be nothing to me.
Let the memory of tongues not unnerve me so that I stumble
    or quake.

But lead me at times beside the still waters;
There when I crouch to drink let me catch a glimpse of your
    image
Before it is obscured with my own.

Preserve my eyes, which are irreplaceable.
Preserve my heart, veins, bones,
Against the slow death building in them like hornets until the
    place is entirely theirs.
Preserve my tongue and I will bless you again and again.
Let my ignorance and my failings
Remain far behind me like tracks made in a wet season,
At the end of which I have vanished,
So that those who track me for their own twisted ends
May be rewarded only with ignorance and failings.
But let me leave my cry stretched out behind me like a road
On which I have followed you.
And sustain me for my time in the desert
On what is essential to me.

THE SPIRIT WITH
LONG EARS AND PAWS

Ever since "Lemuel's Blessing" appeared in the early winter of 1962 in *The New Yorker*, the lonely grandeur of the voice praying and the authority of individual lines and images in it have brought me back again and again to the poem. Yet it remains an enigma. (In a seminar in the Writers Workshop at The University of Iowa I studied "Lemuel's Blessing" with some of the most able and knowledgeable readers of poetry a teacher could want: but we had to admit, after some hard work, that we'd failed to arrive at any stable understanding of the poem. This essay has gone through five or six false starts so far; and as I look at "Lemuel's Blessing" on my desk, it seems more mysterious than ever.) What I find puzzling about this poem is simple yet obscure and even disturbing. There seems to be no question that it is a prayer; yet how does the reader come to some understanding of the enigma which the poem invites him to contemplate: To whom does Lemuel pray? And for what?

Although the answer to the first problem is perfectly clear, it is also enigmatical. Lemuel prays to a spirit to whom he attributes both knowledge of the "way" he wants to follow and power to help him avoid various snares impeding the journey, as well as the resources to sustain Lemuel once he's followed the way into the "desert." What seems mysterious, however, is that this spirit has long ears and paws: indeed, it is a wolf.*

Now, the fact that the spirit has the characteristics of a

---

* Although the poem doesn't explicitly identify the spirit as being a wolf, I think that two clues make a strong suggestion that it must be a wolf. The first clue is of course the epigraph from Christopher Smart which introduces the poem: "Let Lemuel bless with the wolf . . ." As far as I am concerned, this eliminates other canine possibilities such as jackal or coyote. And the second clue eliminates the possibility that the spirit is a dog. Throughout the poem Lemuel makes only the most biting, derogatory references to himself as being "only a dog" when he is without the spirit's assistance. The final possibility—that the spirit is a member of the cat family—is merely fanciful, I think, given the Smart epigraph and the contrast implied between Lemuel as dog and the spirit.

wolf may not at first seem too mysterious. After all, the wolf-spirit might be an alter-ego or totem animal in much the same way that the nagual is often considered as an alter-ego or personal guardian spirit by Central American Indians or that the elanela (which can be either panther or serpent) is viewed as an alter-ego by warriors of the African Fang. North American Indians also prayed to totem animals such as the coyote or beaver; and one hears of private prayers to spirits among the Eskimo, as in this invocation and petition:

> You, gull, up there,
> Steer down towards me.
> Come to me.
> Your wings
> Are red
> Up there in the coolness.

with its implication of: "May I have your virtues, your gifts, your freedom"—and so on.* In other words, Lemuel is praying to an alter-ego or totem animal, asking that he come to possess the wolf's strength, nobility and cunning.

But who is Lemuel? The epigraph from Smart's "Jubilate Agno" identifies him as the Old Testament King of the Hebrews mentioned briefly at the end of the Book of Proverbs. The reader may recall that King Lemuel's short speech (Proverbs XXXI: 1-31) repeats advice on how to be a good and righteous ruler which his mother has given him: "Give not thy strength unto women, nor thy ways to that which destroyeth kings"; avoid

* Anthropologists and scholars of religion and folklore have discovered animal ancestry (or at least, animal aspects and symbolism) in many of the gods, spirits and daemons worshipped by the ancients in the Western tradition. Some scholars even suggest that all gods were originally animal in origin. The Homeric sea-god Poseidon, for one, was originally worshipped as Poseidon Hippius (the Hippopotamus), and the Greek God Dionysus was originally Dionysus Taurus (the Bull). And was the Paraclete or Holy Ghost of the Christian Trinity originally a bird-god? For a more detailed discussion of animal worship and theriomorphic symbolism, the reader can consult Sir Edward Taylor's classic *Primitive Culture* (1871) and of course Sir James Frazer's *The Golden Bough*. And for a brief discussion of religious poetry in general in American literature, the reader might want to refer to Appendix One.

getting drunk; judge righteously when the poor and needy stand on trial before your throne; and find yourself a virtuous wife. In brief, Lemuel seems to be an archetype or model of all that is moral, just and prudent; and he guides his people with law and order. Lemuel is, in effect, the symbol of the civilized community.

Then why does he pray to become like the wolf which traditionally is considered the antithesis of civilized tribal life: solitary, untamed, a predatory killer of livestock, an outlaw in the sense that the dog is not one?

And the sense of paradox only increases when one notices *how* Lemuel addresses the wolf-spirit. Both in the invocation and in the subsequent petitions Lemuel's speech seems deliberately to recall that form of prayer hallowed by centuries of supplication by the children of Israel and by Christians: the Old Testament Psalm. In fact, both the imagery and the structure of the classic Psalm are reproduced liberally throughout the poem.

The metaphor likening the spirit's ears to "cypyruses on a mountain," for example, recalls the Psalmist's frequent mention of such trees and the mountains of the Lord Jehovah; and the haunting image of Lemuel's bones as an "orchestra of flutes" blessing the spirit reminds one of the Psalmist's "All my bones shall say, Lord, who is like unto thee? (Psalm XXXV:10) ; and the stanza beginning "But lead me at times beside the still waters" echoes of course the shepherd Psalm XXIII. In addition, Lemuel uses the same type of humble and self-deprecatory image to describe himself when he is without the spirit—as a dog "lost and hungry,/Ill-natured, untrustworthy, useless"—which the Psalmist often employs to describe himself when he is without Jehovah—as a broken vessel or an owl among ruins.

And Lemuel prays within a structure used by many of the great Psalms—in specific, the Lament Psalm (according to the classification into literary types suggested by the Old Testament scholar Hermann Gunkel). The Lament Psalm usually embodies a structure containing these parts: the introduction consists of a cry for help addressed to Jehovah, followed by the body of the prayer describing the nature of the lament or complaint (often illness or danger of death or old age or the persecution of enemies) ; the lament may often be interrupted by requests invoking a series of motifs to induce the god to intervene; and frequently the Lament Psalm concludes with a vow to offer thanksgiving if the petition is answered. This is almost an exact blueprint of the prayer said in "Lemuel's Blessing." First we hear the invocation and blessing of the spirit; then follows the description of plight and plea for relief and deliverance from enemies and death; several interruptions request the spirit to intervene; and the prayer ends with the pledge of perpetual worship if the plea is heeded and with a reminder of devotion and final request for care.*

Now, what is the paradox contained in the use of the Psalm with which to invoke and petition a spirit who has the characteristics of a wolf? Of all the prayers said in the West the Psalm is probably the most ancient, hallowed and popular form of prayer used in communal worship—whether recited in a Sunday service held last week in a Methodist Church in Peoria or chanted at Matins 500 years ago in a Benedictine monastery in Florence or sung during Yom Kippur 3000 years ago in the Temple of Solomon in Jerusalem. But here the Psalm is used to petition a spirit who seems to embody characteristics which are anti-communal.

The paradox only increases when we consider for what Lemuel prays. What is the "way," for example, which Lemuel desires to find and to follow? He describes it quite clearly. It is a path leading away from the "settlements" and away from

* One also notices a minor stylistic parallel between some of Merwin's lines and what the 18th century English exegete Robert Lowth first observed about many of the lines or parts of lines in the Psalms: they are related in a special way. Lowth called the relationship "parallelism of verse-numbers," of which he suggested three types: synonymous parallelism, where the second line or stich repeats the thought of the first ("Hear this, all peoples!/ Give ear, all inhabitants of the world" (Psalm XLIX:1); antithetic parallelism, where the second stich presents some antithesis to the first ("For the Lord knows the way of the righteous,/But the way of the wicked shall perish" (Psalm I:6); and synthetic parallelism, where the second stich supplements or completes the first ("I cry aloud to the Lord,/and he answers me from his holy mountain" (Psalm III:4). In "Lemuel's Blessing" Merwin makes particular use of the antithetic parallelism in such lines as these:
    Let fatigue, weather, habitation, the old bones, finally,
    Be nothing to me,
    Let all lights but yours be nothing to me.

that which the community calls important or valuable: the "opprobrium of possessed and possessors" and the several "ruths" of the lair, kindness, prepared comforts, approval and known paths. Now, these conditions and virtues are what traditionally makes life worth living in a civilized community; and the subtle ambiguity of the use of the term "ruth" to describe some of them indicates that Lemuel knows only too well that the community with its approval of possession, its promise of home and prepared comforts, and its qualities of kindness, approval and known and tested "paths," is a good if not desirable place in which to exist. ("Ruth" can mean "compassion for the misery of another," and in this sense Lemuel may be feeling pity for those still "trapped" by the values and life of the settlement; but "ruth" also means "sorrow for one's own actions," and in this sense he may be regretting either his former condition as a member of the community or his present action in wanting to leave his lair, the prepared comforts, the known paths—and so on.) Still, it is obvious that Lemuel wants to leave the settlement behind.

And once he's travelled far from it (at least in his desires) he asks to be shown an even more difficult path. It is the path which begins in the stanza "I have hidden at wrong times for wrong reasons . . ." This "path" leads away from Lemuel's former self as a member in good standing in the settlement. His prayer is that he may be delivered from the concerns which that old self may have felt: concern over "fatigue weather, habitation, the old bones, finally," the memory of tongues (his own and those of friends?), concern over his own death and, finally, his own ignorance and failings and concern about those who would follow him, presumably out of desire or what he's now come to regard as "their own twisted ends." What he prays for, in effect, is to become free of the human community, its traditional values, and its definition of who or what he is or should be.

Here, then, is the complete paradox which animates the poem: one who is an archetype of civilized tribal values petitions in a traditionally communal form of prayer that he be allowed to exist outside of civilized communal values, categories, definitions, approval and rewards, and come to share as deeply as possible the nature and characteristics of the wolf.

How are we to understand this paradox? One possible way is to return again to Lemuel. If the speaker in the poem had been, say, Diogenes the Cynic or even Thoreau, the poem would have lacked at least this exciting tension: only one who believes in the traditional values and definitions of civilized society can appreciate what he gives up by turning his back on them. It is one thing to live as a hermit at Walden Pond, never having known or appreciated the success and approval which civilized society can offer; it is another to be a cardinal of the church and then abandon one's power and comfort in order to devote the rest of one's life to helping lepers in Africa. Thomas More's decision to withhold his vote of approval from Henry VIII's remarriage is of course another case in point: More knew what it meant to be not only a millionaire by his own efforts but Lord Chancellor of England and beloved friend of his King. And this accounts for both Lemuel's intimate knowledge of what he now wants to avoid (the details of the several "ruths," for example, are vivid and often tempting) and his disgust and fear of those civilized snares. In short, his former self and life give this present prayer its urgency, intensity, as well as its fierce sincerity.

What exactly does Lemuel want? He longs to escape from any civilized codification (whether it be moral, religious or worldly) and thus perhaps open himself to the unknown possibilities of other realities. The path he wants to follow leads to an existence outside of the community and its values, definitions, laws, morality—and so on.

The only other text by an American I know which resembles "Lemuel's Blessing" is Thoreau's *Walden*. But Thoreau's experience is similar only in its passionate conviction that the farther one can remove oneself from the accepted and comfortable values of the community, the better it shall be for that man. But the reader must search in a far more remote period to find anything that resembles the spiritual dimension of "Lemuel's Blessing." (By "spiritual" I imply the old-fashioned sense of the word: the opposite of the earth, earthy.) We must return, in fact, to the example of the Desert Fathers and the hermits who, during the second and third centuries after the death of Christ, inhabited the desolate areas around the Mareotic Sea, the Thebaid, and the wasteland beyond Antioch, the home only of scorpion, owl, and Egyptian or Asiatic devils. One thinks of Antony the Copt, Simon Stylites and Jerome. Not only did these extraordinary men turn their backs on the community of their day but like Lemuel they sought a way unknown in their desire to become in the image of the Christ. And as we hear the lonely austerity of Lemuel's voice, I wonder if the Christ may have appeared as foreign and inexplicable to those early Christians as the wolf-spirit must seem to a reader of contemporary American poetry. After all, the Christ of the Desert Fathers was not the familiar figure known in medieval Catholic Europe or in 19th century American Protestantism; indeed, he may have seemed to the early hermits and anchorites more like the mysterious presence of the wolf-spirit than the Jesus of later traditional Christian devotion.

A moment ago, I suggested that *Walden* appeared to be the only book in our literature that was at all close in spirit to the experience being explored in "Lemuel's Blessing." I had forgotten that disturbing but memorable passage in "The Dry Salvages" in which Eliot calls on the elders (and himself) to have the courage to abandon "the ruth of the lair" and "the ruth of approval" in order to search for a deeper and uncharted communion with the god:

> Old men ought to be explorers
> Here and there does not matter
> We must be still and still moving
> Into another intensity
> For a further union, a deeper communion
> Through the dark cold and the empty desolation
> The wave cry, the wind cry, the vast waters
> Of the petrel and the porpoise.

But does the Lemuel in Merwin's poem experience the "deeper communion"? Does he reach, in effect, the desert which exists independent of the civilized world and beyond its bound-

aries? The poem doesn't say. In fact, "Lemuel's Blessing" ends
with an enigma even more puzzling than the intricate one with
which it began. The paradox is this: although Lemuel becomes
more like the wolf as the prayer develops (in the sense that
allusions to the derogatory image of himself as "nothing but
a dog lost and hungry" gradually vanish altogether) he still
lacks the wolf's most characteristic and important quality—
namely, austere independence. On the contrary, Lemuel ends by
making one more dependent plea: "And sustain me for my time
in the desert/On what is essential to me."

And the paradox only grows when we wonder about another
question which the poem doesn't clarify: Does the wolf-spirit
answer his prayer? And even more mysterious: Does the wolf-
spirit actually exist outside of the speaker's belief and desire
for escape from the Old Adam in himself? In this sense, the
poem itself disappears into an enigma which recalls the basic,
rich ambiguity which prevades Camus' *The Fall*: Is the narra-
tor speaking to the stranger whom he says he meets in the
waterfront bar in Amsterdam or is he talking only to himself?
The reader never knows for sure because the stranger doesn't
reply even once in his own words.

But the final paradox of "Lemuel's Blessing" only reveals
that the poem is what it describes: an intense longing to be free
from all traditional and known categories and answers, including the answer to questions such as: Does the wolf-spirit really
exist? or Is Lemuel at the end on the way and has he reached
the desert or is he still on his knees in a synagogue or in his own
study? or Is the way and the desert actually inside of him?

Perhaps the best way to think about this final paradox and
its ramifications is to contemplate the image of the visitor with
the fox's head whom Merwin describes in this passage from a
letter written in 1967 commenting on "Lemuel's Blessing":

> When I'd finished the poem, nearly eight years ago, I
> showed it to Ted Hughes. It was the last winter that he
> and Sylvia [Plath] were living around the corner from us
> in London. He told me a story. At Cambridge he set out
> to study English literature. Hated it. Groaned having to
> write those essays. Felt he was dying of it in some essen-

tial place. Sweated late at night over the paper on Dr. Johnson et al—things he didn't want to read. One night, very late, very tired, he went to sleep. Saw the door open and someone like himself come in with a fox's head. The visitor went over to his desk, where an unfinished essay was lying, and put his paw on the papers, leaving a bloody mark; then he came over to the bed, looked down at Ted and said, "You're killing us," and went out the door.*

Appendix One

Both of these problems—To whom is an ostensibly religious poem addressed? and For what does the petitioner ask?—have been present in American poetry almost from the beginning. To whom Edward Taylor's "Huswifery" is addressed, for example, seems obvious: the poet calls on a 17th century Congregational Christ; but what is his Lord's gender? Here is the opening stanza:

> Make me, O Lord, thy Spinning Wheele compleat.
> Thy Holy Words my Distaff made for mee.
> Make mine Afflictions thy Swift Flyers neate
> And make my Soule thy Spoole to bee.

To think of one's self as the Lord's spinning wheel is of course a witty and homespun conceit in the tradition of the Metaphysical Poets. But to let the discussion remain completely within the context of a literary style or school is to miss an odd dimension in this good poem. Let's take the conceit outside of literary fashion for a moment and see that it asks the reader to

---

* The poet continues with the good news that Ted Hughes "changed departments"; and he then offers a fascinating and cryptic comment on both the wolf-spirit in "Lemuel's Blessing" and the animal in the later poem of his called "Totem": "These animals are not *chosen* and refuse to be identified, absolutely, zoologically. They rise, as it were, from dreams, facing away, and no more want that kind of partial identification than the Other wishes to divulge a name." (These passages are from a letter dated November 16, 1967, which helped a lot when I rewrote this essay, and particularly when I decided to leave the poem in the mystery in which it clearly asks to remain.)

view the Lord as a New England housewife and the supplicant as the spinning wheel and spool with which the wife spins "Holy robes for Glory," which the poet will presumably wear in heaven. And for what does Taylor pray? He prays to be saved. But he's asking for special conditions of salvation in which he implies that he wants to continue feeling totally dependent and helpless: he is a passive spinning wheel and spool of yarn. In this metaphor Taylor appears to be asking to return to the condition of a helpless infant, all of whose needs are in the hands of the mother who is the Lord. Even more strange perhaps is this: one can argue that in this poem Taylor ushers in the Blessed Virgin Mary by the back door, as it were, by attributing to the Lord the divine maternal role occupied by Mary down through centuries of Christian devotion. And if this be so, then this poem in its quiet and homey way gives the lie to generations of classic Protestant devotion—including no doubt Taylor's own sermons from the Congregationalist pulpit in Westfield, Massachusetts—which thought that it had banished the Virgin and Maryology forever into a Limbo reserved only for Papists.

Or take a contemporary American devotional poet: the young Robert Lowell of *Lord Weary's Castle* and *Land of Unlikeness*. In poems such as "Christmas Eve Under Hooker's Statue" or "In Memory of Arthur Winslow" or especially in the cycle "Mother and Son," Lowell appears to invoke the Christ of Catholic Europe. But what would English Catholic poets like Francis Thompson, Gerard Manley Hopkins, Blessed Robert Southwell or Richard Crashaw have said about such lines as these?

> Here the Lord
> Is Lucifer in harness. Hand on sword,
> He watches me for mother and will turn
> The bier and baby carriage where I burn.

In fact, Lowell's Christ is less often the Savior of traditional Catholic piety to whom one prays for salvation than he is a curious figure whom the poet summons to act as a kind of avenging angel—one who opposes or who brings fire, brimstone and destruction upon Lowell's parents and upon the Boston Brahman world in which he was born and raised and which he seems to despise and fear in many of his earlier poems.

To explore why most of the American poets who have written "religious" verse invoke such original if peculiar gods as the Lord as New England housewife or the Lord as Avenging Angel and why they ask for such surprising things from the gods is a fascinating, intricate problem. Among some of the poets of the generation we're exploring, for example, one finds surprising testimony of the existence of a supernatural reality which seems to have nothing whatsoever to do with Christian definitions or dogmas. The reader can find discussion of this in the section "Freedom Is a Breakfast Food—and More" in the concluding essay of this book.

KENWARD ELMSLIE

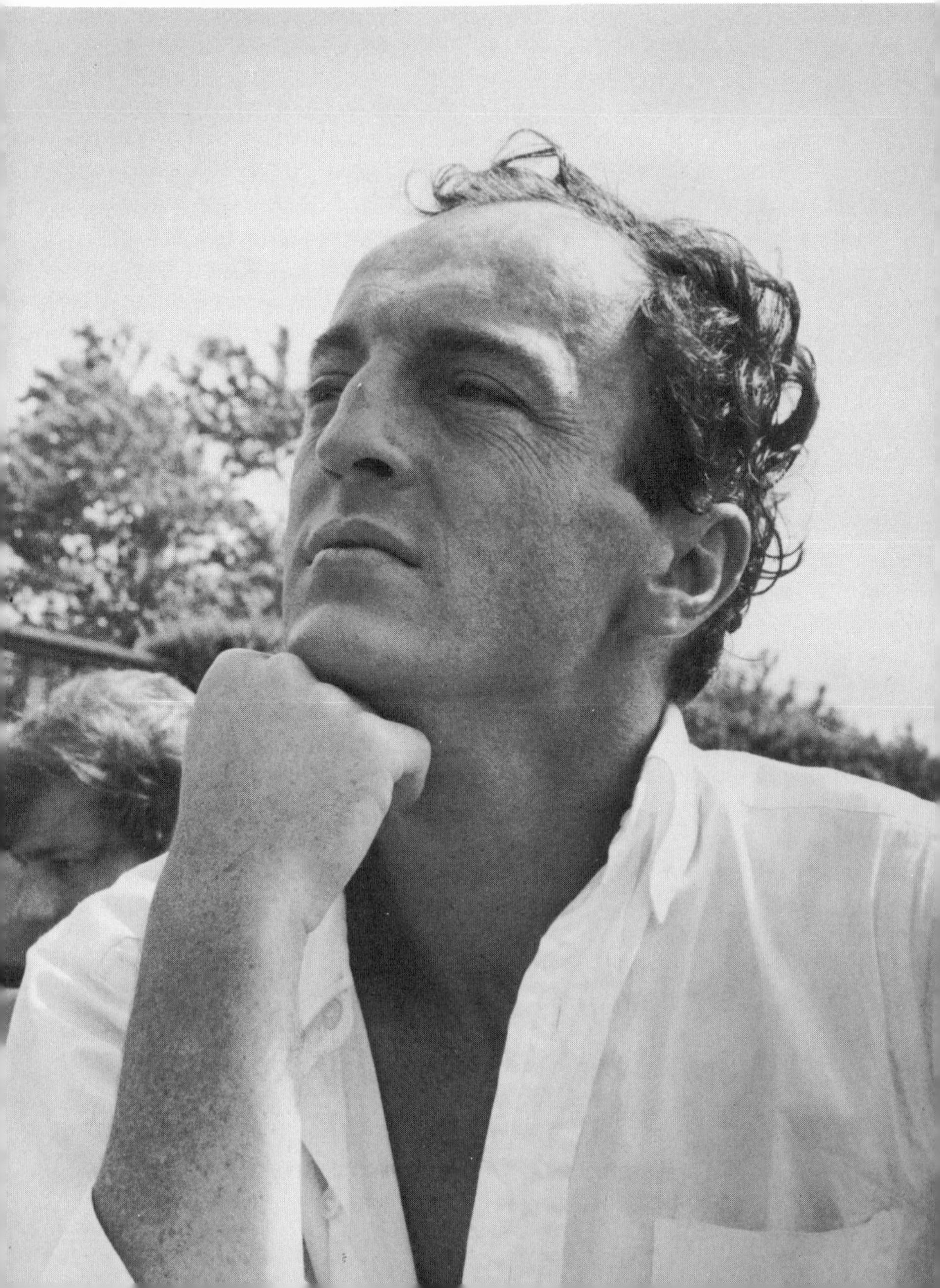

Frank O'Hara

THE DAY LADY DIED

It is 12:20 in New York a Friday
three days after Bastille day, yes
it is 1959 and I go get a shoeshine
because I will get off the 4:19 in Easthampton
at 7:15 and then go straight to dinner
and I don't know the people who will feed me

I walk up the muggy street beginning to sun
and have a hamburger and a malted and buy
an ugly NEW WORLD WRITING to see what the poets
in Ghana are doing these days
                              I go on to the bank
and Miss Stillwagon (first name Linda I once heard)
doesn't even look up my balance for once in her life
and in the GOLDEN GRIFFIN I get a little Verlaine
for Patsy with drawings by Bonnard although I do
think of Hesiod, trans. Richmond Lattimore or
Brendan Behan's new play or *Le Balcon* or *Les Nègres*
of Genet, but I don't, I stick with Verlaine
after practically going to sleep with quandariness

and for Mike I just stroll into the PARK LANE
Liquor Store and ask for a bottle of Strega and
then I go back where I came from to 6th Avenue

and the tobacconist in the Ziegfeld Theatre and
casually ask for a carton of Gauloises and a carton
of Picayunes, and a NEW YORK POST with her face on it

and I am sweating a lot by now and thinking of
leaning on the john door in the 5 SPOT
while she whispered a song along the keyboard
to Mal Waldron and everyone and I stopped breathing

AN IMPURE POEM
ABOUT JULY 17, 1959

"It is 12:20 in New York a Friday/three days after Bastille day . . ." What reader who has been lucky enough to go to school to the New Critics, William Empson or the Neo-Aristotelians wouldn't feel alerted for potential significance by this allusion to Bastille Day in the opening lines of a poem whose title announces that it will probably be an elegy on the tormented life of one of the great artists of American Jazz?

Not only was Billie Holiday hounded and persecuted by police and FBI agents because of her addiction to drugs but she was forbidden in her last, wretched years to work or live in New York City. In an elegy for her, then, the Bastille Day might develop into a symbol similar to what it originally represented to the Parisian mob that stormed it on July 14, 1787: namely, the hated symbol of despotism, the "insolence of office," and the cruel perversions of justice by the establishment in general. In short, the reader might anticipate an exploration of a theme familiar in Western literature since Villon: the artist vs. establishment or middleclass morality.

Behind this natural anticipation is of course the critical assumption that every image—and, in fact, every word—must count by pulling its share of the load in a well-made poem.* Such anticipation by the reader will only be strengthened by the fact that Frank O'Hara in earlier work (such as "To the Harbormaster" or "In Memory of My Feelings") amply demonstrated his skill in the craft. Here is a poet who can write good, traditionally "organic" poems.

Then what is the reader to make of the fact that O'Hara

* The knowledgeable reader will know well such brilliant models of what structural analysis can reveal as R. P. Blackmur's exploration of the image of "the artifice of eternity" in Yeats' "Sailing to Byzantium" and his suggestion that the profound ambiguities in the image may be in an important way what the poem is all about. Mr. Blackmur's essay appears in that excellent collection, *The Permanence of Yeats* (1950).

fails to use or develop the allusion to the French national holiday in any way whatsoever?

It soon becomes clear, in fact, that Bastille Day is mentioned because it happened to fall three days before Miss Holiday's death. No other reason exists for its inclusion in "The Day Lady Died." No ambiguity, no paradox, no tension (in Allen Tate's sense of the term) : no organic reason at all. And it soon becomes evident that all of the other places, events and times exist in the poem for the same reason: each happened (or will happen) on July 17, 1959 in Frank O'Hara's private life.

What kind of an elegy, in short, is "The Day Lady Died"? Only twice is Billie Holiday even mentioned—and then only at the tail end of the poem. The poem encourages the suspicion that she wouldn't have been mentioned the first time if O'Hara hadn't glimpsed her face in a photograph on the front page of the *New York Post* in the tobacco shop in the Ziegfeld Theatre which, in turn, reminds him of the time he heard her sing in *The Five Spot* in Greenwich Village.

"The Day Lady Died" hardly seems to be about Billie Holiday at all. Then what is it about?

"Little more than boring odds and ends," argues one criticism of this poem. Such criticism points out that the reader hears only a prosaic "happening" documenting O'Hara's walk around Manhattan on the afternoon of the day the great singer died. Some poets and some students of mine also dismiss this poem as insipid prose, complaining of claustrophobia and self-indulgence in its autobiographical narrowness. One had to be in O'Hara's circle in the late 1950s, the complaint points out, to know that "Patsy" is writer Patsy Southgate or that "Mike" is her (now former) husband, the Abstract Expressionist Michael Goldberg. And who cares about the bank teller's last or first name? Why mention the name of the *Golden Griffin* and the *Park Lane* liquor store? the Picayunes and Gauloises? Who cares to hear about the whole list of books the poet considers while trying to decide which one to buy for Patsy? Then there's that detail which clearly exists beyond the pale of trivia: the fact that the Hesiod was "trans. Richmond Lattimore"!

Another criticism puts down the poem for being so top-heavy: the first four stanzas could have been deleted and the elegy begun where it should have—with the singer's face in the photograph and the song in the nightclub. Here the charge accuses O'Hara of having tricked the reader. His title promises an elegy on a tormented jazz artist; instead, we hear the banal catalogue of the poet's odyssey around New York City. Still another complaint claims "The Day Lady Died" is an early and perverse Camp poem. It refuses to take seriously the tragic death of Lady Day; instead, lines and whole stanzas are frittered away documenting mundane and ho-hum events. A final criticism damns the poem for being just plain ugly: its language dull chatter; its imagery non-existent; its description bad prose; its rhythms graceless. I agree. Listen to the clodhopper sound here:

> I walk up the muggy street beginning to sun
> and have a hamburger and a malted and buy
> an ugly NEW WORLD WRITING to see what the
>   poets
> in Ghana are doing these days

My strong feeling is that "The Day Lady Died" is excellent *because* of its trivia and ugliness.

Few poems look and sound uglier. But I hope to argue that the poem may have "image of gods" concealed in it once we learn how to read it. Here I am thinking of that description of Socrates given by Alcibiades in *The Symposium*. You'll remember how Alcibiades begins: "And now, my boys, I want to praise Socrates in an image which may seem to him to be a caricature: yet I do not speak to make fun of him but to tell the truth. Socrates is exactly like the grotesque figures of Silenus on sale in the shops of the statue makers. Flutes protrude from their mouths but their stomachs open to reveal tiny figurines of gods hidden inside. The talk of Socrates resembles such a statue. When you first hear him, Socrates sounds ridiculous with his talk of pack asses, blacksmiths, cobblers and tanners of leather. Whoever listens closely, however, learns to open the statue and see what is inside. He will discover that the words of Socrates are the only ones which have meaning."

Let's begin, then, with an obvious question: Why does O'Hara devote only four lines to Lady Day and 24 lines to cataloguing his odyssey among "pack asses, blacksmiths, cobblers and tanners of leather"? And why are even those four lines so unassuming? They contain none of the passion or indignation traditionally associated with an elegy on a great artist's premature and wasteful death.

The most obvious answer argues something like this: "Understatement can often work miracles. By cataloguing commonplaces of one man's afternoon, O'Hara is able to achieve terrific but quiet impact in the final stanza: the reader believes the small, unassuming memory without reservation." And he believes it for the simple reason that the poet hasn't faked. His memory of hearing Lady Day whispering a song along the keyboard to her accompanist becomes a tribute one will not soon forget. On the other hand, I wonder how touching that beautiful final memory ("and everyone and I stopped breathing") would be if O'Hara had preceded it with the emotional tributes and "props" customary in most traditional elegies. In any event, his modest tribute contains more reality and love, in my opinion, than a more conventional elegy might have achieved by using the occasion of her death to express indignation over the lot of the Alienated American Artist—or some similarly predictable theme.

In another sense, "The Day Lady Died" isn't about Billie Holiday at all. It is about the common but sobering feeling that life continues on its bumbling way despite the tragic death of an important artist or some loved one. Trains for Easthampton still depart at 4:19; poets get shoeshines; Miss Linda Stillwagon can be counted on to stand like Cerberus behind her teller's cage; Americans still try to act casual when asking for "exotic" cigarettes—and so on.

And the poem also appears to be "about" how we live inside labyrinths of relationships. Some are dear and significant like the friendship between O'Hara and the Goldbergs; some are comic like the "theatre of the absurd" episode between the poet

and Miss Stillwagon; some are as yet a mystery like the one
between O'Hara and his Easthampton hosts; some are fleeting
but vivid like the "relationship" between the poet and the jazz
singer. The whole poem, in fact, is an example of how a relationship is created: the reader may not feel he's become O'Hara's
friend but he knows and shares a small part of the poet's life.
    All of these possible readings, however, still locate the poem
in the tradition of the organic and well-made work. I'm going
to suggest that "The Day Lady Died" is unique because it also
asks to be read as a work standing on the outside of that
tradition.
    Notice how O'Hara refuses to step away, for example, from
immediate but fragmentary and "unpoetic" experiences by
isolating only those elements which will yield the nugget of
real poetry. In particular, he doesn't isolate the "nugget" of his
memory in The Five Spot from the trivial chaos of events during
the afternoon journey around New York City in which the
memory of Miss Holiday is merely one fragment. Think of what
Pound or Coleridge must have left out of the immediate scene
to create masterpieces such as "The Garden" or "This Lime-
Tree Bower My Prison" and I think the point should be clear.
But "The Day Lady Died" is also a masterpiece in its own
special way. This poem is not only one of the first but it remains
one of the finest examples of what I've come to think of as
"impure" poetry.
    It is an impure poem in several ways. First, there's the in-
clusion of "unpoetic" facts and the indifference to isolating the
traditional poetic nugget from autobiographical experience.
Then there's its "ugly" language and style: the prose words and
rhythms remain mere prose; the man speaking is the same person
who worked as curator at The Museum of Modern Art, met
friends for lunch, talked and gossiped at parties, and lived in the
humdrum world. In brief, he doesn't sound like a poet.
    What is the image of the poet here? O'Hara seems to assume
the role of poet as mirror or tape recorder or movie director in
the sense of Andy Warhol allowing the camera to grind away
for hours on end, filming without editing the top of the Empire
State Building or a man sleeping or eating a mushroom. What

makes this image of the poet so exciting—or at least original? For one thing, the reader meets a poet for whom everything and anything can become part of the poem. What this usually means is: "No sexual taboos." In this poem it suggests something even more novel than that freedom. It means, literally, that everything or anything can be put into a poem in its bare existential reality. Shoeshine and bank account do not have to be "justified": they are not asked to contribute to any organic whole; they simply are there. When we realize that "The Day Lady Died" is probably the first poem to include such unpoetic items as shoeshine and bank balance without asking them to pay their way by contributing to the irony of it all ("I grow old . . . I grow old . . ./I shall wear the bottoms of my trousers rolled./ Shall I part my hair behind?/Do I dare to eat a peach?") we should appreciate how original O'Hara has been here. Reading "The Day Lady Died" can be similar to the exciting, happy experience of having seen for the first time in a museum one of Oldenburg's hamburgers or Warhol's canvas of row after row of *Campbell's* soup cans. In truth, O'Hara has made a new kind of poem.

But if "The Day Lady Died" resembles Stendhal's famous definition—"A novel is a mirror walking down the highway" —one problem remains: In what sense is it a poem at all? How can the poetry of trivia be distinguished from a work which simply lists one man's activities during any one day in any place? Today happens to be December 15, 1967; the calendar on my desk reads: "December 15/Bill of Rights Day."

BILL OF RIGHTS DAY

It is 3:16 in Chicago a Friday
three days after Denise read anti-Viet Nam poems here,
     yes
it is 1967 and I work on this essay
because I have to finish it before
I catch the 10:20 flight with Inara to NYC
where we'll spend Xmas in Red and Mimi's loft on
     Mulberry

—and so on.

What makes "The Day Lady Died" a poem, it seems to me, is the nerve evident in the very act of writing it. Think of it as a poem "about" the excitement of the man writing as he decides to include all of those "unpoetic" existential places, names and events. In short, here is an original "act" in creating a poem. Such audacity is exciting. It's like the story told about Robert Rauschenberg. When art dealer Iris Clert wrote from Paris, asking if he'd accept a commission to do her portrait, Rauschenberg replied by cable: "This is a portrait of Iris Clert because I say it is. Signed: Robert Rauschenberg." One way to view such audacity is to see it as more than Dada or Camp fun-and-games: it is the act of an artist. As the act of an artist, "The Day Lady Died" or the "Portrait of Iris Clert" is more exhilarating and valuable, in my opinion, than a book of well-made organic poems or a gallery full of "good" portraits.

To the reader who may object: "Still, what prevents anybody from doing the same?" I am afraid that my answer might be unsatisfactory: O'Hara's poem was the first. Think of it as an existential fact in itself. Imitation would be without much value.*

But this isn't the whole story. Young poets (and older ones too) can learn a great deal from "The Day Lady Died." One lesson would be to appreciate that this poem finally opens the warehouse dreamt of by many poets: anything, literally, can exist in a poem; and anything can exist in whatever way the poet chooses—as an object which stands in its existential skin without moral or esthetic significance or as one which helps to point a moral or adorn a tale.

Another lesson would be to absorb what Frank O'Hara accomplishes in his figure of the poet as mirror walking around Manhattan. By remaining only a mirror he reflects the surface of what that particular July afternoon in 1959 looked like to him. In the life of the poem that afternoon will remain forever as vivid and present as it once felt to him. Now, this won't sound like too much to the reader who loves Yeats or Eliot or Ginsberg.

* Of course, there may be earlier poems by O'Hara as "impure" as "The Day Lady Died." The point remains, I should trust: O'Hara was the first to write such poems in American literature. See Appendix One for mention of one of the ancestors of O'Hara's type of impure poem.

Yet it is everything in the sense that this poem, finally, offers a superb example of what art alone can accomplish. Art preserves the existential present.

Appendix One

Students of Dada will of course remember similar types of "impure" poetry by some of the Dada poets, in particular "At the Paul Guillaume Gallery" and "Openings" by Pierre Albert-Birot which O'Hara no doubt knew well: his work indicates he felt very much at home in both Dada art and French literature in general. Like many American readers, I first came across the Albert-Birot poems in *The Dada Painters and Poets* (1951) which Robert Motherwell edited. In case the reader hasn't seen this invaluable anthology, here are the poems and Motherwell's note:

"Two poems follow by Pierre Albert-Birot, the editor of *Sic*, a dada review hand-printed by himself, and sent during the first world war gratis to the soldiers on the western front; the translation is by Mme Dollie Pierre Chareau.

(The first poem speaks of a musical afternoon in 1917 during the war at Paul Guillaume's avant-garde gallery; the second poem of the opening day in 1918 of an exhibition by the non-objective painter, Herbin, at Rosenberg's gallery on the rue de la Beaume, and then of the opening of a van Dongen exhibition at Paul Guillaume's. *Cornet à Dés* is one of the major books by Max Jacob, the great 'cubist' poet, and there is a verbal play, in the mention of Satie on the fact that he had created the music for the ballet *Parade*.)

AT THE PAUL GUILLAUME GALLERY

The 13th day of November this year of 1917
We were at Paul Guillaume the negrophile's place
108 Faubourg Saint-Honoré at 8 o'clock
A short time after we were there
Along came Apollinaire
He sat down on a leather chair

And spoke first of a new art that one day he had implied
To be a sort of "technepheism"
To use a very simple term
Which an American had made
A photo had been taken
Between May and October
Of the very first *plâtre à toucher*
Apollinaire descanted afterwards
On poetry not the poets
And the new passionate man
He revealed to us the secrets of the gods
Who thee and thoued him
So that—now—none of us who were there listening
Have the right anymore to say
What's the poem all about I didn't understand a thing
And then we had some Debussy
You see
The poets X Y and Z
And the *Profond Aujourd'hui*
By Monsieur Blaise Cendrars
What the author of *Henriette Sauret* was thinking
I'll tell you when I find out
And then we heard three interludes set to music
Comic
By Auric
And sung by Bertin
These three little pieces were very much liked
And they ran along nicely right to the end
And then and then we had Satie Erik
Who Paraded and disappeared
And Lara who had appeared
Reappeared
And scanned however
Just as she had wished to do
In silence as for prayer
Il pleut by Apollinaire
And we left behind us the light
For the darkness of the night

OPENINGS

The 1st of March 1918 I was
At Rosenberg's where Herbin the painter
Was showing his pictures
Rue de la Beaume
It's a street
Where one sees nothing but stone
And you ask yourself as you go in
Are there people here
You push the little half open door
And you find some
Here's Cendrars Hello
And Soupault   (you arrive)
How are you   (I depart)
Fine Hello Severini
Good day my friend
Good day Max Jacob
Canudissimo Canudissimo
It's pretty isn't it
It's Cocteau who discovered it
He really is smart and witty
I've just read a wonderful book
It's neither of our time nor of
Any other time
Nor on this subject nor on that
To my mind it is simply wonderful
It's the *Journal* of a convert
Gazing on a flower the author
Says I am moved
Why am I moved
Because there is a God
Why have I a notion of God
Because I have faith
And one fine morning
He met Leon Blois
And the next morning
He went to confession
It's a wonderful book

Yes yes oh my dear friend
Let us beat on our breasts
With a Pickaxe
Examine our hearts know ourselves
And we will do immortal works
Be human my brothers
Thus spoke the saint
That I like to see
Still there were some pictures on the walls
    that were there
On purpose to be looked at
And therefore I looked at them
Leaving in other hands
The author of the *Cornet à Dés*
And said to myself
Oil painting
Is a difficult thing
Above all cubism
For there is nothing to be seen
That can take us in
The painter alone is there in each frame
And if he has nothing in him
There is nothing in the frame
Be great cubism
Or do not exist
This painter seems a very charming man
And his pictures are pretty
But not one at least while I was there
Came down from the wall on which it was hanging
And our feet never left the floor
I mean there was no magic
And as my report
Must be true if short
I am forced to state
That Madame André Lhote
Felt sick after clams that she ate

And the 17th
One Sunday of a bloody war week

I took off my slippers
And sauntered down quietly
To the van Dongen show
The Faubourg St. Honoré
Where Paul Guillaume the Eclectic
Keeps shop
Is quite sad on Sunday
Nobody lives in it
Only the houses
Sunday has its reasons
That love does not know . . .

W. D. Snodgrass

APRIL INVENTORY

The green catalpa tree has turned
All white; the cherry blooms once more.
In one whole year I haven't learned
A blessed thing they pay you for.
The blossoms snow down in my hair;
The trees and I will soon be bare.

The trees have more than I to spare.
The sleek, expensive girls I teach,
Younger and pinker every year,
Bloom gradually out of reach.
The pear tree lets its petals drop
Like dandruff on a tabletop.

The girls have grown so young by now
I have to nudge myself to stare.
This year they smile and mind me how
My teeth are falling with my hair.
In thirty years I may not get
Younger, shrewder, or out of debt.

The tenth time, just a year ago,
I made myself a little list
Of all the things I'd ought to know,

Then told my parents, analyst,
And everyone who's trusted me
I'd be substantial, presently.

I haven't read one book about
A book or memorized one plot.
Or found a mind I did not doubt.
I learned one date. And then forgot.
And one by one the solid scholars
Get the degrees, the jobs, the dollars.

And smile above their starchy collars.
I taught my classes Whitehead's notions;
One lovely girl, a song of Mahler's.
Lacking a source-book or promotions,
I showed one child the colors of
A luna moth and how to love.

I taught myself to name my name,
To bark back, loosen love and crying;
To ease my woman so she came,
To ease an old man who was dying.
I have not learned how often I
Can win, can love, but choose to die.

I have not learned there is a lie
Love shall be blonder, slimmer, younger;
That my equivocating eye
Loves only by my body's hunger;
That I have forces, true to feel,
Or that the lovely world is real.

While scholars speak authority
And wear their ulcers on their sleeves,
My eyes in spectacles shall see
These trees procure and spend their leaves.
There is a value underneath
The gold and silver in my teeth.

Though trees turn bare and girls turn wives,
We shall afford our costly seasons;
There is a gentleness survives
That will outspeak and has its reasons.
There is a loveliness exists,
Preserves us, not for specialists.

THE THOREAU COMPLEX
AMID THE SOLID SCHOLARS

Who would want as friend the man speaking in "Paradise Lost" or "The Windhover" or "The Love Song of J. Alfred Prufrock"? Milton sounds like a stern, humorless uncle who thinks he knows everything; one might seek him out for knowledge but hardly for companionship or warmth. And the passionately intense man in "The Windhover" loves only himself and his Christ; in a friendship, his heart would no doubt remain "in hiding." Imagine having dinner every Thursday with Prufrock; he's too self-consciously neurotic to be much fun—I mean, imagine having to sit through his debate about the dangers incipient in ordering a peach for dessert or having to puzzle out whom he means when he confides what "one, settling a pillow by her head," said to him at tea. But what about the man speaking in W. D. Snodgrass' "April Inventory?" Is he the kind of person whom most of us would be glad to know or even call friend?

At first, the answer seems perfectly evident: "Of course he is." Not only is he a man who cares about the perennial loveliness and gentleness in life, nature and in others but he's obviously a good and often stimulating teacher. In addition, he's blessed with a superb wit which he's not averse to turning at times on himself. Moreover, he can admit embarrassing private facts about himself and still keep his dignity: his candor is disarming and enviable.

Due to his warmth, intelligence, wit and candor, then, it would seem that there's little or no doubt to whom the sarcastic reference to "specialists" in the concluding couplet refers: "There is a loveliness exists,/Preserves us, not for specialists." Clearly it's not the speaker; he and, by implication, the reader (who may feel flattered that he too is as warm and candid as the speaker) are the "us" being preserved by the loveliness. The specialists are of course the solid scholars who appear at various times, smiling above their starchy collars, as the very image of all that's routine, plodding, unimaginative, boring: they are the classic square. True, they may be proficient enough in their academic specialty (Early Etruscan Plumbing Systems) but the poem keeps implying that as specialists they can't appreciate the beauty of catalpa, cherry or pear tree, much less the loveliness in others—both of which the speaker appreciates.

But is the poem as black and white as this? Is the battle line as clearly drawn as it at first seems: the engaging young Turk instructor vs. the solid scholars? Let me explain why I even raise such doubts which I feel the poem itself prompts the reader to explore.

Take the question of the speaker's candor. Few poems have been as candid. In the wry, mocking "inventory" of the "little list/Of all the things I ought to know" (in stanza four) and in the almost shocking inventory of personal revelations (in stanza seven) the speaker allows himself a type of candor which hasn't been heard before in American poetry. What seemed so remarkable about the candor when "April Inventory" appeared in 1959 was that it described everyday, "down-home" failures and successes.* The speaker confesses that he's been a flop, for example, when it comes to earning "the degrees, the jobs, the dollars"; and he admits without rationalization or too much embarrassment that it's his own damn fault; and he freely admits, moreover, some private difficulties most men wouldn't dream of mentioning to anybody except perhaps to their psychoanalysts:

> I taught myself to name my name,
> To bark back, loosen love and crying;
> To ease my woman so she came. . . .

* Lately, the "confessional" school of poetry has been given a lot of attention by critics who tend to include in it Snodgrass, along with Robert Lowell, Anne Sexton, Sylvia Plath and Allen Ginsberg. One important distinction, however, seems to have been overlooked: namely, Snodgrass' candor involves confessions of everyday realities, whereas Lowell, Sexton, Plath confess such "glamorous" autobiographical revelations as insanity or nervous breakdown, whereas Ginsberg freely documents his homosexuality. Madness and homosexuality are, after all, extreme experiences beyond the pale of ordinary lives. Large numbers of Americans suffer from mental disease and large bodies of homosexuals live in our cities as well as in Andy Hardy suburbs or small towns or down on the good, old farm; but insanity and sexual inversion remain secret, dark realities to the average American.

However refreshing it sounds—indeed, it's a pleasure to hear a poet finally admit such things without beating around the bush by using metaphor or objective correlative—isn't there also something excessive about the frankness? Why take pains to admit, for example, treatment with a psychoanalyst? And why reveal his woman's difficulty with frigidity? Why spell out so intimately, in fact, one's success as a sexual mate?

One could argue that such frankness only helps to establish the young instructor clearly on the side of the good angels, embracing truth, spontaneity and values which matter, as opposed to the scholars who stand on the side of the bad angels, dedicated to trivial facts, rigidity and values which signify little when all is said and done.

What's odd about the frankness, however, is that the speaker tells far more than necessary to establish this contrast. In fact, the particular items he confesses are irrelevant to the basic contrast established clearly by the witty and often touching items mentioned in stanzas five and six: "I haven't read one book about/A book or memorized one plot . . ." and how he taught "my classes Whitehead's notions;/One lovely girl, a song of Mahler's" and one child "the colors of/A luna moth and how to love." Throughout the inventory of good items the solid scholars appear and disappear much like the Puritans standing in the gloomy forest observing Morton and his merry Indians in Hawthorne's tale "The May-Pole of Merry Mount." But why does the young instructor also mention his analyst and his woman's frigidity? Here he sounds like a bit of a show-off. In fact, his unnecessary exhibitionism translates bluntly: "I'm screwed up enough to need an analyst; but I'm good enough in bed to bring her to the orgasm she couldn't have without me."

What does the confession of these items accomplish? One thing seems clear: they shock when first heard. And the shock may serve as a smoke screen to distract from the speaker's silence about something which, in terms of the poem's fundamental contrast between good vs. false values, is far more important than the revelation of the speaker's analysis and frigid mate: namely, the speaker's real feelings about the scholars. Here I suggest of course that he is not as candid as he at first appears.

How does he feel about the "specialists"? The answer seems obvious: he has nothing but contempt for their deadening, sober rigidities. And he also pokes some fun at them by putting down scholars in a poem which in its formality of uniform stanzas (each containing six lines with identical meter and rhyme pattern) stands solidly in the tradition of English poetry from Chaucer to Yeats. (And is it by accident that "April Inventory" employs the same stanza length, meter and rhyme scheme as that celebrated satire on dull scholarship—Yeats' "The Scholars"?) In other words, the poem against scholars makes fun of them by sounding as if it belonged in their own home territory.

But is contempt moved to satire *all* he feels? Let's find out by looking again at his inventory. Despite the ten previous New Year's resolution lists, he still hasn't earned: 1) his degree; 2) a full-time teaching position; and 3) a good salary. Why not? From what he says, the reader is right to assume he's still either a graduate assistant or perhaps an instructor with the M.A. degree; but he also clearly implies that he's too old to be either: it's time to get the doctorate and be offered a decent academic appointment on the faculty. That he bothers to mention this dilemma is the significant fact, it seems to me: it indicates he's none too happy about his chronic and increasingly demeaning academic lot. But who has the "things of this world" he lacks but deserves, given his obvious intelligence and gifts as a teacher? The solid scholars, smiling above their starchy collars, walk off with "the degrees, the jobs, the dollars." I think it's clear: he's also jealous of the scholars; in fact, he may be chewed by envy even as he pokes fun at them and feels superior.

But this is all implied. The speaker never admits it. Why not? What are we to make of this curious omission by a man who in the rest of the poem can preen himself because of his candor, intelligence, wit and appreciation of genuine values?

The poem itself suggests the answer. In several cunning ways it reveals an attitude held by the speaker which is more complex and ambiguous than the original portrait of him as simply the warm, charming young Turk clearly on the side of the good, the true and the beautiful.

For example, his failure to admit he's probably more than a bit envious of the scholars prompts a second look at his attitude toward scholarship and the vocation of the teacher. What is his attitude?

At first, it seems entirely commendable: he indicates that as far as he's concerned, what matters are not dull, enervating facts or books about books or rote memorization of plots of novels or plays; what matters, he implies, is to teach only what is genuinely valuable: a song of Mahler's, the colors of a luna moth, how to love, and Whitehead's "notions." This is of course the portrait of the good teacher—the Mark Hopkins who devotes himself to exposing students to the truly valuable "wheat" by ignoring the "chaff" of boring facts, enervating details or secondary sources. Such a teacher would rather spend an entire class in reading one poem by Yeats than in lecturing on such secondary sources as Francis A.A.C. Wilson's study *Yeats' Iconography* or even the critical essays collected in *The Permanence of Yeats*.

But there's something peculiar about his attitude—at least, as it's expressed in the description of his class on Whitehead. I'm not qualified to offer an evaluation of Whitehead's philosophy (but from what I understand his "organic philosophy" provides a set of general ideas designed to describe and unify adequately all of the complex components of the universe) ; but I do know that whatever its value Whitehead's thought can scarcely be dismissed as being a collection of mere "notions." Even if the teacher feels that Whitehead is dead wrong, he neglects the job of the teacher by presenting that philosophy as being nothing but a more or less general and vague or imperfect conception of ideas—that is, notions. Here the speaker reveals, in short, that he's patronized the great British philosopher.

And if so, we can also see how he patronizes students. It's as if he says: "You don't deserve to make up your own minds about Whitehead. Take my word for it: his philosophy is nothing but useless notions." And doesn't he also patronize himself? If he hasn't read one book about a book or memorized one plot or remembered one date, he is in all likelihood poorly prepared to do a job of teaching. The same applies if he's also a graduate student, which he may well be: he patronizes both his teachers and himself by not being a good student in the sense of being prepared for classes.

Now, what does this tell about his attitude? It is not simply that he feels superior to the solid scholars; he also has a strong tendency to look down his nose at them, his students, himself, perhaps his teachers, and the vocation of scholarship itself.

Another way in which the poem suggests or reveals the less attractive side of the speaker's attitude can be seen in the look and sound of the poem. We've seen how the uniformity of stanzas might parody the scholars on their home ground; but it might also reveal something about the speaker other than his neat wit. The slightly mechanical rigidity of the uniformity of stanzas, meter and rhyme grates against the grain of what has appeared to be the "point" of the poem: namely, its celebration of the spontaneous and free-spirited, embodied by the young teacher, as opposed to the conformist and hide-bound, typified by the academics. In other words, the look and sound of the poem raise the suspicion that the speaker in his own way might feel as compulsively routine as the scholars. One begins to doubt the extent of the natural freedom of which many of the lines speak or imply. Here the inference seems to be: the speaker implies he's a free soul but feels inhibited (although no doubt largely unconsciously) in what sounds like a fundamental way.

The title itself suggests another variation on the same point. In one sense, the inventory shows him in the black. Stanzas six and seven contain, as we've noticed, several valuable achievements—his successes in a teaching situation with the lovely girl and the child, and those in his private life with himself, his woman and the dying old man. In another sense, the inventory is clearly in the red. He still can't list a degree, good job or salary; moreover, he admits in stanza eight that he's failed to learn four valuable things that would put him in the black—at least, as far as being an adult might be concerned. Notice what the four are:

> I have not learned there is a lie
> Love shall be blonder, slimmer, younger;
> That my equivocating eye

> Loves only by my body's hunger;
> That I have forces, true to feel,
> Or that the lovely world is real.

Here we read a truly candid confession. He exposes how adolescent his attitude has remained, despite the fact that he's now 30 years old. Not only does he still cling to a boyish fantasy of True Love but he admits to being still involved in the adolescent's tense and often harsh denial of the body, as well as in the adolescent's awkward awareness that his strengths and talents remain potential. And, finally, he knows he's still largely ignorant about the world—the poem suggests that "world" here might be translated as meaning: the competition in the academic world for "the degrees, the jobs, the dollars." What does this inventory in the red reveal? Clearly the speaker feels that what might be called good adolescent values are more important than adult ones—in particular, those having to do with competition for jobs and money.

Then what is the portrait of the speaker that has emerged? On the one hand, he remains the personable young man whom we at first liked: candid, caring, "free," and dedicated to sound values in the sense that he knows real teaching means more than mere scholarship and that there is a loveliness and gentleness in life and in others. On the other hand, he's also oddly unattractive: not so candid, "superior," compulsively repetitive, and dedicated to adolescent attitudes and values when he's far too old still to be clinging to them. In brief, he too is a "specialist."

And he not only tells us how he's a specialist but why: he has refused to grow. At 30, he should be well on the road to getting what he wants: a good teaching appointment. Otherwise, why is he still hanging around the university? But he's not on the road; he hasn't even left home; he remains in an important sense adolescent. Even sadder: he's an adolescent corroded by envy of adults who can put to work what gifts they have and walk off with the plums the speaker wants and could earn if only he would get with it.

What accounts for this dilemma? The poem doesn't say; it

does its job by showing the speaker's dilemma for what it is.* Does the speaker himself feel his dilemma? I suspect that he suffers from it. One of the ways in which the poem reveals that he suffers, it seems to me, is through the use of irony. Time and again, the instructor's irony bites himself. For example, notice how the image of the tree becomes (more often than not) the symbol of natural growth as contrasted to the speaker's condition of remaining fossilized in chronic failure to finish work on his degree and thus earn a decent teaching appointment. The opening lines establish this contrast:

The green catalpa tree has turned
All white; the cherry blooms once more.
In one whole year I haven't learned
A blessed thing they pay you for.

The concluding couplet of stanza one encourages the momentary illusion that tree and speaker share a bond in that both have natural growth, although it's a slightly poignant one: "The blossoms snow down in my hair;/The trees and I will soon be bare." But this bond is soon dissolved. In the next stanza the aging instructor's students—the sleek, expensive girls—become a metaphor of the continual renewal and growth of the tree: the students become the annual crop of fruit of cherry and pear. Each year, in fact, brings "younger and pinker" fruit. But the speaker only grows older without growing in the way that counts: he remains sterile—no degree, no job, no dollars. And the wickedly irreverent final couplet puts him in a comic and ironic light: "The pear tree lets its petals drop/Like dandruff on a tabletop." Clearly the implication is that the dandruff refers to his own head which is growing bare. He produces only dandruff,

---

* Due to the fact that the poem doesn't pigeonhole the speaker's dilemma into this or that psychological case history—and by so doing limit the reader's participation to being one of mere "understanding"—the poem can be said to invite the reader to participate in what seems perennial and common about the aging instructor's plight. Many of us have suffered, I suspect, from some of the consequences of his dilemma. Growing up has never been easy for anyone.

whereas the pear tree by shedding petals prepares to bring forth another crop of healthy "girls."

The irony continues to bite the instructor as he watches not only the trees and students grow but the scholars as well (in the sense that they get the degrees, jobs and dollars), whereas he watches himself only grow older.

Obviously he feels irritated, however ironic and witty his remarks about himself and his dilemma. What irritates him is the bald fact that although he's perfectly aware of his gifts in the classroom and in private life, he hasn't been able to put those gifts to work for himself and get the good academic appointment he wants and deserves. Instead of getting that appointment and recognition, he wastes this spring day by looking down his nose at his fellow academics, his students and himself. In this sense, his superiority is a false one. It is quite the opposite of the natural superiority which his intelligence and gifts might claim over the limited brains and talents of the more plodding among his academic colleagues. His dilemma is, in short, that of a man who has the ability to get with it but who wastes his gifts in useless posturing.

The more we examine his dilemma the more I am reminded of a puzzling fact about Thoreau. How was it that a man of such genius for moral realities and for creating great American prose was also such a mean failure in private life?

At everything he tried or seemed to want Thoreau failed: he failed to receive the appointment of instructor when he was graduated from Harvard College; he failed as schoolmaster; he failed as suitor of Miss Ellen Sewall; he failed as lecturer at the Concord Lyceum; and he failed at the one career he seemed to care the most about—that of man of letters. (Niggardly sales and indifferent criticism greeted the only two books Thoreau published during his lifetime—*A Week on the Concord and Merrimack Rivers* and *Walden*.)

What accounts for these failures? It would be romantic to claim that Thoreau's failures came solely as the result of his refusal to compromise his principles; it would be more realistic to try and understand why his contemporaries failed to recognize and reward the extraordinary man he was. In other words: How much of Thoreau's failures were the fault of the traditional villain—the hostile and/or pigheaded square world —and how much were they the fault of Thoreau's own attitude? Everyone knows the shameful history of the square world in its encounters with men of genius such as Thoreau. All too often the square world tries to ridicule or ignore such men who, due to their vivid awareness of the profound capacities of the human spirit, "march to a different drummer" and refuse to get in step with the routine, conventional march of the average man. Such men of genius either criticize or ignore the square world, with its governments, business, culture, manners and religions, which Thoreau dismissed as being nothing more than "restless, nervous, bustling, trivial." One thinks of some of Thoreau's peers in this respect: Socrates, Diogenes the Cynic, Christ, Buddha, Nietzsche, Freud. Clearly the square world of 19th century Concord was not about to shower recognition or prizes on Henry Thoreau who kept reminding that world there were deeper and more exciting scenes for a man to enjoy than the accumulation of cash, clothes and conventional geegaws.

But how much of Thoreau's fate as a chronic loser also resulted from that sour, unhappy side of himself which encouraged him to act like a skulker (as Robert Louis Stevenson was the first to suggest)? The implication of Stevenson's criticism is that Thoreau skulked because the world refused to admit the genius which at the time only he knew he possessed. As a result, he wasted a lot of time and energy in looking down his nose at his fellow citizens. In particular, he looked down on two important qualities which make one's life a success (at least in the common sense of the term). Everyone knows what those qualities are: the desire to earn what one wants; and the ability to force one's contemporaries to recognize achievement in having earned what one wants. Instead of putting his considerable gifts to work to earn what these qualities can achieve, Thoreau chose to skulk and remain a loser.

I am looking at three photographs of Thoreau. The middle photo depicts the oval crayon drawing by Samuel Rowse—the earliest authentic portrait of Thoreau, drawn in 1854 when its subject was 37 years old: Thoreau is beardless, dignified, youthful—and arrogant. Flanking the drawing are the familiar daguerreotype made in 1856 in Worcester, Massachusetts, and the

ambrotype made five years later in New Bedford: both show
Thoreau bearded but still dignified, youthful—and arrogant.
All three photos seem to testify to the suspicion that the man
who lived day after day, week after week, and year after year in
Concord felt like a skulking, unappreciated adolescent, even as
he knew that he was capable of writing one of the classics of
world literature in *Walden*.

The Thoreau Complex, then, is one which embodies the
sour jealousy and quiet desperation of a man of great or strong
gifts who refuses to put those gifts or strengths to the test by
earning the success he deserves.*

What I imply should be apparent: the speaker in "April
Inventory" feels much like Thoreau might have felt as he walked
around Concord on a day in spring in the 1840s or 1850s. As the
speaker walks around the campus during a season when everything is growing but himself, he skulks and looks down his nose
at the solid scholars, smiling above their starchy collars, busy
about earning the degrees, the jobs, the dollars. The scholars
resemble the butcher, the baker and the candlestick maker of
Thoreau's Concord; or more accurately: the scholars are like the
selectmen.

And the irony is of course that one who peers down his long
nose at them but who has failed to win their respect is as much
a "specialist" in envy, skulking and ill will as the scholar is a
specialist in that he devotes this spring day to digging up one
more fact about the plumbing construction among the Etrus-
cans. In this sense, both the young instructor and the solid
scholar deprive themselves of sharing in the "gentleness" which
survives despite their myopia and in the "loveliness" which exists and preserves us despite their sad addiction to either the
Thoreau Complex or the equally enervating dead-end alleys of
"useless" scholarship.

But the final irony might be at the expense of the skulking
side of the speaker's Thoreau Complex. The skulker may have
talked himself out of a job, as it were.

Where does the speaker get the knowledge, for example, to

*See Appendix One for James Russell Lowell's analysis of the Thoreau
Complex.

recognize the limitations of the "specialists" whom he mentions so derisively in the final stanza? And where does he obtain the freedom with which to appreciate the loveliness and gentleness around him? Both may have come from his growing awareness of how enervating and adolescent is the skulker and his sour attitude—his "specialty" in feeling superior to but envious of men who at least put to work what talents they possess.

In brief, he may have realized that the "specialist" inside himself is his own worst enemy: it only encourages him to indulge his jealousy and false superiority and to waste both his time and gifts. In these final lines—which are as memorable, it seems to me, as any in contemporary American poetry—the speaker not only turns his irony against the skulker in himself but he transcends that enervating attitude. The reader might even be encouraged to think that if the young Turk in "April Inventory" can speak other poems which have anything near the genuine candor, wit and skill evident in this poem, then he may indeed banish the skulker for good. Such poems might earn him literary recognition; and thus he can be in a good position to obtain the jobs and dollars.

The genuine candor in this poem, then, is the speaker's courage to allow the skulker to have his say. In this sense, "April Inventory" performs one of the immemorial functions of poetry: it exorcises an evil spirit by bringing it into clear, hard light where the spirit stands finally revealed for what it is.

And this brings us back to the original question: How many of the men speaking in "Paradise Lost," "The Windhover," "The Love Song of J. Alfred Prufrock" or "April Inventory" would you want as a friend? Any man who has been able to exorcise the crippling attitude which has prevented him from being the person he could be is one I know I might want as a friend, especially if he is a man who is also as honest, witty, intelligent, gifted and caring as the instructor in "April Inventory."

Appendix One

Nobody has explored the skulker in Thoreau's attitude as thoroughly as James Russell Lowell in his essay "Thoreau," published in 1865, three years after his subject's death at 44. (Mr. Edmund Wilson has complained that the Lowell paper is "not merely grudging but surly"; and it is; but it also offers a brilliant analysis of why Thoreau failed and skulked, despite his manifest gifts.) The backbone of Lowell's argument seems to be contained in his observation that "a greater familiarity with ordinary men would have done Thoreau good, by showing him how many fine qualities are common to the race. The radical vice of his theory of life was that he confounded physical with spiritual remoteness from men. A man is far enough withdrawn from his fellows if he keeps himself clear of their weakness. He is not so truly withdrawn as exiled, if he refuses to share their strength."

Cupidity, hypocrisy, duplicity, the betrayal of ideals, the lust for slaughter in war, and that hardcore cynicism often cloaked by terms such as "practical" or "realistic": these were some of the weaknesses in men Thoreau despised. And rightly so. But what strengths did he refuse to share? The strength of love earned and sustained by a husband and wife; the strength of creating and rearing children, earning one's living, paying the rent, making laws, building museums, publishing newspapers, editing a definitive scholarly text of Thoreau's works—and so on. In brief, Thoreau refused to share or admire the strengths of the adult, practical man.

Those of Thoreau's townsmen in Concord who did succeed in their private and/or professional lives must have put to work whatever talents they had and earned what they achieved. But Thoreau might have expected Concord to genuflect whenever he walked by simply because he was Henry Thoreau and not because of anything he'd done to earn their respect. And he must have skulked when Concord refused to genuflect. Lowell puts the finger on this part of his attitude when he observes that Thoreau was forever talking of getting away from the world but "he must always be near enough to it, nay, to the Concord corner of it, to feel the impression he makes there . . . This egotism of his is a Stylites pillar after all, a seclusion which keeps him in the public eye."

One begins to question, in fact, the celebrated statement that "the mass of men lead lives of quiet desperation" in that one wonders how much of the statement also applies to Thoreau himself. He probably felt frustrated if not desperately unhappy at times when it became clear that the world wasn't about to honor the genius only he and a few others (Emerson was one) knew he had but which he refused to show in any revealing way or to put to work in order to earn the recognition he seemed to have craved. Instead, he kept aloof from others. Thoreau must have spent a lot of time looking down his nose at those who in every other way were his inferiors except that they earned what they wanted to get. "The dignity of man is an excellent thing," Lowell observes, "but therefore to hold one's self too sacred and precious is the reverse of excellent."

James Wright

AS I STEP OVER A PUDDLE AT THE END OF WINTER, I THINK OF AN ANCIENT CHINESE GOVERNOR

> *And how can I, born in evil days*
> *And fresh from failure, ask a kindness*
> *of Fate?*
> — Written A.D. 819

Po Chu-i, balding old politician,
What's the use?
I think of you,
Uneasily entering the gorges of the Yang-Tze,
When you were being towed up the rapids
Toward some political job or other
In the city of Chungshou.
You made it, I guess,
By dark.

But it is 1960, it is almost spring again,
And the tall rocks of Minneapolis
Build me my own black twilight
Of bamboo ropes and waters.
Where is Yuan Chen, the friend you loved?
Where is the sea, that once solved the whole loneliness
Of the Midwest? Where is Minneapolis? I can see nothing
But the great terrible oak tree darkening with winter.
Did you find the city of isolated men beyond mountains?
Or have you been holding the end of a frayed rope
For a thousand years?

THE LONELINESS OF A THOUSAND YEARS
OR THE POET AS EMMETT KELLY

Few readers will fail to respond to the increasingly anguished loneliness embodied in James Wright's "As I Step over a Puddle at the End of Winter, I Think of an Ancient Chinese Governor." Seldom has the desolation of being alone without a loved one, friend or family been captured as piercingly as in the concluding lines, beginning with the question, "Where is Yuan Chen, the friend you loved?" and ending with the bleak, memorable "Or have you been holding the end of a frayed rope/For a thousand years?" Given the poem as a whole and the facts of the old Chinese poet's life, Po Chu-i could only reply: "Yuan Chen died many years ago. No, I never reached the city beyond mountains —and it wouldn't really have mattered if I had. Yes, it feels as if I've been left holding the end of a rope for a thousand years." Loneliness like this is painful and depressing; it certainly isn't normally considered amusing. Then how can we account for the suspicion of comedy which occurs throughout this otherwise melancholy poem?

Ever since the poem first appeared in *Harper's* in 1961, I've admired it but I tended to read it as the depressed and humorless poem it seems to be until very recently when the final lines raised the suspicion of an undercurrent of comedy which, in turn, prompted another look at other parts of the poem, including the title. The comedy in the final lines is quiet; it is foxy; but it's there.

It emerges when one allows the image of Po Chu-i to recall the earlier image (in stanza one) of his boat being towed up the rapids toward Chungshou. Who is towing his boat? Although the poem doesn't make it clear—it might be some type of a tugboat—the image of the frayed rope (and the earlier mention of bamboo ropes) suggests that coolies are doing the job, towing by rope as coolies have done in the Orient for centuries. The towing coolies, in turn, encourage the suggestion that in the final image Po Chu-i becomes a coolie too as he

stands holding the end of a frayed rope. Now, this may not seem
funny at all; but it is, in an ironic or dark humor kind of way,
when one remembers that Po Chu-i was not only one of the
great classic poets of China but he also distinguished himself as
a statesman during the late phase of the Tang Dynasty.*
Think of what the effect would be (assuming the feeling of the
poem stays just as it is) if instead of the Chinese poet, the man
addressed were T. S. Eliot who instead of being transformed
into a coolie became a Cockney taxicab driver in the concluding
lines. Who wouldn't laugh?

And when one looks again at the title, it too reveals a streak
of the comic. Why is the puddle mentioned, for example? Why
take pains to include such trivial detail? Why not have the
title read, simply: "At the End of Winter, I Think of an Ancient
Chinese Governor"? What the mention of the puddle accomplishes, it seems to me, is an almost mock heroic tone: the poet
spoofs himself a bit.** Think of those ads prominent a decade
or so ago: "They laughed when I sat down at the piano during
Jill's birthday party," confesses Jack; but then, thanks to his
correspondence music lessons, he astonishes the skeptical guests
by his sensitive rendition of "Night and Day." Doesn't the figure
of the poet stepping over a puddle and thinking of an ancient
Chinese statesman have a similar comic effect: "They laughed

* The comic irony becomes more acute when one remembers that Po Chu-i
came from a background as wracked by poverty as that of any coolie. Not
only did he surmount it to earn honors as a poet and statesman but he was
also one of those fortunate poets to enjoy vast recognition during his lifetime. The eminent translator of Chinese literature, Robert Payne, reports
how Po Chu-i earned such fame that "his verses were sung by plow boys
and peasants, as well as by the emperor and the men of the court," and
how the old poet found delight in discovering poems of his written on the
walls of inns, temples, village schools and the cabins of ships.

** I suspect that the knowledgeable reader may have overlooked the possibility of comedy here for much the same reason I did at first: namely,
James Wright wrote this poem. Due to the prevailing gravity and dignity
in most of his work, we're not encouraged to expect comedy or farce in a
new poem by him. Here it might help to think of the title by pretending
that its author isn't James Wright but a relatively unknown poet. On the
other hand, I assume that the "I" speaking in this poem and Mr. Wright
are one and the same: I see no reason to consider the voice speaking a
persona in the way in which, say, Lemuel clearly is one in Merwin's
"Lemuel's Blessing."

as I stepped over a puddle at the end of winter and thought of Po Chu-i—until they read this poem."

And there's this curiosity too in the title: Why doesn't Wright say, "I think of an ancient Chinese poet"? After all, the world remembers Po Chu-i because he wrote superb verses and not because he was governor of Hangchow and Honan and finally president of the War Board of the Emperor. Again, it's as if Eliot were the distinguished poet addressed by the title: "I think of a British publisher." Or as if the title read: "I think of an Elizabethan actor"—meaning Shakespeare. Or "I think of a French diplomat"—meaning St.-John Perse. Or "I think of an Advertising Executive"—meaning James Dickey. What's the effect of addressing Po Chu-i as governor instead of as great poet? One tends to feel it's somehow funny—in an ironic or probably joshing way.

But so what? In a moment, I hope we'll see how these minor comic touches (we'll find more) make sense only when seen as an undercurrent within what is the prevailing heartbreaking experience of this poem. But the comic undercurrent is important. It helps to create an experience of loneliness which is deeper, more bitter and funnier than the description of mere depression or desolation. In fact, I suspect that when the comic and tragic elements can be seen as united into "the yoke and shell of the one egg" (to borrow a figure from Aristophanes) we will know a total experience of loneliness which could be unforgettable.

So let's look at the comic elements within the context of the poem as a whole. What happens, for instance, when the title is read as an integral part? What's accomplished by the mock heroic tone in the opening dependent clause? and by the odd choice to identify Po Chu-i as governor?

We'll discuss the appellation of governor first. By identifying Po Chu-i with his political job, Wright prepares the reader for the intimate, bantering humor of the opening salutation: "Po Chu-i, balding old politician,/What's the use?" Politician? Governor or Secretary of War would be more appropriate. And more accurate. The fact is that Po Chu-i was distinguished for his political integrity. In a tradition notorious for corrupt court favorites and politicians, he was an honest official and, according to Payne, he was more reserved and Confucian than his fellow poet-statesman Yuan Chen; indeed, Po Chu-i was "more deeply imbued with conceptions of morality, possessing a fundamental dislike for Taoism and a still more fundamental dislike for court displays," intrigues and bribes. But to call a man a politician is to suggest if not actual duplicity, then certainly self-seeking aggrandizement in his character. Is Wright being flippant here? If the rest of the poem were a parody of Po Chu-i, then he certainly is being flip and sarcastic; but the tone of subsequent remarks about the old Chinese poet and the questions asked of him reveal that the speaker in this poem feels deeply about Po Chu-i; and, in fact, he talks with him as one talks with an old and cherished friend.

Compare the way in which Wright addresses Po Chu-i with the malicious way John Berryman (or his persona Henry) talks about Frost in the first of the cycle "Three Around the Old Gentleman":

> His malice was a pimple down his good
> big face, with its sly eyes. I must be sorry
> Mr. Frost has left;
> I like it so less I don't understood.

And although Berryman-Henry ends the "elegy" on a note of tribute, it is niggardly: "Gentle his shift, I decussate and command,/stoic deity. For a while here we possessed/an unusual man."

Wright's address is the opposite. By calling him "governor" and "balding old politician," he's teasing his friend a bit: he knows perfectly well that Po Chu-i is a renowned poet. And the explosive abruptness of "What's the use?" is exactly the exasperated tone in which one can talk with a friend with whom one has shared a lot. With a friend one can be perfectly blunt. If you're fed up or depressed, you can say so without worrying about the effect. Friendship offers possibilities of candor and directness often impossible or severely restricted

between husbands and wives or lovers. At the same time, I
don't think that the abrupt, angry "What's the use?" conceals
an attack on the friend the way it well might if a beloved or
wife were being addressed. Isn't the bantering but affectionate
tone of "governor" and "balding old politician" much the same,
in fact, as if Ezra Pound were to begin a poem addressed to his
old friend Eliot: "Old Possum, what's the use?"

The humor in addressing Po Chu-i as governor and balding
old politician lies, then, in the joshing, bantering tone one often
uses with a friend. It is not a parody of a venerable poet by a
younger one. That both men are poets is almost irrelevant in
this poem. Unless the reader happened to know who Po Chu-i
was (I admit I had to do some research in Payne's anthology
The White Pony) he couldn't tell from the poem that Po Chu-i
was a great poet or even a minor poet. In the context of the
friendship between the young American poet and the old
Chinese one, this is as it should be. Good friends who are poets
do talk about poetry and literary gossip but not as much as one
might think. What they often do talk about are the essentials
important to any two men: "How's it going? Feeling good?
How's the old heart and its adventures?" And this is what the
speaker in Wright's poem talks about with Po Chu-i: "What's
the use? We're born alone; we live alone; we die alone. Old
friend, I know how you felt in your old age as you went from
one political job to the next. Loneliness is hell."

And notice how the subtle fusing of images relevant to both
men draws them into a deeper intimacy as the poem develops.
Even the most cursory reading suggests how the two are united
by the central image of water. For Po Chu-i, water is the rapids
of the Yang-Tze and the river or rapids implied by the final lines
when the old poet becomes a river coolie. For the speaker, it is
the "black twilight/Of bamboo ropes and waters" and the
miraculous sea that once solved the loneliness of the Midwest.
Both men are also associated with cities: Minneapolis and the
ancient Chinese city of isolated men beyond mountains.

Most important, both poets share images of exacerbated
loneliness. For example, notice how both seem frozen in a
timeless world of desolation. Loneliness for Po Chu-i is the
memorable final image that he's been alone for a thousand

years.* Loneliness for the speaker is embodied primarily in two images: the prehistoric sea that "once solved the whole loneliness/Of the Midwest" which, although its waters vanished centuries ago, is also timeless in its presence in the poet's mind in 1960; and the curiously timeless "great terrible oak tree" which stands rooted in eternal winter—the only thing seen by the poet in the end. Notice how both title and the line stating that "it is 1960, it is almost spring again" tell us that the poem occurs in late March or early April; yet the oak is "darkening with winter" without ever having known springtime. Both prehistoric sea and oak combine, in turn, to suggest a loneliness as timeless as the 1000 years of Po Chu-i. All of the images of loneliness blend finally to suggest one figure of man as alone in 1960 in Minneapolis as he was in 800 A.D. in China: loneliness *per omnia saecula saeculorum.*

The humor in addressing Po Chu-i as governor, then, has a double edge. Its good humor is obvious: the poet joshes an old friend. The second edge is blacker and cuts deep. It's as if the speaker says: "Loneliness gnawed your vitals too. What difference did it make that you were a great poet? Best to call you by an official title: it's more faceless; there's less room for personal feelings that break the heart."

Now, let's return to the mock heroic part of the title in which the speaker makes quiet fun of himself as the poet who writes a long and grave title. After the composite figure of the eternally lonely man, the tone of this clause probably sounds like a serious blemish. And it would be—but only if the reader fails to respond to the irony in the mock heroic pose.

Why does the poet make fun of himself? In the context of the poem, the answer is somewhat elusive but it is there. It will help if we wonder about another question first: Why does he talk with Po Chu-i in the first place? In the world of his poem he has no other friend: he's terribly alone. The mock heroic irony may come, then, from the suspicion that his one friend is, after all,

* Notice here how the image of the old Chinese poet as river coolie suggests an unmentioned metaphor which contributes to the burden of Po Chu-i's loneliness: the boat which the rope towed. It could be accurate to view the absent boat as having contained things once precious but now lost forever to the old poet: most important among them, Yuan Chen.

only a ghost in an anthology of classic Chinese literature. In other words, he will end as he began: and the irony is that he knows it but as early as the title, he cannot help but speak with such passion to a ghost because his loneliness is excruciating and he must try anything to relieve or exorcise it. At the risk of being overly ingenious, I think that we can also see the mock heroic pose as a kind of protection against the possibility that his friend will fail him and he will end lonelier than when he began. It's as if he says: "If I can laugh at myself, then it's not that serious; and the chance that my loneliness will only increase as I try to talk with Po Chu-i won't be as bad as it might be if that talk fails."

And does it fail? At first, it seems that it will succeed because the poet is able to call over the centuries to one who knew a similar loneliness and wrote of it in lyrics like:

EARLY AUTUMN: LONELY NIGHT

Thin leaves flutter on the Wu-T'ung tree
near the wall.
Amid the thumping of the washerwomen
autumn begins its song.
I find a place under the eaves
and fall asleep,
alone. Waking, I watch
the bed, half-
filled by the light of the moon.

But no answer comes. The questions become increasingly desolate and desperate in the final stanza; and after the final question, the speaker is left standing on stage, as it were, surrounded by only the ghosts of his own questions. He appears as alone as Anthony Quinn on the beach at sunrise in the final scene of *La Strada*. The implication is poignant and heartbreaking: there's nobody he can talk with; his one friend will remain forever mute.

I'm sure I don't have to labor the point that this is a tragic image. But it's also comic. It is comic in much the same way that a great clown like Emmett Kelly is comic. Here the figure of the poet is, in fact, that of the classic clown who laughs at himself while his heart is breaking; and in this figure the poet is a microcosm of the poem itself: both are tragic and comic at once.

Exactly how does he laugh at himself? We've seen how he parodies himself as poet in the mock heroic part of the title. He also appears to poke fun (in an extremely subtle way) at the main image of water he's created. A moment ago, we explored some of the ways in which this image is tragic in that it embodies several of the more poignant feelings of desolation—the prehistoric sea, the vanished Chinese river of the final lines, and so on. But isn't there also something a bit ludicrous both in the sequence of shapes the image assumes and in the crazy sequence of time in which it exists?

Beginning as a trivial puddle in a Minneapolis street in 1960, the image expands into the dangerous rapids of the Yang-Tze as it swirled along over 1000 years ago; then the water returns to the present in Minneapolis but now it's almost invisible in the "black twilight"; but it abruptly balloons again, swelling into the vast prehistoric sea which, although only a memory, is terribly visible and present in the poet's mind; and, finally, the water evaporates in the final lines where its presence is merely implied by the figure of the old Chinaman holding the bamboo rope on the bank of an invisible river centuries ago.

To follow these swellings, contractions and eventual disappearance as the water appears and disappears in different centuries is comic, it seems to me, in that it suggests the sleight-of-hand trick of a magician: "Now you see water. Now you don't."

By deflating or poking fun at his basically tragic image of water the speaker seems to be playing his role of heartbroken clown. Out of fierce desolation and unhappiness he makes jokes.

A part of his humor, finally, might come from two ironies implied by his situation. The first we've noticed: the poet is capable of the love and affection which destroys loneliness but the person for whom he feels affection was buried over 1000 years ago in distant China. The second is as telling: he has written a good poem about loneliness. In memorable speech, he's been able to describe the condition of suffering caused by being alone; his poem has the ability to reach others and earn their attention and perhaps even their love. But the final irony is that he won't know who reads his poem. Like a clown or mimic on stage, he can't see the faces in the darkened theatre.

In what sense are these ironies comic? They are funny, it seems to me, for the most basic reason: the joke is on the speaker. One thinks of course of Chaplin's face in the final scene of *City Lights;* or of Grock about to begin his recital, extracting from an enormous gladstone bag a tiny toy fiddle.

I end by offering a final picture of the poet as clown: he can and at the same time he cannot surmount his loneliness. His paradox is at once farcical and heartbreaking.

Appendix One

In its subtle mixture of tragic and comic, Wright's poem approaches as near in spirit as any I know to that famous but puzzling definition of the true poet given by Socrates in *The Symposium*: "Aristodemus was only half awake and he missed the beginning of the talk, but the chief thing he says he remembered was how Socrates was compelling Aristophanes and Agathon to admit that the genius of comedy was identical with that of tragedy and that the true poet of tragedy was also a poet of comedy."

I'd like to explore this curious definition not in terms of its theory of poetry but in its relationship to the dialogue itself. As far as I know, the definition hasn't received much attention from commentators on Plato and yet I suspect that it contains a fascinating example of the subtlety of Plato's art. The definition of the true poet occurs, you will recall, at the tail end of the banquet when all of the other guests either have passed out or have gone home. What Socrates suggests about poetry seems to have nothing whatever to do with the talk about Eros which has dominated most of the dialogue. Then why does Plato include it?

Some commentators on Plato suggest that the final episode merely adds a graceful conclusion to the general portrait of Socrates which is the real heart of the dialogue. R. G. Bury puts it this way: the dominant factor in the dialogues is "nothing less than the personality of Socrates, as the ideal both of philosophy and of love, Socrates as at once the type of temperance and the master of magic." Thus, the dialogue ends with a minor but charming touch: Socrates takes care to see that his sleeping friends are comfortable and then refreshes himself with a bath at the Lycium before beginning his day "as usual" in conversation about the eternal verities with his fellow Athenians.

I incline to see the final episode as more crucial than that. In truth, I suspect it contains the final word by Socrates on the nature of Eros. The question is: What is Socrates *complete* view of human love?

The most obvious answer—and the traditional one—directs the reader to the speech Socrates gives half way through the dialogue. It is the magnificent definition of the ladder of love which leads to the Beatific Vision of the "single science of Beauty everywhere." But this great definition contains only half of Socrates' attitude about the nature of human love; the other half is embodied in the curious suggestion that the true poet must be both tragic and comic; and I suspect that the second half is more important in the end than the more celebrated first.

But first, let's follow Socrates as he builds his definition of the ladder of love which leads to the eternal "ocean of Beauty." He begins with characteristic mock humility. "My opinion about Eros," he tells his fellow guests, "is merely a recitation of the lesson I learned at the feet of that wise old woman, Diotima of Mantineia." But he doesn't fool us for long. He uses the mask of Diotima in order to sift the wheat from the chaff in the previous definitions of Eros. Speaking through the mouth of the mask of Diotima, Socrates is free to expose through irony and considerable charm and wit the sugary sentimentality of Agathon, the hard-core nacissism and pederasty of Pausanias, the cloddishness of Phaedrus, the pedantry of Eryximachus, and the corroding cynicism of Aristophanes. What Socrates retains, on the other hand, is the basic premise used by several of the preceding speakers: namely, the knowledge of Eros begins with the relationship between an older teacher and a beloved pupil.

This relationship starts, Socrates explains, when the teacher instructs his pupil how to appreciate specific beautiful forms in other people (including handsome boys) and in the world around him. The next rung on the ladder is reached when the pupil comes to contemplate and love the beauty of laws, institutions and works of great art. Then he ascends to the third rung where he learns that all beautiful forms are only part of one whole, which is described by the figure of an immense sea of Beauty everywhere. Once he comes to know and love the whole, he is ready to create a multitude of "fair and noble thoughts" of his own until finally he's at the top of the ladder. There he knows the vision of "the single science of Beauty everywhere."

And on this noble note Socrates ends. But *The Symposium* doesn't. On the contrary, the banquet turns into a merry and eventually drunken homosexual party.

What tips the scales from a lecture on the philosophy of love to a gay party is the boisterous entrance of Alcibiades in the company of some tipsy companions and a flute girl. What follows is the most charming episode in the dialogue: Alcibiades' witty, slightly ironic yet deeply affectionate tribute to Socrates. Alcibiades seems to be a bit high as he begins by explaining that he will praise Eros by praising Socrates. He recalls how Socrates was always teaching him to stop neglecting the "needs of my soul" by wasting time in courting popularity among the Athenians; and how he once tried but failed to seduce Socrates. (To the other guests this last confession must have sounded ironical indeed. As everybody knew, Alcibiades could have had as lover any man, boy or woman in Athens.) Alcibiades concludes his encomium amid the merriment of all over his frankness—especially because he sounds as if he were still half in love with Socrates. With affection and wit, Socrates chides Alcibiades for only pretending to be drunk in order to blow up a quarrel between Agathon and himself and thereby keep both in love with Alcibiades. More revellers crash the party; most of the guests pass out or leave, including Alcibiades; and the dialogue ends with the small scene in which Socrates spells out his *ars poetica* to a sleepy Agathon and Aristophanes.

But why doesn't the dialogue conclude on the brilliant level of Socrates' description of the ladder of love? Why the intrusion of everyday "impurities" (as Lionel Johnson would have called them)? In other words, what contribution to the total definition of Eros can the two parts of the dialogue be said to offer?

In the ladder of love speech, Socrates spells out clearly that the ascent must begin with the love between an older teacher and a beloved pupil: he makes it perfectly clear that the ascent cannot be made alone. Now, Socrates is obviously the ideal older teacher in this dialogue. But who is the beloved pupil? A quick look at the roster of guests eliminates all but one. Our host Agathon is a vapid, self-indulgent pretty boy; Pausanias is brighter but he'd use sophisticated encomiums about "spiritual love" only to attract the lad with whom he wants to engage in homosexual acts of sodomy or fellatio; Phaedrus is a well-intentioned but dull clod; the physician Eryximachus sounds like such a stuffed shirt that he'd bore Socrates to tears; and Aristophanes is just too cynical and, besides, he'd prove an impatient pupil—he's already found his own hilarious and mocking way of viewing life.

Obviously the answer is: Alcibiades. Not only is Alcibiades the most handsome young man in Athens but his speech shows he's brilliant and capable of appreciating Socrates and what he has to teach.

And here is where the comic side of love occurs. The one guest capable of ascending the ladder of love reveals that he's fundamentally incapable of devoting himself either to his teacher or to the contemplation of any beauty other than the beauty he's found and loved in his own person. The comedy here is of course ironic. And the irony is also at Socrates expense. Although he knows of the Ideal Love and how to achieve the vision of it, he also "learns" in the dialogue that his one potential pupil adores only himself.

More heartbreaking is the tragic side of the knowledge of the limits of love. To appreciate some of its quality we should look at this dialogue and its characters in their historical context.

Most Plato scholars agree that good reason exists to think that *The Symposium* takes place on an evening in the spring of 416 B.C. That was the year in which Agathon won first prize for tragedy in the annual competition staged each spring in honor of Dionysus. More important is the fact of the profanation of the sacred Hermae one evening during that same spring—an event which was to trigger a series of bitter and brutal episodes which led to disaster for both Alcibiades and Athens. Earlier in that year, Alcibiades had been elected to lead the Athenian expedition against Sicily, according to Thucydides and Plutarch; but on the eve of his departure somebody (or as Plutarch suggests, a band of revellers) defaced the statues of the Hermae which stood in many of the temples and front doors of the city. The citizens were outraged. Enemies of Alcibiades began to fan public opinion by accusing him of having profaned the statues. Eventually, he was relieved of his leadership and summoned home to stand trial. Alcibiades chose to flee to Sparta.

His biography now becomes the coarse and melancholy tale of his betrayal of Athenian military and defense secrets to the Spartans which helped in great measure to bring about the final collapse of Athens; and then his betrayal of Sparta to the Persian king, followed by his betrayal of Persia to the Athenians— and so on and on. When one remembers the glorious promise of his youth, his assassination at 46 in a farm house in the Troiad by killers hired by the king of Persia is almost Elizabethan in the bleakness of its tragedy.

I suggest this: *The Symposium* occurs on the same night that the Hermae were mutilated. The Alcibiades whom we see at the banquet is at the very summit of his powers: everything lies before him; he is like a god. But those of Plato's circle who heard or read *The Symposium* when Plato finished it around 385 B.C. would also have fresh in mind the subsequent career of duplicity, betrayal and consummate perversion of his gifts which make Alcibiades the Lucifer of the Greek world.

And here at last the tragedy and comedy of Socrates' definition of the true poet merge: Alcibiades is both the only and the least potentially beloved pupil. What is Socrates' final definition of love? Human love is both comic and tragic because of the paradox that the one man capable of learning the vision of the Ideal Beauty and Love has devoted a lifetime to the most crippling and eventually destructive adoration of himself.

FAIRE, FOUL AND FULL
OF VARIATIONS:
THE GENERATION OF 1962*

1

Barbarians Inside the City Gates

"None of us can say who will succeed, or even who has or has not talent," Yeats remembers having observed to his fellow young poets in the Rhymers Club one evening in the 90s in the Cheshire Cheese in Fleet Street. "The only thing certain about us is that we are too many," was his wry conclusion.

I am happy to say that only the first of these points applies, in my opinion, to this generation of American poets. Who will succeed? still remains largely an open question: most of these poets are still in their early 40s. Ten or twelve of them, however, have established themselves as leading members of the generation. One or two of them show the signs that they may well mature into major talents. In addition, one can read at least a dozen others whose works are not only the genuine article but who grow as poets in important and often surprising ways.

What all of the members of this generation share is the excitement of creating a body of work far more "faire, foul and full of variations" than anyone could have hoped for back in the grim, nervous years of the first Eisenhower Administration, when we were all young, trying to learn how to write and count-

---

* I want to thank Robert Bly for having suggested the arithmetic by which this date was found. Bly says that a good way to find the year with which to identify our generation would be to begin with the obvious date of 1917 for the Eliot-Pound-Williams generation and then to add 15 years for each succeeding generation. It works out well. In 1932 Hart Crane committed suicide—perhaps the most important single event in the Crane-Tate-Warren generation. (How startling to realize that if Crane had chosen to live he'd be 70 today.) In 1947 Lowell's *Lord Weary's Castle* won the Pulitzer Prize—still the best book of the Berryman-Lowell-Shapiro generation. And in 1962 Allen Ginsberg was in India learning from gurus; and such important volumes as John Ashbery's *The Tennis Court Oath* and James Wright's *The Branch Will Not Break* were published.

ing rejection slips, and scrutinizing with awed but invidious eye the oval photographs of poets only a few years older than ourselves—such as Karl Shapiro dressed in GI jacket or Delmore Schwartz looking mysteriously pensive and intense—whom one discovered in the gallery at the back of the 1946 edition of Oscar Williams' *A Little Treasury of Modern Verse.*

To a young poet the scene in American verse in the late 1940s and early 1950s seemed much like walking down 59th Street in New York for the first time. Elegant and sturdy hotels and apartment buildings stand in the enveloping dusk, mysterious in their power, sophistication, wealth and inaccessability. One of the most magnificent buildings houses Eliot, his heirs and their sons; other tall, graceful buildings contain e. e. cummings, Marianne Moore, Ezra Pound, Wallace Stevens, William Carlos Williams. The doormen look past you but you are noted if you walk too near: No Admission.

Civilized, verbally excellent, ironic, cerebral and clearly bearers of the Tradition, the poems admired as models included: the Eliot of "The Love Song of J. Alfred Prufrock" and *Poems 1920* and "The Waste Land," the Ransom of "The Equilibrists" and "Bells for John Whiteside's Daughter," the Tate of "Sonnets at Christmas" (*not* "Ode to the Confederate Dead"), the Warren of "Bearded Oaks," and of course the Auden of "In Memory of W. B. Yeats," "September 1, 1939" and "Musée des Beaux Arts."* Then came the sons: the Lowell of *Lord Weary's Castle,* the Delmore Schwartz of "For Rhoda" and "In the Naked Bed, In Plato's Cave," the Shapiro of *Person, Place and Thing* and *V-Letter,* the Wilbur of "A Black November Turkey" and "Love Calls Us to the Things of This World."

Pound was, as always, a special case. To many of us who

* How many poems were hatched in the early 1950s while their author hunted through art museums or galleries for that painting or sculpture which might inspire something which sounded like the most envied opening lines of those years: "About suffering they were never wrong,/The Old Masters: how well they understood/Its human position . . ."

What is surprising in this context is that the finest poem about "art" to come from the new poets is "The Artist" by Kenneth Koch—that droll and wildly funny prophecy written in the late 1950s which, in a mysterious way, describes so accurately so much of what indeed is happening on the art scene ten years later.

grieved at the spectacle of a great poet locked in a hospital for the insane he seemed almost like a Lear lost on the heath amid the storm. (Rumor reached us, however, that he'd kept his humor. An editor of one of the little magazines—was it Cid Corman?— reported that in reply to a request for poems Pound had scribbled on a postcard: "Birdee in cagee/No singee. EP.") Almost every young poet admired "this side idolatry" such magical early lyrics as "Cino," "The Garret," "The Garden," "Alba," "In a Station of the Metro," and of course the translations— the Propertius cycle, "The River-merchant's Wife: A Letter," "The Jewel Stairs' Grievance," and "Exile's Letter" (shall we ever see their like again?) *The Cantos* were like trying to think about Freud's metaphor that the unconscious is a Zuyder Zee impossible ever to drain completely. Young poets read feverishly in the poem, admiring individual cantos or passages but despairing over ever understanding much. Most admired were "The Pisan Cantos," although one dared not hope to try and imitate the harsh, wounded voice which rasped and sang in such passages as the "O Lynx, my Love, my lovely lynx" in Canto LXXIX and throughout the entire Pull Down Thy Vanity Canto LXXXI—in many ways the finest poetry in English in our century.*

Then there were the other poems widely read and respected as models: "pity this busy monster manunkind," "buffalo bill's

---

* Hart Crane was another special case. Was there any young poet who read "Voyages II," "Praise for an Urn," "Repose of Rivers," "At Melville's Tomb" or "Legend" ("As silent as a mirror is believed,/Realities plunge in silence by") without loving the complexity, intensity, the incandescence of the images? And although we heard from such respected critics as Tate and Yvor Winters that "The Bridge" was a San Simeon of noble but disastrous intention, we found unforgettable city poetry in such sections as "To Brooklyn Bridge," "The Harbor Dawn," and "The Tunnel." (And I suspect every young poet felt the wound in lines Crane wrote about memory: "Is it the whip stripped from the lilac tree/One day in spring my father took to me?/Or is it the Sabbatical, unconscious smile/My mother almost brought me once from Church/And only once, as I recall?") But Crane seemed, as Robert Lowell says, "the Shelley of my age": a poet of the first rank probably but not to be imitated. Although we felt devotion to the poems and the legend of *Catullus redivivius,* we knew his voice was finally too personal, insular, and remote to be an influence in practical ways that mattered. Finally, there was that sad qualification: Crane had been dead 20 years; he didn't seem part of the living scene.

defunct," "in just spring" and "somewhere i have never travelled" by cummings; "Spenser's Ireland" and "Poetry" by Marianne Moore; "Esthetique du Mal," "Sunday Morning" and
"Thirteen Ways of Looking at a Blackbird" by Stevens (what
young poet has not suffered gloom when trying to write a poem
as pure as the Blackbird?); and "The Red Wheelbarrow" and
"Tract" by Williams.

Clearly all of these are fine poems; and it was a pleasure to
know them. To a beginning poet, however, the legacy of such
examples often appeared almost too rich: in fact, it often was
enervating. Our problem was of course the ancient one of the
son trying to enter the same business or political party in which
his father had found success, power, wealth and respect: How
to find one's own way of viewing feelings and experience and the
world around one and a voice of one's own in which to tell it?

To many of us it seemed as if the poetry scene in this country
were as much a board of directors' meeting or closed shop as the
New York art world must have looked to a young painter around
the same period. Pollock, Kline, de Kooning and Hofmann:
these were giants; one could foresee only refinement within the
basic premise of Abstract Expressionism. And so when I suggest
that American poetry in those years seemed to be settling into
successful and comfortable middle age, I imply no sarcasm. All
of the major poetic discoveries and innovations had been accomplished—or so it seemed—and the scene looked, in truth,
often as dull as Easter Sunday around 5 or 6 p.m., the roast lamb
long since eaten, the adults visiting or napping, Aunt Marie
petulant behind the Easter lilies beginning to droop, the movie
playing at the local Bijou one you'd already seen twice, and
Jack Benny and Rochester grinding out stale gags over the
radio inside its American Gothic wooden box. One did not
know that the barbarians were already inside the gates of the
city.

By barbarian I imply nothing more than the alien or the
enemy of prevailing contemporary standards of correctness or
purity of taste. Some literary historians and critics might date
the invasion of the barbarians as occurring in 1956 when
Lawrence Ferlinghetti published in his City Lights Pocket
Poets Series the small, hardboiled-looking, funeral-black bor-

dered edition of *Howl and Other Poems* by young Allen Ginsberg. Everybody remembers how that book and its subsequent
victory in court over the accusation of obscenity by the San
Francisco police department helped to move into merry high
gear the San Francisco poets soon to be discovered and chris-
tened "beat" by Henry Luce, as Gregory Corso once quipped.
To date the advent of the barbarian with *Howl*, however, would
be mere journalism. Equally important and radical innovations
were being explored at the same time by poets as alien to the
San Francisco poets as well as to one another as John Ashbery
in Paris, Robert Creeley in Majorca, James Dickey in Atlanta,
Isabella Gardner in Elmhurst, Illinois, John Logan in South
Bend, W. S. Merwin in London, Frank O'Hara in New York,
W. D. Snodgrass in Iowa City, and James Wright in Minneap-
olis—and at least a dozen other equally gifted poets.

All of these poets were barbarians in this sense: they shared
a concern with trying to write types of poems either alien or
hostile to the poem as defined and explored by Eliot and his
heirs and their sons, as well as to types of poems created by the
other leading writers dominating the scene ten or fifteen years
ago. In the next section—"Ten Poets in Their Skins"—I talk
about the poets whose works were discussed in the essays; and in
the final section—"Freedom Is a Breakfast Food—and More"—
I hazard some generalizations about the work of the generation
as a whole.

2

Ten Poets in Their Skins

John Ashbery is the Sphinx of the generation. Not only are all
of his poems enigmas or simply impossible to understand but
they appear to promise esoteric wisdom one finds nowhere else
in America poetry. Fellow poets, critics and students admit to
despair at ever discovering the key (if one exists) to the riddle
of the poems in *The Tennis Court Oath* (1962) and *Rivers and
Mountains* (1966). Often I feel exactly the same: the difficulty
we experienced in trying to read "Leaving the Atocha Station"
may still be a wound for some readers; and even if my reading

makes sense, it holds no guarantee that one has found the key to unlock any other Ashbery poem. Each one proves cryptic, puzzling, unique.

One quality most of Ashbery's poems share, on the other hand, is something like the peculiar excitement one feels when stepping with Alice behind the Looking Glass into a reality bizarre yet familiar in which the "marvelous" is as near as one's breakfast coffee cup or one's shoes being shined by an angel in the barbershop. In an Ashbery poem the marvelous is, in fact, the cup and the shoes—and the angel. His gift is to release everyday objects, experiences and fragments of dream or hallucination from stereotypes imposed on them by habit or preconception or belief: he presents the world as if seen for the first time. But the problem is: each poem is the first time in its own way unlike any past or future Ashbery poem. One way to read an Ashbery poem, it seems to me, might be to remember all one has felt or learned about poetry, including his poems—and then forget it and let the poem at hand do its own work.

But what accounts for the peculiar, chilly absence of feeling in almost everyone of his poems? One receives no sense or awareness of the man whose voice one hears. The Sphinx is invisible. Yet the effort and energy in the act of editing or suppressing personal feeling is terribly evident. At times, this act seems almost heroic. Ashbery appears to silence or make a sacrificial victim out of the traditional poet in himself (he is perfectly capable of writing good traditional verse as his first collection *Some Trees* (1956) demonstrates) in order to present a reality for our contemplation which is the everyday one but seen by an angel who has no emotional investment in either people or fried bats or blind dogs or Italian hair or air pollution or forestry or slacks or peaches or poems. The puzzling thing is: angels love, it is said. In many of Ashbery's poems, one hears only elusive intimations that his angel may be looking for love—but of what kind or from whom one cannot know.

You get some of this feeling when hearing the poet read in public or when spending time in his company. Dressed in tweed jacket, slacks and necktie, Ashbery recites fantastically original poems in a straightforward manner without explanation or hermetic intonation as if the poems were the most conventional ones of the season. In his person, the poet is civilized, shy, witty—and remote if he doesn't happen to know you well. Frequently Ashbery looks at you and the scene around him as if he suddenly found himself in the middle of one of his own poems. "How odd that this glass of wine is here at all," he seems to say. "And a window too! Taxis and lunch hour on 56th Street. My, my . . ."

*   *   *

On the back dust jacket of *For Love: Poems 1950–1960* one finds a photograph of **Robert Creeley** looking like an elegant Jean Lafitte. With one wry, cold but concerned eye, he stares directly at you; the other eye is a slit. A dignified wooden crow stands in profile on the table at which the poet sits. The photograph has always seemed to me to be a mirror of Creeley's close-to-the bone, personal lyrics. One of the qualities which stamped him as an original and which, as it turned out, also stamped him as a leader of the generation, was this incessant personal voice, unmistakable, stingy at times, stuttering, often perverse, the budding lyricism clipped. At first, I inclined to think his poems were whittled from too dry a stick: they wanted blood; later, I came to see that Creeley's insistence on ignoring the basics— metaphor, imagery, descriptions of landscape or surroundings, analogies of sensibility discovered by observing animals—came from a courage to follow the mind as it observes with caustic, lucid comments the behavior and moods of the irrational heart.

Above all, Creeley is a poet of love, talking and stuttering half aloud, half to himself, of those few essentials which matter to a lover: "Who is this woman? Who am I when I say I love her? What do we share?" Whereas cummings is a troubador of Romantic Love, Creeley's work seems closer in spirit to Catullus at his bald, biting best. The man who wrote:

> *Odi et amo. quare id faciam, fortasse requiris.*
> *nescio. sed fieri sentio et excrucior.*

("I hate: I love. You're curious perhaps how this can be? I don't know. I feel it. Excruciating.")

is brother to Creeley's "The Business":

> To be in love is like going out-
> side to see what kind of day
>
> it is. Do not
> mistake me. If you love
>
> her how prove she
> loves also, except that it
>
> occurs, a remote chance on
> which you stake
>
> yourself? But barter for
> the Indians was a means of subsistence.
>
> There are records.

This was the voice we heard. It is authentic. Only occasionally Creeley's determination to talk absolutely straight, without elaboration, appears a bit adolescent: the "sincerity" becomes obvious, banal, boring.

Another quality in Creeley's best work is the odd, interesting combination of cool hipness and an almost courtly dignity. The man is like this. Wearing a trim Vandyke and a dark blue blazer, he moves as easily among the young poets on the Lower East Side as one assumes he does among some of his academic colleagues educated at Harvard Yard.

*   *   *

Although **James Dickey** arrived late on the scene, he's more than made up for time lost. When his first collection *Into the Stone* appeared in 1960, he was already 37; but in less than ten years he's become one of the most celebrated poets of the generation and some critics such as Peter Davison wonder if he may not be the most interesting and powerful poet in the nation. In addition to having earned most of the major poetry awards, Dickey is also a critic noted for his independence of judgment, common sense, and abiding love of the art of poetry in such collections as

The Suspect in Poetry (1964) and *Babel to Byzantium* (1968).
What is stunning about Dickey's poems is the imagination often evident in the sudden radiances of joy or tenderness or empathy felt amid such familiar situations as climbing stairs to say goodnight to his sons, hunting and camping in North Georgia or Virginia, visiting an ailing father in the hospital, observing caged animals at the zoo. Even more stunning is how joy and tenderness often mingle in the same poem with a vein of cruelty, malevolence or violence.

Astonishment over the familiar tempts Dickey at times to ramble on too long: the lines and stanzas begin to rattle like a Model T Ford driven by moonshiners over the back roads of Georgia. At other times, he tends to lose a poem because of an inclination to censor or hesitate to explore the uglier, less robust areas in his experience which might qualify the image of the poet being presented in the poem as hearty American male.

Recent works of Dickey have, happily, ignored this last tendency. In poems like "Slave Quarters," "The Firebombing," "The Fiend" and "The Sheep Child," he explores disturbing secret lusts and an appetite for brute violence and power which troubles certain fellow poets and critics who seem to approve only poems which embody the pieties of the Northern White Liberal. What distinguishes such poems is the power of the imagination at work, which only seems to increase as the poet matures. No other poet of the generation could have imagined or written the speech of the sheep child "only half/Sheep
like a wooly baby" pickled in alcohol in a bottle standing in some back corner in a museum in Atlanta. Here is what the sheep child says:

> I am here, in my father's house.
> I who am half of your world, came deeply
> To my mother in the long grass
> Of the west pasture, where she stood like moonlight
> Listening for foxes. It was something like love
> From another world that seized her
> From behind, and she gave, not lifting her head
> Out of dew, without ever looking, her best
> Self to that great need. Turned loose, she dipped her face

Farther into the chill of the earth, and in a sound
Of sobbing   of something stumbling
Away, began, as she must do,
To carry me. I woke, dying,

In the summer sun of the hillside, with my eyes
Far more than human. I saw for a blazing moment
The great grassy world from both sides,
Man and beast in the round of their need,
And the hill wind stirred in my wool,
My hoof and my hand clasped each other,
I ate my one meal
Of milk, and died
Staring. From dark grass I came straight

To my father's house, whose dust
Whirls up in the halls for no reason
When no one comes   piling deep in a hellish mild
      corner,
And, through my immortal waters,
I meet the sun's grains eye
To eye, and they fail at my closet of glass.
Dead, I am most surely living
In the minds of farm boys: I am he who drives
Them like wolves from the hound bitch and calf
And from the chaste ewe in the wind.
They go into woods   into bean fields   they go
Deep into their known right hands. Dreaming of me,
They groan   they wait   they suffer
Themselves, they marry, they raise their kind.

Masculinity, ambition, exuberance, humor, and deep, conflicting feelings of affection and depressed brutality under control are one's general impression of Dickey as a person. Exuding
classic Southern charm, he is an accomplished raconteur and
can be a boon companion. Often in everyday situations both the
man and the poet are visible. In December 1962, Dickey and I
were strolling through the Lincoln Park Zoo on Chicago's North
Side when suddenly he stopped to study with what appeared
reverence the huge gray timber wolf pacing back and forth in
an outdoor cage. "Isn't it a privilege," he asked quietly, "to live

in the same universe with such a magnificent beast?" One felt
close to the source of his best poems. Another time, Dickey was
gazing out of large glass windows in a Mies van der Rohe apartment high above Chicago when he broke a long silence by con-
fessing: "Sometimes, I swear, I feel thick glass separates me from
other people." There's that too in his work. Some of his poems
such as "Faces Seen Once" or "Them, Crying" or "The Sheep
Child" seem desperate attempts to describe or break that glass.

* * *

Of all the poets of the generation **Isabella Gardner** is best at
exploring the mystery, ugliness, pain and sexuality of human
relationships. What distinguishes her poems of relationships
such as "The Widow's Yard" or "Mea Culpa" or "Zei Gesund"
or "To Thoreau on Rereading Walden" in *West of Childhood:
Poems 1950–1965* is how the relationship is experienced in its
own existential terms: she refuses to gloss over either the twisted
or the graceful or erotic by letting the relationship stand for
this or that "significant" message or moral.

Much the same occurs when the poem delineates relationships between people and animals or birds. "That 'Craning of
the Neck'" and "Part of the Darkness" are old favorites of mine.
In long, ragged couplets "Part of the Darkness" tells how a
mother and children vacationing in Wisconsin stop at a garbage
dump in the hope of observing wild bears feeding. When the
bear who does come turns out to be tame and, finally, after
rooting in garbage, slinks away amid a choir of booing children,
the mother confesses: "I also was reluctant to concede that there
is no wild honey in the forest and no forest in the bear." The
reader too is left inside a fresh experience of the eventual, nagging disillusion at the niggardly boundaries of the real world
with which we all must come to terms. And because the bear
remains only an animal lacking the glamor of savagery it can be
felt to embody what in life turns out to be—despite our imagination, desires, fantasies, the poetry is in us—simply what it is:
no more, no less. At their best, her poems bear witness to the
exhilerating reality of things-as-they-are.

In addition, Miss Gardner has that Celtic "lovely gift of
the gab" which often makes her poems a pleasure to read aloud.

They sing. Once in a while, the lyricism waxes overly lush or mawkish. But when she keeps control of her good ear, she's capable of sounds which seem to come from some more verdurous Elizabethan season:

LINES TO A SEAGREEN LOVER

My lover never danced with me
Not minuet nor sarabande
We walked (embracing) on the sand

My lover never swam with me
We waded to our ankle bones
And winced and shivered on the stones

My lover never flew with me
We stared at sea birds slicing space
And cried What freedom Look what grace
But under my ailanthus tree

I wish my love had lain with me
Not on the sand beside the sea

In the winter of 1954, I happened to hear Miss Gardner at what was her first public reading, which took place in a somewhat dilapidated library in a high school in South Bend, Indiana. Wearing a formal gown, she recited her verses in a voice beautifully modulated, lyrical, and eminently Boston patrician, seemingly unperturbed by the drabness of the room. And over the years, I've continued to admire Miss Gardner's steadfast sense of the vocation of the poet. As she says, "A poem is a kind of witness; a clue to and proof of the poet's feeling toward, as Unamumo said, 'the man of flesh and bone; the man who is born, suffers, and dies . . . the brother, the real brother'; and a poem should bear witness to the poet's own particular joy and pain."

*   *   *

Howl and Other Poems (1956) by **Allen Ginsberg** is one of the milestones of the generation. Although these poems offer an excitement coupled with fury over contemporary America, the voice we heard also had some of the toughness and quality of familial piety and sweetness of some Jewish immigrant burdened by centuries of suffering and lamentation at the Weeping Wall of European ghettoes and also the exhilaration of loony Hasidic revelation: "The universe is a new flower. America will be discovered. Who wants a war against roses will have it. Fate tells big lies, & the gay Creator dances on his own body in Eternity." Some of Ginsberg's work is redundant, ungrammatical, prosy, boring, and smug: the most poorly written of any potentially major American verse since Whitman. Those poems that are Ginsberg classics, however, not only provide a primer of techniques and embody with compelling authority intimate angers, hopes and anxieties but they reveal a poet who appears to be of that company of whom the Evangelist of the Book of Revelation spoke: "From the days of John the Baptist until now, the kingdom of heaven suffereth violence, and the violent bear it away."

During the next ten years, *Howl and Other Poems* was to sell some 100,000 copies. Ginsberg became the most famous poet of the generation—and certainly the most photogenic. One was delighted to come across photographs of Ginsberg in *Esquire*, the Ganges swirling about his naked body while the poet prayed among the sacred cows; or wearing a tiny 5 & 10¢ Uncle Sam hat, looking solemn but patient at some Viet Nam protest rally; or stark naked, staring like a rapt fakir, in a chic book of portraits by Avedon; or in *Life*, beaming behind an immense beard, magnificent as some Old Testament patriarch.

Obviously Ginsberg relishes his fame and enjoys clowning a bit with it. Nothing could be farther from the truth, however, than the popular cartoon of Allen Ginsberg as a nutty, rabid, naughty wild man from Borneo who carries a Black Magic kit which will blow up Madison Avenue or the Pentagon. Actually, he is bone-serious, erudite, intelligent and, most of all, a poet deeply involved in the problems of his craft and in the literary scene. In truth, Ginsberg strikes me as that rare person: the committed artist. No member of the generation—with the exception of Bly—has done more to help hack away polite literary junglerot and to promote a lot of the good contemporary American writing. His energy and generosity are legendary. From his apartment in a Lower East Side slum, Ginsberg conducts his campaign. He is forever giving away money or staging some benefit reading somewhere in an effort to raise funds for a little magazine or a small press devoted to poetry; forever writing mountainous letters crammed with insight and common sense in an effort to push what he believes is the new literature and to convert the infidel; forever talking poetry, poetry, poetry; forever scrapping hard for what he holds dear or valuable— whether it be literature, repeal of narcotics laws, Viet Nam protests, or expansion in personal freedom on all fronts. As I suggested earlier, there is a generous portion of the tough, shrewd Jewish immigrant in his makeup: he fights for what he wants.

When Ginsberg reads, he is great. When he was in his late 20s and early 30s, he would stand on stage, slight and often bristling or incandescent with anger, but with a compelling aura of intelligence and sweetness, wearing lumberjacket shirt or black turtleneck and soiled blue jeans and owlish Columbia University intellectual glasses. Looking very Jewish, nose prominent, lips thick, head shaggy but prematurely balding, and clutching an endlessly unfolding scroll of poems, he'd begin to recite "Howl" or "Kaddish" or "Death to Van Gogh's Ear," hunching forward, thrashing a simian arm pointed straight at the audience, weeping, haranguing, caressing as he built and built and built the long locomotive stanzas, his oddly boyish, grating New York voice hammering away until suddenly, magically, something seemed to explode and you felt transported: the poet had revealed part of his soul. This was the Ginsberg who became notorious for both his courage and his absence of shame. During one reading in the late 1950s in Los Angeles, a heckler hooted, "What the hell are you trying to prove?" and when Ginsberg shot back, "Nakedness," the heckler responded, "What's that?" whereupon the poet took off all his clothes and stood calmly on stage. And in front of 1000 people at a benefit in Chicago to raise money for the first issue of *Big Table*, Ginsberg answered a hostile question from one of the audience— "Mr. Ginsberg, why is there so much hostility and hate against women in your poems?"—with the blunt reply: "Because I'm queer."

Since he has become a guru and the most famous living American poet, Ginsberg seems to have allowed more of the sweetness and love to dominate his recent public readings attended by overflowing crowds. Candor, power and authority are still strongly evident; but one also often feels in the presence of a holy man as Ginsberg, now bald but with abundant beard and wearing Hindu robes or dark business suit, recites poems and chants the Hari Krishna mantra on the stage.

Allen Ginsberg has both the talent and the ambition to become a major American poet. Sometimes, I feel he cannot fail to become one; at other times, I wonder if in order to write major work about the eternal human verities, a poet must also allow himself to know what it's like to love one's own woman for herself and to appreciate what many men experience daily in the worlds of business, politics, science and education when they accomplish something valuable which benefits themselves and also others. So far, Ginsberg's work doesn't indicate he cares about such realities. I hope it's clear that I say this with respect for a man who is one of the princes among the poets of his generation. Whatever the direction his future work will explore, in fact, Ginsberg may become the first American poet to win the Nobel Prize.

*   *   *

While teaching in the early 1950s in the shadow of the Golden Dome of the Blessed Virgin Mary at Notre Dame University, John Logan was writing out of such intimate traffic with the saints that his poems announced a new sensibility in American poetry. One was startled to find Mother Cabrini, Augustine, Antony the Copt or Blessed Robert Southwell sitting in his living room or on the Chicago South Shore & South Bend train, talking, as familiars, with the poet. Out of such familiarity with the "lust for the absolute" came poems like "Spring of the Thief" in which one of the radiant moments of poetry in the generation occurs: "The name of God is changing in our time./What is his winter name?/Where is his winter home."

Even when Logan abandoned Catholicism and explored the truths of the flesh discovered in himself, his students, friends and children, there was a sense in which his work remains defined by what John Crowe Ransom calls "the secular priesthood" of the poet. In most of his poems, Logan confesses and attempts to absolve or exorcise the vagaries, postures, fetishes, lusts, primitive needs and furies of his heart and often our own. When I read in manuscript *Ghosts of the Heart* (1960) in a garish, loud restaurant on Michigan Avenue in Chicago, I slowly became aware that these poems—confessional, anguished, honest—seemed to give tongue to mute but enduring emotions of the men, women and children sitting at counter or table amid the trivial babble. And this quality is perhaps why Logan's poems are so moving: the best of them describe our common humanity, "crawling between heaven and earth," and that part of our condition in which we seek that which Yeats reminds us bluntly once was but now is gone for good: "Man is in love and loves what vanishes,/What more is there to say?" In poems such as "Monologues for the Son of Saul: I," "Lines for Michael in the Picture," "To a Young Poet Who Fled," "Love Poem" and "On a Photograph by Aaron Siskind," Logan bears witness to the fact that even if Yeats' phrase be true we cannot help but continue the search for "the freshness/nothing can destroy in us—/ not even we ourselves": our need to love and be loved in return. Only a poet of the first order could have written such a passage as:

> After some miserable disaffection
> of the only human heart and human hand
> we'll ever have, we move to this pictured glove
> or hand (ghostly absence) of Aaron Siskind,
> a small spirit by image, able to shape
>
> eloquently in the air—as though
> to tell "a man stands here"—able to meet
> a handsome and beloved guest, or turn
> so tenderly on a wife's face and breast.

When a Logan poem fails, it is due to a softening of such tenderness and clarity: the poem disintegrates into sentimentality. Tears flow for his and our longings as copiously as the lachrymose bath at the beginning of *Alice in Wonderland.*

When he was in his 30s, Logan was incredibly energetic, wiry, with sharp Germanic features and intensely gentle eyes. Although sophisticated in taste, he was very much a lad from Iowa in his manner and appearance. Meeting with him for a drink or dinner, you were likely to listen, fascinated, as he mentioned a passage he had just read in, say, Harvey's *On the Circulation of the Blood,* switched to an analogy from one of John Chrysostom's homilies, then dipped into some raw, recent experience, and he might end—somehow pulling it all together into a good intuition—with an analysis of the poet as oral masochist. What was unique about such talk was how it circled its subject like some bird drawn by Morris Graves but at the same time it was concrete, meat-and-potatoes talk.

Now in his middle 40s, Logan wears an abundant, bushy mustache which, combined with long, long hair and recent girth, gives him the felicitous appearance of some early American woodsman. A great deal of the intensity has been channelled, mellowed and put to work to serve his abiding passions: poetry and teaching. Of the many poets in our generation who are also teachers Logan is probably the most gifted. Devoted gangs of students follow him as if he were the Piper wherever he happens to be lecturing: the love is mutual and enduring. Although Logan has mellowed and has fathered nine children and seems to be on his way to becoming one of the sages of poetry, there remains a deep part of him that remembers and shares in the youth he was. You can see it vividly when he reads in public. Swaying slightly, his face twisting in odd, shy grimaces, with abruptly jerking gestures and embracing, loving movements directed at his audience, Logan recreates the hard, brilliant, lonely isolation of the adolescent, although his poems are those of a complicated man.

*   *   *

When *A Mask for Janus* by **W. S. Merwin** miraculously appeared in 1952 as the Yale Series of Younger Poets selection, many of the young poets probably shared my admiration and envy: here clearly was the prince of the new poets. At twenty-five, Merwin was already writing with "an intimate ease, as though he knew it all from inside." And through the years he continues to create interest as book after book appears, the most current of which—*The Moving Target* (1963) and *The Lice* (1967)—contain his finest work.

When Merwin does not abandon himself to a peculiar type of Luciferean contemplation of parts of himself known only to him, the bulk of his poetry is both rewarding and disturbing in the manner of truly original verse. In many of his most recent lyrics, one feels as if taken into a country where all is poetry—pristine, totally natural, miracles everywhere. Listen to this brief poem called "Dead Hand":

> Temptations still nest in it like basilisks.
> Hang it up till the rings fall.

Or hear the beginning of the prose poem called "Lost Month": "The light of the eyes in the house of the crow. Here the gods' voices break and some will never sing again, but some come closer and whisper. Never their names." For some reason I'm at a loss to explain, the Merwin of the best of these recent poems recalls the Lucretius of the chilly, translucent passages about the immortals and the vision at the opening of Book III of *De rerum natura* when "the gates of the universe fly open" and the poet finds himself gazing into the eternal.

In addition, he is, hands down, the most reliable and interesting translator of the generation. One always trusts a Merwin translation to be both faithful to its original and good poetry.

In his person, Merwin is an original. Exceptionally handsome and charming, he is brilliant and independent in both his opinions and way of life. Along with Ginsberg, Dickey and Ferlinghetti, he commands the most presence on stage during a public reading. In the early 1960s, he usually wore a Navy pea-coat and watch-cap, thick Clancy Brothers sweaters, and corduroy trousers; but the appearance of being a Chelsea bohemian was contradicted by his manner which suggested nothing so much as an aristocrat whose ancestral manor or chateau unfortunately had been lost amid the changing currents of history. Of all the members of the generation Merwin involves himself least in the literary scene or in the traffic of literary politics. Since the late 1940s, he has lived abroad in Majorca, London, and now on a farm near Lot in the South of France. He remains a prince among the poets.

* * *

No one could have guessed ten years ago that the poems of **Frank O'Hara** would be among the most seminal influences on the work of the youngest generation of American poets now in their 20s. So much of the work collected in *Meditations in an Emergency* (1957) and *Lunch Poems* (1965) appeared at first flat, prosaic odds and ends of commonplace events, thoughts, gossip, locations and clichés. A typical O'Hara poem would be addressed to friends such as "Adieu to Norman, Bon Jour to Joan and Jean-Paul" and begin and remain on such a chatty level as:

> It is 12:10 in New York and I am wondering
> if I will finish this in time to meet Norman for lunch
> ah lunch! I think I am going crazy
> what with my terrible hangover and the weekend coming
>   up
> at excitement-prone Kenneth Koch's
> I wish I were staying in town and working on my poems
> at Joan's studio for a new book by Grove Press
> which they will probably not print
> but it is good to be several floors up in the dead of night
> wondering whether you are any good or not
> and the only decision you can make is that you did it

Today, one has come to see why such poems are considered pioneering classics not only by the young but by some of O'Hara's contemporaries. Such poems are classics for the obvious reason: O'Hara was probably the first poet to ignore taking the traditional step away from undigested daily experience in order to refine it into formal art. In brief, he was the first and he remains the best of the poets of the impure (which will be discussed in detail in the next section).

Once one learned how to appreciate this impure quality, the

reading of an O'Hara poem was usually like trying on a new pair of glasses. What had been dim or ignored out of habit or prejudice or preconception suddenly became incandescent with poetry. O'Hara seems to say: "There is *nothing* that cannot find a home in the poem." Instead of simply talking about such an exciting possibility—as Marianne Moore does in "Poetry"—O'Hara allows "the immovable critic twitching his skin like a horse that feels a flea, the base-/ball fan, the statistician," business documents and school books to exist in all of their existential impurity cheek by jowl next to lines containing nuggets of pure poetry such as "(sometimes I think I'm 'in love' with painting)" or the final stanza of "The Day Lady Died."

Wit is another part of his example and legacy. Again, O'Hara's edgy, sometimes corny but always very genuine wit is as commonplace as the time of day or the mildly good high one can feel at a cocktail party. It is, as he might say, "real."

At other times, however, O'Hara hides behind a kind of adolescent Wow! and smarty-pants posturing and fails to get at or get across the complex of feelings which clearly originated the poem. Instead, he remains entangled by New York chic and hysterical activity—an acting-out of feelings on the page instead of an exploration into their reality. But at his best, the man speaking in many of O'Hara's poems possesses that rare quality: charm.

O'Hara's tragic death in August 1966 saddened us all. (A beach taxi blinded by oncoming headlights swerved and ran over him on Fire Island, where he was on vacation. As his friend Arnold Weinstein said, bitterly: "Frank was killed by a car on an island where there are no cars.") Most of the poets knew and liked Frank O'Hara; and some loved the man. Everybody admired his generosity, his intelligence, and his excitement about being alive and on the scene. His friend Kenneth Koch remembers: "Frank's presence and his poetry made things go on around him which couldn't have happened in the same way if he hadn't been there."

*   *   *

Autobiographical candor gives strength and authority to many of the best poems of **W. D. Snodgrass**. Few poets dare the type of confession we read in "April Inventory" and when his first collection *Heart's Needle* (which earned the Pulitzer Prize) appeared in 1959 it seemed as if Snodgrass had opened a whole new Indian territory. It isn't merely that he writes about such immediate and often painfully revealing experiences as the skulker in himself who hides behind the flattering mask of the young Turk instructor or the embarrassing but cozy feeling of being helpless when a patient in the hospital or the grim charade one acts out when visiting the folks back home. Older poets such as Lowell and Shapiro have written about similar experiences. Rather, it is that Snodgrass refuses to posture or play the traditional poet when exploring such events: he tells it like it is for one man who happens to be named William Dewitt Snodgrass.

In addition, what impresses me is how American his poems are: the best are straight and well-made. Occasionally, his concern with homey vocabulary and nuances of technique get in the way, however, coercing the poem to conform to dull talk or some preordained stanzaic or rhyme pattern until the lines begin to jingle-jangle-jingle like verse canned by Muzak. "Ten Days Leave" and "At the Park Dance" are examples. Take these lines from the first poem: "His folks

> Pursue their lives like toy trains on a track.
> He can foresee each of his father's jokes
> Like words in some old movie that's come back.
>
> He is like days when you've gone some place new
> To deal with certain strangers, though you never
> Escape the sense in everything you do,
> "We've done this all once. Have I been here, ever?"

When the gift for American talk and technique work for and not against him, Snodgrass can write that touching cycle "Heart's Needle" where with directness comparable to "April Inventory," he delineates the nuances of what it feels like for a young father to make the annual visit with his small daughter now separated from him by the sword of divorce. Without once forcing the comparison, the cycle becomes an annual but poignantly brief return to an Eden after the Expulsion. In lines like these one reads Snodgrass at his best:

> You raise into my head
> a Fall night that I came once more
>   to sit on your bed;
> sweat beads stood out on your arms and fore-
>   head and you wheezed for breath,
> for help, like some child caught beneath
> its comfortable woolly blankets, drowning there.
> Your lungs caught and would not take the air.
>
> Of all things, only we
> have power to choose that we should die;
>   nothing else is free
> in this world to refuse it. Yet I,
>   who say this, could not raise
> myself from bed how many days
> to the thieving world. Child, I have another wife,
> another child. We try to choose our life.

Over the years, I've not seen Snodgrass as often as I would have liked but the few times we've been together I felt that the man and the poet were the same. He is indifferent to postures. When he was in his 30s, he sported a square-cut mustache which gave him the appearance of a good-looking Groucho Marx; recently, he's cultivated a luxuriously bushy beard which he wears with the verve of some Irish man of letters of the old school. His enthusiasm for good literature, which he conveys with considerable charm, is animated and infectious.

*   *   *

After some recognition as a poet grounded in the style of Kenyon College, **James Wright** suffered a sea change which resulted in 1963 in one of the masterpieces of the generation: *The Branch Will Not Break*. These piercing lyrics come from primeval emotions. Although contemporary, their voice is that of a shaman

who recalls or reveals that we live in a miracle of air, earth,
water and fire, and that the soul has been known to leave the
body and then return again to inhabit it. Here is the voice:

TRYING TO PRAY

This time, I have left my body behind me, crying
In its dark thorns.
Still,
There are good things in this world.
It is dusk.
It is the good darkness
Of woman's hands that touch loaves.
The spirit of the tree begins to move.
I touch leaves.
I close my eyes, and think of water.

Only rarely the voice falters by coddling an overly precious
image which intrudes into the poem an Aubrey Beardsley
estheticism: "This cold winter/Moon spills the inhuman fire/Of
jewels/Into my hands." When the voice retains its purity, it
speaks of a world beneath the crust of our daily one of income
tax returns, DC jets, computers, personnel directors, Great
Books discussion groups and Richard M. Nixon. This is that
world beneath where the soul remains rooted in gentleness, rage,
lust, cold loneliness, love and an abiding awareness of the verities handed down by Homer and the Book of Genesis: "Of all
the creatures that creep and breathe on earth none is more
wretched than man:" and "The Lord God formed man of the
dust of the ground, and breathed into his nostrils the breath
of life; and man became a living soul."

Certainly you sense this wretchedness and grandeur when
you hear and watch Wright read in public with his electric, all
but unbearable intensities or when you spend time in his company. Few could or perhaps would want to sustain his daily
pitch of intensity and his consuming love of poetry in all its
shapes. As Robert Bly puts it: "Deep in [Wright's] personality
is the plower who does not look back. Everyone recognizes this

in his work instinctively, and it is probably one reason for the great affection people have for his work. His instinct is to push everything to extremes, to twist away and go farther. It is obvious that out of devotion to poetry, he would leave any job in the world, with no notice, or live in any way." Early one Sunday in 1966 after a long, exuberant dinner party—during which Wright delighted everybody by his spirited recitations from memory of what was literally an anthology of Irish pub and curse songs, American Indian runes, Housman lyrics, and impersonations of Wilkins Micawber and other Dickensian characters—I was awakened by the sound of his voice reciting aloud to himself in the hallway between his guest room and our bedroom the entire sonnet by Allen Tate, "Ah, Christ, I love you rings to the wild sky." I was astonished: it was as if poetry were the air he breathed, the dreams he had dreamt.

One aspect of Wright which one only comes upon in very recent work but which is abundantly evident in the man himself is an infectious, bubbling, lopsided humor. Suddenly in the midst of a grave conversation about literary politics or Viet Nam, Wright, stocky and deadpan, might break into a classic 1930s amateur hour pose, declaring: "By day, a humble butcher in the Bronx; by night—a fabulous tapdancer!" which he then demonstrates with gusto.

3

The War of the Anthologies

That not all of the poets of this generation admire one another's work goes without saying: it is a literary commonplace that Byron detested Keats, dismissing the *Odes* of 1820 as the scribblings of a Cockney; or that Keats harbored little affection for Shelley either as a poet or as a man; or that Robert Frost disliked (and perhaps envied) Eliot and Pound— and so on. Moreover, it seemed at first that this generation, more than any previous one, could be divided into two distinct and hostile camps. Even before Donald M. Allen's anthology *The New American Poetry* appeared in 1960, it had become a stock-in-trade among literary journalists and some of the poets themselves to pit the Black Mountain/Beat writers represented in the Allen collection against those whose work had become prominent three years earlier in *The New Poets of England and America* edited by Donald Hall, Robert Pack and Louis Simpson.

Not one poet appeared in both anthologies, which surely must be some kind of bizarre literary record, and certain broad differences were obvious. No poet in the Hall-Pack-Simpson collection admitted in verse to having smoked marijuana or spent time in jail or read the *Diamond Sutra* or taken seriously Charles Olson's poetics spelled out in his 1950 essay "Projective Verse, or Composition by Field." Few poets in the Allen anthology, on the other hand, admitted to having been inside an art museum or university classroom or having been married or fathered children or having heard of Eliot's theory of the "objective correlative" or seen poems in which a new line begins with a capital letter. The model of older poets was also apparent. The Allen poets seemed to have absorbed the example of Pound, Williams, cummings, Olson and Louis Zukofsky more enthusiastically than the writers of the earlier anthology, many of whom obviously admired Eliot, Stevens, Auden, Ransom, Marianne Moore, Tate, the Pound of "Hugh Selwyn Mauberley," Shapiro, Lowell, Wilbur and Stanley Kunitz, and who preferred more formally organized metrical stanzas as distinct from the short/ and very long line breath units favored by the majority of the Allen anthology poets.

These differences were fairly clear; and I remember reading in book reviews and letters vitriolic, patronizing remarks made by poets from each anthology; and hearing wisecracks which circulated along the literary grapevine putting this poet down for being a Beat nudist or that one for inhabiting a grey flannel mind: but the war of the anthologies seemed largely a cardboard affair in which I found I had little lasting interest because poems in both collections had moved me deeply. Moreover, I mistrust attempts to corral poets into movements or schools. All this accomplishes, it seems to me, is the manufacture of subtle but rigid preconceptions which limit or damage one's ability to face an individual poem on its own terms.

Ashbery, Koch and O'Hara, for instance, have been called New York Surrealists. It is probably accurate to suggest that each of these writers has admired Lautréamont's famous simile which became a dogma among the Surrealists: "He is as handsome as . . . the accidental encounter upon a dissecting table between an umbrella and a sewing machine." However, Ashbery would perhaps break the phrase into fragments which would reappear oddly but freshly in different stanzas of one of his poems; Koch might include the name and address of the Cincinnati manufacturer of sewing machines or expand the metaphor in several comic directions like a kind of sophisticated Keystone Kop chase; while O'Hara might quote the sentence exactly in a stanza depicting him being New York busy at a cocktail party in Easthampton, Long Island, gossiping excitedly with the painter Jane Freilicher and Janice and Kenneth Koch.

Much of the same type of distinction might be made about other groups or schools into which some of these poets have been herded by critics, literary historians and, in some cases, by the poets themselves. The Black Mountain poets, for one, are supposed to honor William Carlos Williams and Charles Olson by writing in taut lines or in stanzas constructed out of "fields" of units of breathing; and, indeed, Paul Blackburn, Creeley, Ed Dorn, Robert Duncan, Denise Levertov, Joel Oppenheimer and John Wieners all have testified to their admiration of the examples of Williams and Olson. But the fact remains that a characteristic Creeley poem is in its exploration of the complexities of love closer to many of Logan's poems than to a Duncan poem like "Four Pictures of the Real Universe" which in its adventure into the spiritual is in important ways nearer to some of the later lyrics of Merwin or Wright. So too for the Beat poets. In his occasional tremendous acts of imagination, Ginsberg is closer to Dickey than to Corso or Ferlinghetti.

All of these comparisons, however, are more than odious: they are useless when we turn to our real task of trying to talk about this particular poem or that particular poet. Obviously a classic Beat poem like Ferlinghetti's "Dog" has much in common with another classic like Ginsberg's "Sunflower Sutra": but they are only as similar as the dreams of Siamese twins.

4

Freedom Is a Breakfast Food—and More

Everyone who reads modern poetry has been amused if not educated by the merry ironies in the cummings poem "as free-dom is a breakfastfood." To many of the poets of 1962, however, it must seem that as far as poetry is concerned freedom is even more than what the cummings poem implies. Freedom can be, in fact, a breakfast food; and "truth can live with right and wrong." An almost intoxicating variety of freedoms is, it seems to me, the prevailing characteristic of the body of work created and still being created by this generation.

All of these freedoms seem, in turn, part of the attitudes of this generation to the fundamental problem which each generation solves in its own terms: namely, What is a poem? To put the question in more practical terms: What are the attitudes with which many of these poets view experience and that existential trinity of person, place and thing?

Now, everybody knows that our attitudes originate and often end in feelings stored in our unconscious; and that those feelings walk, as it were, through this existential world, calling this scene or person black and that one bonny; and, finally, that we also learn through experience, the sweet and the sour of it, in our journey through this world, which is "incorrigibly plural," as MacNeice put it; and that such experience helps to shape the forms which our attitudes finally assume. And poetry is of course one of the most precious testaments to such realities. In poetry, one is free, as perhaps in few other situations, to explore one's feelings and experience of the world as honestly and memorably as one can. And the question each new generation of poets must ask of course is: How best view this "sad, bad, glad, mad" reality in which we find ourselves?

I rehearse such commonplaces because I want to stress that this generation of American poets is on the high, happy adventure of creating and innovating a complex of new ways in which to view our common condition—an adventure which in its abundance, freshness and originality is, in my opinion, as interesting as any since the Olympians of 1917. Consider, for one example, the attitude with which many of these poets view the urban scene.

Since Blake and Baudelaire, the modern city has been seen by poets as a Babylon of alienation and anonymity infested by demons of industry and technology. Existence in the city is an enemy of the human spirit in much the same sense in which Plato believes the body is a prison or tomb which for a brief period ensnares the pilgrim soul on its journey to the shores of the ocean of beauty everlasting. After Blake and Baudelaire, the great texts in this tradition of course are: Francis Thompson's prose describing the hag masses in the London of the 1880s; the Unreal City of *The Waste Land* and its grim suburbs among "the gloomy hills of London"—Hampstead and Clerkenwell, Campden and Putney, Highgate, Primrose and Ludgate— in "Burnt Norton;" the Bosch-like subway ride of *The Bridge;* and the Boston of *Lord Weary's Castle* where "serpents whistle at the cold."

Almost the sole exceptions seem the Manhattan of Whitman and the Chicago of Sandburg. (But both were largely unread by most of the young poets back in 1950. Ginsberg is the exception here.) At first, Delmore Schwartz and Karl Shapiro also appeared to see the city as a potential Jerusalem—a place in which *some* human happiness and fun might be found. "For Rhoda" opens with a celebration of the urban scene in Central Park—"Calmly we walk through this April's day,/Metropolitan poetry here and there"—which once enchanted me because it was the first poem which agreed that Jackson Park at 57th Street near The University of Chicago, where I read so many of the modern poets for the first time, was as exciting and real as I knew it was. But the Schwartz poem soon turns into a poignant nightmare about human transiency in which New York bursts into consuming flames. One also admired Shapiro's "Drugstore" and "Auto Wreck": but both occur in what finally is a malevolent city.

What seems remarkable about the new poets is how many of them simply *ignore* the hallowed tradition of the city as Babylon. Many celebrate the city, in fact, in all of its vulgarities, elegance, icons of Pop or Op Art, violences, sidewalk trees, traffic, shop windows, sandhogs, helicopters and subways. In "The Avenue Bearing the Initial of Christ into the New World," Galway Kinnell has a hymn to the contemporary Melting Pot on the Lower East Side; O'Hara is a master at communicating excitement over the existential facts of Manhattan—as is Ferlinghetti over some of those of San Francisco. Paul Blackburn, Denise Levertov and Kenneth Koch simply view the city as where a lot of the action in their poems occurs and not as cause for moral indignation or spiritual acedia. Ginsberg and Wright, it is true, often experience the city as if it were Babylon or the Court of Pharoah: but that the city no longer need be evil for poets is indeed news, and God knows (as Creeley might say) such news is good.

Hallowed attitudes in poetry die as hard as they do in anything else. When an attitude once profound but now arthritic in the sense of having hardened into dogma as the City as Babylon is buried by poets of a new generation, then we should slaughter the black bell-sheep and break out the new wine. Every reader who loves poetry knows that a significant new attitude can only open more doors of perception for everybody. There is no end to our understanding of reality. (What I've just suggested about the fresh attitude to the city, however, doesn't imply that a poet of this generation or any young poet to come can't despise the city and write out of that hate. All I mean is that, thanks to the poets of 1962, he doesn't *have* to hate the urban scene.)

Another freedom of attitude I find intriguing, although I don't understand it, is the testimony to the existence of another and possibly supernatural reality evident in poets as varied as Brother Antoninus, Dickey, Duncan, Ginsberg, Levertov, Logan, Merwin and Wright.

What's impressive is how once again these poets (with the exception of Antoninus and the young Logan) seem indifferent to the traditional attitude toward experience one was taught to call religious: namely, *Quem dicunt homines esse Filium hominis?* Jesus asked his disciples: Whom do men say the Son of Man is? If one answers with Peter: "Thou art the Christ, the Son of the Living God," then the Christian faith clearly is the true one. Everyone knows the memorable poems by Americans embodying the anguish both of the question and of the possible answers: the Melville of "Father Mapple's Hymn" and the pilgrimage to the Holy Land in "Clarel," the Eliot of "Journey of the Magi" and "Ash Wednesday," the Stevens of "Sunday Morning" and "A High-Toned Old Christian Woman," and the Lowell of *Lord Weary's Castle.*

Once again on the contrary, the young Americans ignore not only the question of Christ but also the attitude which favors that answers to it are viewed within a Christian context which names one either Christian, heretical or heathen. Zen Buddhism, medieval alchemy, worship of totem animals, Hinduism, experiments with psychedelic "drugs" and other stimulants, Hasidism, prayers to Hermes Trismegistus, invocation of archetypes from Jung's Collective Unconscious, "natural" mysticism and magic: these are some of the contexts within which the new poets explore spiritual experience.

One of the most mysterious of these poems is Robert Duncan's "Four Pictures of the Real Universe" in which the poet strives to become an illuminated alchemist by conjuring the invisible and supernatural with four Tarot cards. "By magic we may arise and speak with spirits without knowing ourselves," warns the motto at the beginning of the poem. Here is the "picture" of The Pasture:

> The Great Sun Himself comes
> to eat at my heart, asks
> that I return myself into Him.
>
> And the white body, a Moon,
> in the precincts of the Earth
> revolves. How
> the Dead draw the Sea after them!
>
> But the Living, the immortal corpuscles,
> sail without shadow
> toward the pyres of the Sun.

One also finds intense "spiritual" joy in some of James Wright, as in the well-known final lines of "A Blessing": "Suddenly I realize/That if I stepped out of my body I would break/Into blossom." Logan bears a like witness:

> Ekelöf said there is a freshness
> nothing can destroy in us—
> not even we ourselves.
> Perhaps that
> *Freshness* is the changed name of God.

In poems such as "The Vegetable King," "Fog Envelopes the Animals," "The Heaven of Animals," "The Sheep Child" and "The Owl King," Dickey journeys with almost ecstasy into that world of totem animals, spirits and daemons as if he were some Druid priest come back among the hills and pines of Georgia. At other times, his intense and exhilarating communion is with the dead; at still other times, he is the first American poet, as far as I happen to know, to explore and to explore with delight the experience of the possibility of the ancient dream of reincarnation.

Certainly Ginsberg often communicates comparable exhilaration over the existence of an eternal realm, evident in the "loony" Hasidic revelation quoted earlier: "The universe is a new flower . . . Fate tells big lies, & the gay Creator dances on his own body in Eternity." Of all the poets Ginsberg seeks most relentlessly and passionately the countenance of the Godhead:

> Nameless, One faced, Forever, beyond me, beginningless, endless, Father in death. Though I am not here for this Prophecy, I am unmarried, I'm hymnless, I'm Heavenless, headless in blisshood I would still adore
> Thee, Heaven, after Death, only One blessed in Nothingness, not light or darkness, Dayless Eternity—
> Take this, this Psalm, from me, burst from my hand in a day, some of my Time, now given to Nothing—to praise Thee—

But his search is not always such celebration. In the four pentecostal poems at the end of *Kaddish*—"Lysergic Acid," the fierce

"Magic Psalm," "The Reply" and "The End"—it's closer to agony. In these poems, Ginsberg performs the ancient ritual: Invoking of the God. These poems are both invocation and confrontation. In them, the poet asks and gives no quarter. One must take them as literal, experienced visions, or not at all. What was hard to bear when one first read them in 1960 or 1961 was the shock of witnessing a contemporary American poet struggling like a Hebrew prophet with his god. The God whom Ginsberg invokes, hates, adores, mocks, and with whom he wants to copulate and in front of whom he weeps on his knees: this God is terribly present. The God of Eliot, by contrast, is one honed from the tomes of the Patristic Fathers and Elizabethan divines; the God of Ginsberg is the one who exists before defini- tion by the civilized sensibility: the barbarous deity who speaks from the Burning Bush.

Everybody knows that Ginsberg is also one of the poets who bear testimony to the spiritual experiences allegedly created or made possible by the use of such natural drugs as marijuana, hashish, peyote and yagé and such artificial psychedelics as mescaline, LSD and psilocybin and such synthetic stimulants or ampethamines as dexedrine, benzedrine and methedrine. The poet tells us, in fact, that the final three pentecostal poems above attempt to document "visions experienced after drinking ayahu- casca—an Amazon spiritual potion." Ferlinghetti in the recent "After the Cries of the Birds" (and in his note on that poem "Genesis Of"), Philip Lamantia, Michael McClure and Gary Snyder also have written poems which testify to the "worlds unrealized" available when under the influence of LSD or pey- ote or mescaline.

Experiences of "moving about in worlds unrealized" are also explored by poets as different from those who write of hallucinogenic states as they are from one another: the Ashbery of "The Swimmers: Part II," Robert Bly, Denise Levertov and W. S. Merwin. The prayers to totem animals by Merwin in "Lemuel's Blessing" and "Totem" I find especially moving and mysterious.

To indicate that Antoninus differs from contemporaries such as these because his faith is Christian certainly sounds odd (at least to one who was once Catholic too).* Brother Antoninus is the Apostle of this generation. At their best, his poems—such as "Zone of Death," "A Siege of Silence" and his masterpiece "Annul in Me My Manhood" ("Annul in me my manhood, Lord, and make/Me woman-sexed and weak/If by that total transformation/I might know Thee more")—bear anguished witness to the ancient Christian view of the fury and the mire of human veins: "I am crucified with Christ."

If Antoninus stands alone among his contemporaries as the only poet who testifies to the continuing validity of the Christian view of reality, then who are the models (if any) for some of the other ways of articulating the experience of the "worlds unrealized"? One is clearly the Roethke of "In a Dark Time," "Once More, the Round" and "The Abyss"; and behind Roethke stands the Yeats of the visions and intimacies with the spirits. And Blake.** And I wonder how many of the poets have reread with profit the Shelley of "Ode to the West Wind" and the Wordsworth of the great ode and "Tintern Abbey" and the Dylan Thomas of the druidic incantation, "The Force That

---

* In the event that the reader may not happen to know: Antoninus is a Dominican friar. After some years as a lay brother with renewable vows, he recently took his final vows, becoming a religious, and now lives in a monastery at San Rafael in California.

To keep the record accurate: Ned O'Gorman and Samuel Hazo also tend to view the experiences being explored in their poems in a Catholic light. Philip Lamantia has also written what some call "Catholic poetry"; but I incline to see his poems like "Still Poem 8" and "Cool Apocalypse" as documents of a kind of "mystic in a savage state."

** Indeed, Ginsberg in a moving passage tells of having a "mystical" experience in 1948 when he was living in Spanish Harlem during which he heard a "very deep earthen grave voice in the room," which "woke me further deep in my understanding of the poem" (he'd been reading Blake's "The Sunflower" and had just masturbated to ejaculation) because "the voice was so completely tender and beautifully . . . ancient. Like the voice of the Ancient of Days." And he continues: "the peculiar quality of the voice was something unforgettable because it was like God had a human voice, with all the infinite tenderness and anciency and mortal gravity of a Living Creator speaking to his son." The poet explains that he "immediately assumed, I didn't think twice," that the voice "was Blake's voice; it wasn't any voice that I knew." One can read the complete account of Ginsberg's experience in his interview conducted by the young poet Tom Clark "The Art of Poetry VIII: Allen Ginsberg" in *The Paris Review #37*.

Through the Green Fuse"? Everybody will know the masters of poems of hallucinogenic states: the Coleridge of "Kubla Khan," Gautier, Baudelaire, Rimbaud, and Artaud and the Surrealist poets. In any event, I think it's clear that some of the best poets of this generation are embarked on a voyage into what may be another reality than the pragmatic one of earth we know, and in which some of them may discover the perennial wonder of that greatest and most frightening of truths: "There are more things in heaven and earth, Horatio,/Than are dreamt of in your philosophy." At the very least, one can mark that some of these poets seem like those souls described in the lines of Virgil:

> *stabant orantes primi transmittere cursum*
> *tendebantque manus ripae ulteroris amore*

("They stood praying to be the first to cross/and stretched out their hands, longing for the farther shore.")

Or take the freshness and freedom with which many of these poets view the hoary problem: Should the poet be concerned in his art with everyday political realities?

Let's recall the attitude to this question evident in previous generations. What is the roll call of great American political poems? "Frescos for Mr. Rockefeller's City" by Archibald Macleish? Little more than sentimental liberal doggerel. "Aeneas at Washington" by Tate? Remote allegorical verse more interested, it would seem, in trying to sound like Eliot's "Difficulties of a Statesman" than in exploring nitty-gritty New Deal realities. "Bryan, Bryan, Bryan, Bryan, Bryan" by Lindsay? Cotton-candy populist pieties. (The poem's one virtue, however, lies in its good, sweaty use of 1896 talk as heard at the State Fair in Springfield, Illinois.) And where were the poets of 1947 when Joseph McCarthy conducted his inquisition or when two Eisenhower administrations bumbled along, insanely escalating the nuclear arms race? And Frost? No political poem of consequence. His well-known "The Gift Outright" isn't political poetry: it's 7th grade propaganda.

The bald fact seems to be that the prevailing attitude among the older American poets sounds something like this: convictions about contemporary political realities belong in prose; poetry is too "pure" to contain them.*

Nothing could be more alien to this attitude than the exploration of political convictions, prejudices, outrages and indignations by many of the new poets. Muscular and direct political poems have been written by such men as Bly, Duncan, Louis Simpson, Ferlinghetti, Ginsberg, Robert Hazel, Wright and George Starbuck, whose "Of Late" is, in my opinion, the finest anti-Viet Nam poem to come from this generation. Most of their poems voice the outrage felt by an increasing number of citizens at the aggression and continuing escalation in Viet Nam by the Johnson Administration.** Does it take an outrage of this dimension to "hurt you into poetry?" Perhaps it does.

Not all of the political poetry of this generation, on the other hand, is particularly good. Much the same might be said of it as could be said about the bulk of Romantic poetry or Beat verse: its origin is more in the desire to be famous by being contemporary than in the deeper necessity which creates the effort to write poetry. Calling Lyndon Johnson bad names, in brief, is not poetry. Nor is righteous indignation against the Pentagon hawks. Exploration of why Johnson may be an evil man; or what the realities and implications are behind the claws and lust for blood of hawks: these might make poetry.

In any event, due to the example of these writers, the presence of politics in poetry has become and I trust will continue to be a distinct possibility for poets today and to come. American poetry may even someday produce a Mayakovsky or Neruda for whom the question, Is the poem a proper vehicle for politics?

---

* Exceptions of course exist: cummings' "i sing of olaf glad and big" and "Thanksgiving" (1956) and *The Cantos*. Everybody likes the Olaf poem but it's not, strictly speaking, political; it's an assault on the collective military beast by way of tribute to individual guts. And I don't like the protest against America's failure to help the Hungarian Freedom Fighters in the Thanksgiving poem because the satire is just too cute, smug, smart-ass. The politics in *The Cantos* only illustrate, it seems to me, Gertrude Stein's comic valentine about the less attractive side of Pound: "he was a village explainer, excellent if you were a village, but if you were not, not."

** See Appendix One for mention of the read-ins created by many of these poets and of the example of Robert Bly.

is as fatuous as it is absurd. Almost ten years ago, Lawrence
Ferlinghetti spoke out in contempt and with good sense when
he challenged the bromide that artists must not dissipate energy
by writing about nitty-gritty brutalities on the political scene.
In an important way, his statement speaks for many poets in
the generation. Here it is:

> I am put down by Beat natives who say I cannot be beat
> and "committed" at the same time, like in this poem
> ("Tentative Description of a Dinner Given To Promote
> the Impeachment of President Eisenhower"), man. True,
> true. William Seward Burroughs said, "Only the dead
> and the junkie don't care—they are inscrutable." I'm
> neither. Man. And this is where all the tall droopy corn
> about the Beat Generation and its being "existentialist"
> is as phoney as a four-dollar piece of lettuce. Because
> Jean-Paul Sartre cares and has always hollered that the
> writer especial should be committed. Engagement is one
> of his favorite dirty words. He would give the horse laugh
> to the idea of Disengagement and the Art of the Beat
> Generation. Me too. And that Abominable Snowman of
> modern poetry, Allen Ginsberg, would probably say the
> same. Only the dead are disengaged. And the wiggy
> nihilism of the Beat hipster, if carried to its natural con-
> clusion, actually means the death of the creative artist
> himself. While the "non-commitment" of the artist is
> itself a suicidal and deluded variation of this same
> nihilism.*

The freedom with which many of the poets create comic
verse, laughs, gags, even occasional slapstick or standup comic

---

* Some poets and critics complain that Ferlinghetti's celebrated broad-
sheets—the Eisenhower impeachment, "One Thousand Fearful Words for
Fidel Castro," and "Where Is Vietnam?"—are no more than doggerel. On
the contrary, the Eisenhower broadsheet is, in my opinion, a contemporary
classic. As distinguished from "Aeneas at Washington," no question exists
about whom Ferlinghetti attacks and why: the *directness* in the act is where
one finds the poetry. This directness gets sidetracked by superficial praise or
lampoon, however, in the Castro and anti-LBJ poems, it seems to me, and
weakens both. That somebody finally wrote about such realities in poetry
is important: I only wish he'd written about them with more depth.

routines is clearly another good achievement by this generation.
What was the humor like among the poets of 1947? or 1932? or
1917? Satirical, often sour or nasty, cerebral, and "witty" in the
metaphysical manner learned from Eliot, Auden and the Pound
of "Hugh Selwyn Mauberley" and the Stevens of "Le Monocle
de Mon Oncle." Everybody who cares about modern poetry
knows how neat this wit is:

> I shall not want Capital in Heaven
> For I shall meet Sir Alfred Mond.
> We two shall lie together, lapt
> In a five per cent. Exchequer Bond.

*

> It is for nothing, then, that old Chinese
> Sat tittivating by their mountain pools
> Or in the Yangtse studied out their beards?
> I shall not play the flat historic scale.
> You know how Utamaro's beauties sought
> The end of love in their all-speaking braids.
> You know the mountainous coiffures of Bath.
> Alas! Have all the barbers lived in vain
> That not one curl in nature has survived?
> Why, without pity on these studious ghosts,
> Do you come dripping in your hair from sleep?

*

> Winter is icummen in,
> Lhude sing Goddamn,
> Raineth drop and staineth slop,
> And how the wind doth ramm!
> > Sing: Goddamn.
> Skiddeth bus and sloppeth us,
> An ague hath my ham.

*

> as freedom is a breakfastfood
> or truth can live with right and wrong
> or molehills are from mountains made

—long enough and just so long
will being pay the rent of seem
and genius please the talent gang
and water most encourage flame

*

A pantheist not a solipsist, he co-operates
With a universe of large and noisy feeling-states
    Without troubling to place
Them anywhere special, for, to his eyes, Funny-face
    Or Elephant as yet
Mean nothing. His distinction between Me and Us
Is a matter of taste; his seasons are Dry and Wet;
    He thinks as his mouth does.

Still his loud iniquity is still what only the
Greatest of saints become—someone who does not lie . . .*

Humor among the new poets is usually more spontaneous, buffonish, ebullient and immediate, everyday, funny. Instead of wry, cerebral amusement, one laughs loud and clear at the comedy in such poems as Kenneth Koch's "The Artist," Ferlinghetti's "Underwear," Gregory Corso's "Marriage," Creeley's "Naughty Boy," and in such lines as:

Though lovers stand at sixes and sevens
While civilizations come down with the curse,
Snodgrass is walking through the universe.
                    —SNODGRASS:
                        "These Trees Stand . . ."

*

Quick! a last poem before I go
off my rocker. Oh Rachmaninoff!
Onset, Massachusetts. Is it the fig-newton
playing the horn?
                    —O'HARA:
                        "On Rachmaninoff's Birthday"

---

* In the unlikely event the reader doesn't know this poem: It is "Mundus Et Infans" by Auden. The poet is describing a baby.

I dreamt I went shooting fish in my bare chest
—STARBUCK: *Title of poem*

*

When she introduces me to her parents
back straightened, hair finally combed, strangled by a tie,
should I sit knees together on their 3rd-degree sofa
and not ask where's the bathroom?
How else feel other than I am,
often thinking Flash Gordon soap— . . .

And the priest! he looking at me as if I masturbated
asking me Do you take this woman for your lawful
    wedded wife?
And I trembling what to say say Pie Glue! . . .

And when the milkman comes leave him a note in
    the bottle
Penguin dust, bring me penguin dust, I want
    penguin dust—
—CORSO: *"Marriage"*

*

And the sign in McAlister Street:
"IF YOU CAN'T COME IN
SMILE AS YOU GO BY
    L♡VE
    THE BUTCHER
—WHALEN:
    "Sourdough Mountain Lookout"

*

And here's a brief poem by Creeley called "The Family":

Father
and mother
and sister
and sister
and sister.

*

I, as an aging phoney, stale, woozy, and corrupt

from unattempted dreams and bad health habits,
am comforted: the skunk cabbage generates its
frost-thawing fart-gas in New Jersey and the first
crocuses appear in Rockefeller Center's Channel
       Gardens:
Fall, it is not so bad at Dugan's Edge.

                —DUGAN: *"Letter to Donald Fall"*

*

who copulated ecstatic and insatiate with a bottle of beer
a sweetheart and a package of cigarettes a candle and fell
off the bed, continuing along the floor and down the hall
and ended fainting on the wall with a vision of ultimate
cunt and come eluding the last gyzym of consciousness

                —GINSBERG: *"Howl"*

*

I wish eastern standard
time, etc. rang the
changes in our hearts.

                —OPPENHEIMER: *"Blue Funk"*

Humor bubbles throughout Ferlinghetti. Much of it comes
from viewing with an irreverent but good-humored eye sacro-
sanct or taboo subjects such as "Chagall is a Master of Modern
Art" or "One never mentions underwear or urination in a
poem." Here's a Ferlinghetti poem which makes me laugh
everytime I teach it or hear the poet read it:

Don't let that horse
             eat that violin

    cried Chagall's mother

                   But he
           kept right on
               painting

And became famous

And kept on painting
                The Horse With Violin In Mouth

And when he finally finished it
he jumped up upon the horse
                        and rode away

        waving the violin

And then with a low bow gave it
to the first naked nude he ran across

And there were no strings
                        attached

Of all the poets Kenneth Koch comes nearest to being a
comic genius. "Taking a Walk with You," "The Artist," "Thank
You," "Lunch," "Fresh Air"—the list could multiply for days—
are comic poetry of the first order. No American poet has written better. What distinguishes Koch is not only the sophistication but the ebullience, freedom and intelligence of his comic
imagination. In some ways, it often seems closest to the intricate
and terribly funny quality in the "nighttown" episode in
Ulysses, although Koch explores none of the darker or heartbreaking quality of the comedy in that episode. In brief, Koch
is the opposite of Ogden Nash or what's called light verse. The
more familiar one becomes with *Thank You and Other Poems*
(1962) the more one feels delight, surprise and that kind of truth
only comedy can offer. Here is Koch:

And thank you for the chance to run a small hotel
In an elephant stopover in Zambezi,
But I do not know how to take care of guests, certainly
        they would all leave soon
After seeing blue lights out the windows and rust on their
        iron beds—I'd rather own a bird-house in
        Jamaica:
Those people come in, the birds, they do not care how
        things are kept up . . .
It's true that Zambezi proprietorship would be ex-
        citing, with people getting off elephants and com-
        ing into my hotel,
But as tempting as it is I cannot agree.

> And thank you for this offer of the post of referee
> For the Danish wrestling championship—I simply do not
>   feel qualified . . .

What about the bawdy promised by the quotation from Burton in the title of this essay? Much of the world's best poetry concerns, as everybody knows, depiction of sexual desires, anxieties, pleasures, furies, anguish, sublimations and fun; and the ancient preoccupation with the god or devil of the loins is as noticeable in the work of this generation as in any other; but what seems their particular achievement in working such well-plowed fields is, again, the freedom of directness or candor with which many of these poets explore sexuality.

The line by W. D. Snodgrass in which he tells how he learned "To ease my woman so she came" could stand as motto for much of this candor. In everyday language, these poets spell out what they are talking about when describing passions heterosexual or homosexual or bestial or inverted or neurotic.

In addition, there are the happy or profound delights of sex which some describe in their lines. One remembers with no sense of nostalgia the Adam and Eve of previous generations of American poets: the "young man carbuncular" and his bovine girl friend in *The Waste Land*. What a grim pair. On the contrary, eroticism and sensuality are explored lyrically by Isabella Gardner—the best poet in the generation to celebrate the richness of sexual desire—in such poems as "Summer Evening," "Cock-a-Hoop" and "Lines to a Seagreen Lover"; and by Ferlinghetti in poems like "In Paris in a loud dark winter," "It was a face which darkness could kill," "Sarolla's women in their picture hats" and "Dove sta amore" in which the poet sings of "couples going nude into the sad water/in the profound lasciviousness of spring/in an algebra of lyricism/which I am still deciphering."

"Fuck Ode" and "A Garland" by Michael McClure attempt to describe in popular language the excitement of intercourse and fellatio, cunnilingus and analingus. That somebody *finally* did so in American verse is certainly welcome news; but both poems seem more preoccupied with shouting the taboo words than with embodying the sexual experiences. For good sexy poetry, I'd still rather read cummings' "she being Brand" and "i like my body when it is with your."

Both Creeley and Dickey write directly and openly about desire for women, although Creeley appears more preoccupied by the intricate checks and balances in the relationship than in describing the physical acts, and Dickey in poems such as "Cherrylog Road," "Sun," "Adultery" and "The Fiend" explores the feeling before or after intercourse, in particular, those of Adam banished from the Garden. "The Fiend," which describes with compelling empathy and dignity a voyeur, and "The Sheep Child," which is about bestiality, are the first poems in our poetry about these taboo experiences and Dickey deserves our praise for that.

Homosexual desire and love are described by Ginsberg and John Wieners: both write memorably and often sadly about the love which until this generation had "dared not speak its name." Clearly Wieners' "A Poem for the Old Man" is one of the finest and most touching depictions of the love of a youth for an older man.

Behind all of these freedoms is of course the freedom implied in the view of these poets of the fundamental problem of any poet or generation: What is a poem? How much of raw autobiography should or can be included or edited out? What is a "well-written" poem?

Now, it's obvious that most of the best poems to come from this generation offer as reply the traditional answer: a poem is an organic whole embodying in memorable language one's view of experience, person, place and thing. Moreover, the poem embodies one *whole* experience, however complex, ambiguous or simple; and all of the technical elements—imagery, metrical pattern, title, use or absence of rhyme, the look of the poem on the page or its sound when read aloud—contribute to creating the organically whole experience. Clearly "Howl" or "The Sheep Child" or "April Inventory" are as traditional in this organic definition as "That Time of Year Thou Mayest in Me Behold" or "When Lilacs Last in the Dooryard Bloom'd." When you begin to read and to try and understand them, you have no trouble about locating where at least to begin. You begin with the tacit assumption: a poem is an organic whole.

The more I became familiar with some other good poems from this generation, however, the more I began to suspect something totally fresh and unique might be happening for which I knew no critical precedent. Two poems written in the late 1950s, in particular, puzzled and even annoyed when I first read them: "Message" by Allen Ginsberg and "The Day Lady Died." What puzzled and annoyed me was a certain intrusion of what looked like inorganic or arbitrary imagery within what I assumed were traditionally organic poems.

The Ginsberg poem begins and ends like most traditional love lyrics: the poet is in Paris writing to his lover "gone in NY/ remembering me good" and he admits how lonely and frustrated he feels without his beloved.* Suddenly four images occur in the midst of the lover's direct talk.

Ocean liners boiling over the Atlantic
Delicate steelwork of unfinished skyscrapers
Back end of dirigible roaring over Lakehurst
Six women dancing on a red stage naked

Clearly the first image is organic: the ships represent the voyage the poet hopes either he or his lover will take which will end in reunion. But what about the other three? How are they organic?

If the three images ended the poem, they could be seen as embodying a moment of irrationality caused by the intensity of the poet's anger over the separation. But the poem ends with the same kind of straight love talk with which it began: "The leaves are green on all the trees in Paris now/I will be home in two months and look you in the eyes."

When I first heard Ginsberg read "Message" in early 1959, its intensity and candor impressed me but I also felt puzzled by the intrusion of the images of skyscrapers, dirigibles and dancers.

* Although "Message" doesn't identify the beloved as Peter Orlovsky, I don't think it's necessary to pretend that Ginsberg is talking to anybody else. At the time the poem was written, it was an open fact that the two had been lovers for some years and Orlovsky had just returned to New York after a Wanderjahr in Europe with Ginsberg. Also, the reference in the poem to the beloved's "drunk brothers" clearly refers to sad but known facts about some of the Orlovsky brothers.

Like most members of my generation, I'd learned from the New Critics and Neo-Aristotelians and from examples such as "Sailing to Byzantium," "Mending Wall," "Sunday Morning" and "Auto Wreck" that a poem is an organic whole to which any image in it contributes. Moreover, we learned that when an image fails in the last analysis to contribute to the whole, it's usually a danger sign that the poem too is a failure.

Now, I'll spare the reader by not spelling out my attempts to discover how the skyscrapers or dancers might be understood to contribute to the central experience of homosexual love in the poem. The point will be evident when I mention that possible readings—such as: "The skyscraper could be part of the Manhattan skyline seen from an ocean liner on which the poet longs to be" or: "They're a metaphor for 'unfinished business' between Ginsberg and Orlovsky"—seemed pretty silly in the end. But I was stuck. Of course, I could have forgotten about the poem and gone back to read and teach such traditionally organic poems as "Howl" or "Sunflower Sutra"; but I liked "Message" and I felt it contained genuine poetry: I wanted to understand it.

Trying to teach the poem a few weeks later in a workshop at Loyola University, I found that the last two images were even more puzzling than the skyscrapers. Attempts by the students and myself to "justify" the images and thus begin to "understand" them only turned up such rather pretentious analysis as: "The Hindenberg is an ironic image of the journey the poet wants to take home to his lover; the irony is that the dirigible explodes at Lakehurst and the poet isn't in reality on that trip home." Another attempt went something like this: "The dirigible is a sodomy image ('back end of dirigible'). Or an embodiment of longing accelerated into explosive anger over the fact of separation." The six women proved as baffling. If the dancers were grotesques—females wearing garish carnival masks like in an Ensor painting or serpentine, castrating temptresses like in an Edvard Munch—then a good case could be made that the image is organic in that it's an image of malice against women and their sexuality: "Message" is, after all, hardly a hymn to heterosexual ardor. Nothing in the image, however, suggests malice. In fact, the image is sexy—and heterosexual.

In the end, it was the dancing women that suggested the key which can unlock the problem, How are the three images organic? I still recall how it felt something like a perfect spring day when it finally dawned: "Why not just leave alone the image of the dancers? Let it exist as it seems to ask: as a fragment of heterosexual desire. And why not let all three images be only what they are? Why not enjoy the delicacy of the steel of the unfinished skyscrapers as a purely esthetic urban fragment? the explosion of the Hindenburg as an apocalyptic image from a nightmare of the 1930s? and the naked dancers on the red stage as naked dancers on a red stage?" And why worry about their interrelationship? See them as independent from any relationship. See them even like three haikus as independent from each other as from the poem as a whole.

Then what have we? An "impure" poem.* Its impurity exists in the lack of organic function or justification of the three images: the images are simply there. But in what sense? One of the exciting things they accomplish, it seems to me, is to offer a fresh image of a man writing a poem. In the midst of writing a conventionally organic love lyric, Ginsberg suddenly forgets or ignores his natural tendency as poet to edit or refine material floating from his unconscious. Instead, he allows the mystery of other parts of himself to float for a moment into the poem; and he ignores all the rules of creative writing by allowing them to stay. What we see, in truth, is a homosexual love poem which also contains a small but vivid revelation of the complexity and irrationality of the poet's unconscious.

One final point. If Ginsberg had continued to free associate, permitting more and more impure images to float into the poem, "Message" would become another kind of poem entirely. Such a flood of inorganic images, in fact, might tend to negate the poet's earlier message of love; the reader would begin to suspect that Ginsberg was more fascinated by his unconscious than by

---

* Let me stress that by impure I mean a wider range than the term at first may suggest. Impure here implies neither foul nor obscene nor adulterated. Impure means, broadly, the intermixture of foreign or incongruous elements within an otherwise traditionally organic poem. Obviously I'm not using the term in the sense defined by Robert Penn Warren in his well-known essay "The Pure and the Impure in Poetry." By impure Warren means, roughly, bad poetry.

Peter Orlovsky. But of course this doesn't happen. On the contrary, we're left with a good impure poem.*

Inorganic or irrational imagery has of course been a commonplace in French poetry since Jarry, Apollinaire and Max Jacob; and in Spanish and South American writing there's probably an even older tradition encouraging its use. As far as I know, "Message" is the first example of the inorganically impure image in American verse. And the point of course is: the three impure images are not Dada or Surrealist poetry. On the contrary, skyscrapers, dirigible and dancing women exist within an otherwise perfectly traditional organic poem. That is the impure quality.**

In order to clarify what I mean by the impure image, here are a few other examples of it in work by the new poets:

My misunderstandings: for years I thought "muse bello" meant "Bell Muse," I thought it was a kind of

* To what extent Ginsberg had any or none of this in mind is of course another matter. In a letter he sent me during the summer of 1959, however, his explanation of how the three inorganic images got into "Message" bears out the possibility that he was trying to write an impure poem. "In both ["To Lindsay"] and Ocean Liner poem ["Message"] the rapid shift of imagery comes from despair [sic] what to say in the middle of the poem & sudden shift of mind to transcription of disparate, seeming discordant images running thru head at the moment. The poems are accidents," he explained. "The art is in trusting such natural accidents to produce a point. But it's an art of accident, almost as much as Schwitters shaking words up in a paper bag—I shake up images in the bag of my head."

** To suggest how radical "Message" is, in fact, we have only to look to a classic example of organic imagery: Lowell's "Christmas Eve Under Hooker's Statue." Throughout this poem the imagery fits so intricately that it looks like highly complicated parts of a beautiful machine. Take the stone statue of Union General Hooker at which the speaker in the poem is looking in stanza one. In stanza two the statue comes to life in the personification of the god of war: ". . . once again/Mars meets his fruitless star with open arms,/His heavy sabre flashes with the rime,/The war-god's bronzed and empty forehead forms/Anonymous machinery from raw men . . ." In the final stanza Mars becomes, in turn, Santa Claus: the ironic symbol of peace on earth. All of the images introduced in stanza one, in fact, (with the possible exception of the Horn of Plenty) come to life in malevolent ways in the final two stanzas as the poem expands into a grinding, anguished experience of universal war: the war inside a man; the war between father and son; the war between brothers; and the eternal war in which mankind has slaughtered its own, fouling the earth since the days of Cain.

Extra reward on the slotmachine of my shyness in the
    snow when
February was only a bouncing ball before the Hospital
    of the Two Sisters of the Last
Hamburger Before I Go to Sleep.

KOCH: *"Taking a Walk With You"*

*

Another time, if I need it,
Create a little wind like a cold finger between my shoul-
    ders, then
Let my nails pour out a torrent of aces like grain from
    a threshing machine.

MERWIN: *"Lemuel's Blessing"*

*

I am a Hittite in love with a horse. I don't know what
    blood's
in me I feel like an African prince I am a girl walking
    downstairs
in a red pleated dress with heels I am a champion taking
    a fall
I am a jockey with a sprained ass-hole I am the light mist
    in which a face appears
and it is another face of blonde I am a baboon eating a
    banana
I am a dictator looking at his wife I am a doctor eating a
    child
and the child's mother smiling I am a Chinaman climb-
    ing a mountain
I am a child smelling his father's underwear I am an
    Indian
sleeping on a scalp
                    and my pony is stamping in the
                        birches,
and I've just caught sight of the *Niña*, the *Pinta* and the
    Santa Maria

O'HARA:
"In Memory of My Feelings"

This evening I offer you the easy aspirin of death
Boots on the golden age of landscape
You don't understand when I've
Smelled the smell of . . . I don't know
Now from opposite sides of the drawing
The nut of his birthday

ASHBERY: "Night"

*

Between two walls,
A fold of echoes,
A girl's voice walks naked.

WRIGHT:
"Snowstorm in the Midwest"

*

Evil is sty in eye of universe
hung upon a coughing horse
that follows me at night
thru a hollow street
wearing blinders
Evil is green gloves inside out
next to a double martini
on a cocktail table

FERLINGHETTI:
"Big Fat Hairy Vision of Evil"

Isolated from their poems, these images—some terribly funny, others exciting in their arbitrary free association—sound no doubt like translations from Dada or Surrealist texts. But the fact is—and it's a crucial fact—these images occur in traditionally organic poems rooted, as all good American poems have been, in the pragmatic, the concrete, the intelligible. The impure image exists, in truth, solely on its own two or three feet.

But with what result? Clearly the impure image offers the possibility of expansion of areas of reality and consciousness within the organic poem. In a moment, we'll look at this possibility in more detail. Here I want to talk about two other impure aspects I find as exciting as the impure image.

Both of them depend—like the impure image—on the intrusion of material traditionally edited out of the well-made organic poem. The difference is: whereas most inorganically impure images clearly come from the poet's unconscious, these two elements come from his everyday (more or less) rational life. The elements I have in mind are: the inclusion of undigested or raw autobiography; and the profuse inclusion of specific localities in poems when the poem organically does not need or "want" such specific localities spelled out. We might call both of these elements: the prose of the impure.

Both elements are evident of course in "The Day Lady Died." Let's look at the first one: the inclusion of direct or raw autobiography. You'll remember how O'Hara refuses to step away from the catalogue of mere prosy autobiographical odds and ends in order to extract the traditional "essence" from personal experience which, in turn, animates the creation of metaphor or character in a dramatic monologue which embodies much of the original autobiographical event or emotion. Clearly the young T. S. Eliot must have suffered some of the sexual inhibitions voiced by J. Alfred Prufrock: but Eliot is not Prufrock. Homosexual love and alcohol were two of the bedrocks of Hart Crane's emotional life: nowhere in his verse are either mentioned as such.* The point I suggest is obvious. Traditionally, the poet never lays bare his heart in verse by including mention of a hangover or that his mistress or beloved is named Anne Boleyn or Jeanne Duval.

On the contrary, the new American poets spell out clearly in verse the immediate experiences which their poems explore. If one gets drunk, one says so without the comfort of protection afforded by mask or metaphor—as Wright does with force in "Two Hangovers" and in the first of his two elegies on Harding or as Alan Dugan sets it down in "Elegy for Drinkers" or as O'Hara often admits in a poem. If you are in treatment with a psychoanalyst, you mention it plainly: Snodgrass and Dugan have done so. Or if you've been committed to an insane asylum, you describe it without disguise like Anne Sexton in "The

---

* I'm not suggesting that "Voyages II" isn't one of the masterpieces of homosexual literature or that "The Wine Menagerie" isn't fairly good verse about the clarity of vision induced by a certain state of intoxication. When reading both poems, however, you'd never know that Crane was in love with a young sailor absent on a Caribbean voyage when he wrote the first or that he was often tragically drunk.

Double Image" and Edward Marshall in "Leave The Word
Alone." If you favor homosexual love, you say so without circum-
locution—as Ginsberg lays it on the big table in "Howl" or in a
line like "America I am putting my queer shoulder to the
wheel" or as Wieners reveals in "A Poem for the Old Man."*

In other words, these poets would applaud T. S. Eliot's
celebrated description of the poetic process:

> When a poet's mind is perfectly equipped for its work,
> it is constantly amalgamating disparate experience; the
> ordinary man's experience is chaotic, irregular, fragmen-
> tary. The latter falls in love, or reads Spinoza, and these
> two experiences have nothing to do with each other, or
> with the noise of the typewriter or the smell of cooking;
> in the mind of the poet these experiences are always form-
> ing new wholes.

But many of the new poets would also be interested in the fact
that the poet has fallen in love with Mary or Peter or Paul or
that it is Spinoza's *Tractatus theologico-politicus* he happens
to be reading or that a Remington Rand typewriter clacks or
that it is the odor of turnips or spring lamb he smells: some or
all of which facts could conceivably be put in the poem in their
existential impurity.

Now let's look at the other example of the prose of the impure: the practice of many of these poets to locate poems in
specific localities on the map. Midwestern rural areas and towns
crop up by name in many poems by Bly, Logan and Wright.
An entire directory of states and cities gives "Howl" much of its

---

* "Confessional" poetry is the current critical term in fashion for such
candid inclusion of autobiographical material in poetry. I dislike the term
not only because it implies a hint of exhibitionism and bad manners but
because it suggests that poets in the past weren't confessional and that this
somehow was admirable because they were more concerned with creating
art than with exorcism or seeking absolution. This is of course hogwash.
Few poems are more "confessional" than the Sonnets. Most of them are
shameless, in fact, in both their exhibitionism of Shakespeare's ability to
attract both the young gentleman and the Dark Lady and in their delineation of his masochism. Instead of "confessional," then, I suggest we see the
revelation of private facts as being one aspect of the impure and leave it
at that.

punch and authenticity. The De Kalb Avenue stop on the BMT, 55th Street, the tobacconist's shop in the Ziegfeld Theatre near 6th Avenue are named specifically in lines by Blackburn, Koch and O'Hara. Hunting spots and automobile graveyards and U.S. highways are catalogued by Dickey. Amid particular California coastal areas Brother Antoninus undergoes spiritual agonies.

Naming localities has been a potential tradition in American verse since Whitman of course but with the exception of some Lindsay, Sandburg, Masters and Lowell the tradition has been restricted to such fancy exercises as Benét's "American Names." What distinguishes the 1962 generation isn't simply the abundance of concrete localities: it is the way in which many of the poems take pains to spell out a location because that is where the poem *is*. The poem isn't merely on the page. It is in the Shreve High football stadium in Martins Ferry, Ohio; or near Highway 106 near Cherrylog Road in North Georgia; or in Indian Gully near Red Oak, Iowa where a high school picnic occurs during the late 1930s; or in a pasture near Rochester, Minnesota; or in a Brooklyn/Manhattan subway station; or in a Volkswagen entering the outskirts of Wichita; or on Grant Avenue in San Francisco along which careens the parade celebrating Chinese New Year.

Here I imply nothing esoteric. All I suggest is that the pinning-down of experience to the locality where it happened when the poem as a whole doesn't require that the locality be named lets in a curious and extremely American sense of reality I happen to find invigorating. It's something like that immediacy, that sting of truth one always recognizes when a spouse or friend is talking about genuine experience. All good poems of course have his quality; but the spelling out of name places when the localities are not organically necessary only adds to the reality of the poem and—Eliot's warning that "human kind/Cannot bear very much reality" notwithstanding—the more awareness of reality the happier for us and our children and our children's children.

What do both of these prose aspects of the impure accomplish? Clearly it's much the same as what the impure image

accomplishes: they open unexpected doors previously locked
and allow more reality than ever to enter into the poem.*

Exactly what kind of reality? Obviously it's a complex kind.
On the one hand, there exists the possibility of including in a
poem multiple (and until now irrelevant) parts or fragments of
the poet's personality, as our discussion of the impure images in
"Message" revealed. But it should be stressed that not all of
these parts need be inhabitants of the poet's unconscious. Concrete autobiographical facts from past and present can also be
included. On the other hand, there's the possibility of including
as much of everyday reality as one chooses. Names of specific
regions, towns, cities or streets are only one element here; the
poet can also include by name the Sunday supplement of *The
New York Times*, say, or the brand of the cigarette mentioned,
the first and/or last name of one's beloved or friend, the color
of the taxi, the title of the book the poet is reading while he
waits, fitfully, for "the appointed hour."

What are some of the implications created by these possibilities? For one, the hoary and honored distinction between the
separate but equal powers which are poetry and everyday life
becomes blurred and in the end requires a new and more
catholic definition. In addition, a poem need no longer be one
tailored organic whole. Sections of it can be as organic as it lies
within the poet's skill to create; other sections can be as impure
or arbitrary as he chooses. The entire poem, in turn, can be as
simultaneously rational and irrational, coherent and chaotic,
"lovely" and "ugly," significant and banal as life itself. In this
sense, the impure, it would seem, might be an innovation of the
first order in the art of American poetry.

A final question remains: Where does the impure come from?
Some critics and literary historians will argue, no doubt,

* I trust no one will misunderstand what I'm suggesting: this is not a
blueprint of How to Write an Impure Poem in Five Easy Lessons. It should
go without saying that the impulse to create an impure poem—and there
are many kinds—is the same type of impulse which in all events created
"The Rape of the Lock" or Horace's Ode II:xiv *"Eheu fugaces, Postume."*
When elements of the impure are "dragged into prominence by half poets"
the result is the same as when Ambrose (Namby Pamby) Phillips sat down
to write a Pindaric Ode: "the result is not poetry."

that the impure is basically an extension of poetic attitudes created and explored by the Dada and Surrealist poets and also by some of the great modern poets who write in Spanish or Russian. And indeed, this generation of American poets has been singularly lucky to have had good (or even passing) translations of Apollinaire, Breton, Char and Max Jacob; Raphael Alberti, Lorca, Antonio Machado, Neruda and Vallejo; and Serge Essenin and Mayakovsky. From those among these foreign poets who came from Catholic cultures, the young Americans could learn to trust the irrational on its own terms because the irrational ("spiritual" would be the more comfortable term) contains everyday miracles. Five Latin words transform a piece of bread into the body and mind of the Creator of the universe whom one can eat whole with one's mouth; angels talk with men in dreams or on a Paris streetcorner; ghosts of saints inhabit the "visible" world through which we like to fancy we walk; the god is a bird: "What if everything in the Beyond," André Breton asserted in 1930, "is actually here, now, in the present, with us?" And from the Bolshevik poets and Vallejo and the Apollinaire of "Zone," the Americans could learn how a poet can construct a stage out of the commonplace occurrences in his autobiography on which he might dramatize himself without apology or the disguise of masks or dramatic monologues. In that agonized poem "You and Me," Mayakovsky, for one, includes the telephone number of his mistress, street names, snatches of official propaganda, and so on; in "The Day Lady Died" O'Hara mentions that the tobacco shop where he buys the two cartons of cigarettes is located in the Ziegfeld Theatre near 6th Avenue.

But the differences in how the young Americans explore and develop paths marked by the foreign masters are even more interesting than the similarities. No American poet tried to duplicate, say, the famous image in "Zone" of the Christ as the original aviator who during the Ascension breaks the world's altitude record because the Christ of Catholic Europe has never been a lasting reality on this side of the Atlantic. What an American might create, on the other hand, is an image in which the spiritual may be embodied in a machine. In a memorable image of spiritual evil in contemporary America, Ginsberg says: "Moloch whose mind is pure machinery! . . . Moloch whose breast is a cannibal dynamo!" And no American poet (with the possible exception of Ginsberg) has used the autobiographical impure to construct a stage of the dimension of Mayakovsky in "You and Me" or "At the Top of My Voice" or a narrow, bitter stage like the late poems of Vallejo. (Or is John Wieners our Vallejo?) Instead, the Americans seem more interested in everyday, less dramatic autobiography.

Finally, the freedom evident in the creation both of the impure elements and in the other freedoms we've seen is equally apparent in the way in which these poets write, as well as in the language they use. The evidence of their works points to a happy fact. From now on, an American poet can write in any style or combination of style and in any idiom he chooses. There exists no one correct or best style; and there exists no idiom or language which cannot appear in the poem.

Obviously these possibilities came into being because of the achievements and innovations of previous generations extending back to our father Whitman. Without the example of Whitman and possibly Sandburg, for instance, the powerful locomotive stanzas of "Howl" or "Kaddish" would probably not have taken the exciting and important form they did; and without the intricate constructions with which to embody spoken speech patterns created by Williams or cummings or Roethke, many of the lyrics of Logan, Creeley and Levertov would probably not have been as successful as they often are. And so on. What looks exciting is the spectrum of style among these poets. At one end are tightly-controlled lyrics which depend on delicate, harsh tensions created by varying line lengths—a technique worked with success by Wright, Blackburn, Logan, Creeley, Merwin, Oppenheimer, Snyder and Bly, among others. At the other are the lumbering lines of Brother Antoninus which often move like Pacific Ocean breakers punishing the coastline and Dickey's recent experiments with extended pause within lines of ten or even fifteen feet as in "May Day Sermon to the Women of Gilmer County, Georgia by a Woman Preacher Leaving the Baptist Church" and Koch's prose passages in "The

Artist" or Ginsberg's long, sweaty stanzas in "Kaddish" and "Wichita Vortex Sutra."

Abundance and variety occur too in the language. Whitman, Masters, Lindsay, Eliot, Sandburg, Pound, cummings, Williams, Marianne Moore, Shapiro, Roethke, Lowell: they taught us how not to be ashamed or afraid to use everyday words, syntax and speech patterns—that pragmatic, physical American talk which remains in a vivid way a frontier vocabulary because it describes how something or somebody *works*. But the spectrum of idiom remains as broad as possible, extending all the way from Ashbery's vocabulary made from the prose of the best art journals, newspaper prose, clichés, Harvard Yard slang and diaries and letters written by civilized people; to Ferlinghetti's diction built on the hip idiom of North Beach coffee houses, parodies of Hearst editorials and drugstore paperback sociology, including a generous dose of literary allusions and puns; to the talk of Logan and Snodgrass which is homey Midwestern frequently contorted by anguish, like the talk of Sherwood Anderson's characters in *Winesburg, Ohio*; to the straight conversational prose employed by Dugan and Starbuck which is occasionally spiked by recondite words dear to the lust of a lexicographer.

Years ago, Ezra Pound laid down the law: "Make it new." The poets of the generation of 1962 have done just that; and as they mature I suspect they will continue to accomplish just that with even more originality and excitement than they generated in their youth.

Appendix One

Many of the poets have taken vigorous part in read-ins held all over the nation in protest against the continuation of involvement by the United States in the Viet Nam civil war. Robert Bly has been one of the more active. His courage and guts literally to put his money where his mouth is have earned the admiration and respect of most of his contemporaries. In September 1967, Bly refused a $5,000 grant from the National Foundation on the Arts and Humanities awarded to his The Sixties Press with this statement: "Since the Administration is maiming an entire nation . . . it is insensitive, even indecent, for that Administration to come forward with money for poetry . . . there could be no pride in such an award." And in February 1968 at the celebration in Lincoln Center for the National Book Awards, the poet handed the $1000 prize money given for his collection *The Light Around the Body* to a young student named Mike Kempton and counseled him "not to enter the U.S. Army now under any circumstances." In handing over to Kempton his prize money, Bly asked that it be used "to find and counsel other young men to defy the draft authorities and not destroy their spiritual lives by participating in this war." It was a heroic act of civil disobedience. In commending Bly's acts, *The Nation* said that his "extensive and impressive work in opposing the war through the formation of American Writers Against the Vietnam War, culminating in his splendid action in Lincoln Center, are exemplary for our times."

ACKNOWLEDGEMENTS

Acknowledgments are gratefully extended to the following authors and publishers for their kind permission to reprint the poems or excerpts from poems:

ASHBERY, John—for "Leaving the Atocha Station," Copyright © 1961 by John Ashbery and for the excerpt from "Night," Copyright © 1960 by John Ashbery. Both reprinted from *The Tennis Court Oath*, by John Ashbery, by permission of Wesleyan University Press.

CREELEY, Robert—"The Business" (Copyright © 1959 by Robert Creeley) and "The Wicker Basket" (Copyright © 1959 by Robert Creeley) are reprinted with permission of Charles Scribner's Sons from *For Love* by Robert Creeley.

DICKEY, James—for "The Heaven of the Animals," Copyright © 1961 by James Dickey and for the excerpt from "The Sheep Child," Copyright © 1966 by James Dickey. Both reprinted from *Poems 1957-1967*, by James Dickey, by permission of Wesleyan University Press.

GARDNER, Isabella—for "The Widow's Yard" and "Lines to a Seagreen Lover" from *West of Childhood*, Copyright © 1965 by Isabella Gardner. Reprinted with permission of Houghton Mifflin Company.

GINSBERG, Allen—for "Wichita Vortex Sutra," Copyright 1966 by Allen Ginsberg. Reprinted with permission of *The Village Voice* and Coyote Books, San Francisco. And for the excerpt from "Howl" from *Howl and Other Poems*, Copyright © 1956 by Allen Ginsberg. Reprinted with permission of City Lights Books. And for the excerpt from "Kaddish" from *Kaddish and Other Poems*, Copyright © 1961 by Allen Ginsberg. Reprinted with permission of City Lights Books.

LOGAN, John—for "A Century Piece for Poor Heine," from *Ghosts of the Heart*, Copyright © 1960 by The University of Chicago. Reprinted with permission of The University of Chicago Press. And for the excerpt from "On a Photograph of Aaron Siskind," Copyright © 1961 by John Logan. Reprinted from *Spring of the Thief*, by John Logan, by permission of Alfred A. Knopf, Inc.

MERWIN, W. S.—for "Lemuel's Blessing" and "Dead Hand" from *The Moving Target*, Copyright © 1960, 1961, 1962, 1963 by W. S. Merwin. Reprinted with permission of Atheneum Publishers. And for the translation of the Eskimo Poem "You, Gull."

SNODGRASS, W. D.—for "April Inventory" and the excerpts from "Ten Days' Leave" and "Heart's Needle" from *Heart's Needle*, Copyright © William Snodgrass, 1959. Reprinted with permission of Alfred A. Knopf, Inc.

WRIGHT, James—for "As I Step Over a Puddle at the End of Winter, I Think of an Ancient Chinese Governor," Copyright © 1961 by James

VIKING PRESS—for the excerpt from *Finnegans Wake* by James Joyce, Copyright © 1939 by James Joyce.

WITTENBORN, SCHULTZ, INC.—for the excerpt from Tristan Tzara and the two poems by Pierre Albert-Birot and note by Robert Motherwell from *Dada Painters and Poets* (Documents of Modern Art, Volume 8). George Wittenborn, Inc., New York, New York.

THE POEM IN ITS SKIN

Two of the essays originally appeared in somewhat different form in the following periodicals and the author thanks the editors for their permission to reprint them in this collection: "Was Frau Heine a Monster?" appeared in *The Minnesota Review;* and a substantial part of "Faire, Foul and Full of Variations: The Generation of 1962" was printed in *Choice # 5.* In addition, passages of "Faire, Foul and Full of Variations" were first published in reviews written for *Big Table, Evergreen Review, The Nation* and *Poetry.* The author is also grateful to John Logan, who read the entire manuscript and offered incisive advice; and to Allen Ginsberg and W. S. Merwin for information and suggestions for variant readings which helped a lot when I rewrote the essays on their poems; and to Inara Carroll for her discerning comments on John Ashbery's "Leaving the Atocha Station."

10/9